recht/et
crim

RETHINKING LEGAL NEED

Rethinking Legal Need

The Case of Criminal Justice

PAUL ROBERTSHAW

Cardiff Law School
University of Wales

Dartmouth

Aldershot · Brookfield USA · Hong Kong · Singapore · Sydney

Published by
Dartmouth Publishing Company Limited
Gower House
Croft Road
Aldershot
Hants GU11 3HR
England

Dartmouth Publishing Company
Old Post Road
Brookfield
Vermont 05036
USA

A CIP catalogue record for this book is available from
the British Library and the US Library of Congress

ISBN 1 85521 207 2

Printed in Great Britain by
Billing & Sons Ltd, Worcester

Contents

Note:

The text does not cover material and developments after
1990. In particular it does not refer to Robert
Martineau's evaluative, and highly critical, study
'Appellate Justice in England and the United States'
William Hein, Buffalo 1991, discussed by Professor Zander
NLJ 12/4/1991, 491. In addition there are continuing
developments in the Law Society of England and Wales,
especially a new Guide to Client Care 3/1991.

P.E.M.R.

Preface

This book has been a long time brewing. Such work
requires, develops, patience (some) and stamina. Stoic
virtues these may be, but they inspire little pleasure in
recollection. Such pleasure is to be recollected and
gratefully acknowledged to a variety of persons, helpful
in different ways at different times, only some of whom
can be mentioned here. In particular I am happy to
single out the examiners of the thesis from which this
book derives: Professors Martin Partington and Michael
Zander. It is an honour to record your combined
qualities of charity and judiciousness. In return I can
say, and you can see, that I have taken your advice to
restructure and reshape totally to heart. Of those whose
intelligence, good humour and skill overcame my
incompetence in preparing the thesis and book for
publication, I especially acknowledge Carol Black and Zoë
Selley; it has been a pleasure working with you. By the
happiest of coincidences a former student, Nia James, was
between Criminal Legal Aid articles and solicitor in the
South Wales Crown Prosecution Service when the book
required literary criticism and painful amputation for
excessive length. Your surgery was excellent; I await
your first novel. Finally, but by no means least, I can
take this opportunity to thank the publishers. Dartmouth
have taken a risk that others would not, or whose
accountants make their publishing decisions for them.
May you flourish.

P.E.M.R.

1 Introducing the Problem of Legal Need

Introducing the Problem of Legal Need

Suppose that someone has a problem; is in trouble. How do we know that he, or she, has a problem; is in trouble? Is it because we think that they are, or because someone else says that they are, or because they themselves state that they are? For example our 'someone' has been charged with theft from a store, has been granted bail, and is due to answer the charge before the magistrates.

From a 'commonsense' or nominalist point of view it is difficult to deny that these are 'legal' situations. We might therefore not go beyond this way of describing these problems and conclude that such problems can only be resolved by legal, lawyer, solutions. We might be prone to reach such conclusions if we are ourselves lawyers, or if we do not stop to reflect. The lawyer or the unthinking person are not necessarily 'incorrect' in their reflexes; indeed their reflexes have powerful support from the official definition of the situation. To put it another way, we would likely say that someone who advised the accused to seek the help of a cab driver, themselves need psychiatric help? But would we have same reaction if the accused was advised to seek psychiatric help, or if the accused insisted on coping with the situation personally?

There are situations which are officially defined as legal, where practically everyone has some kind of legal representation, such as defendants in the Crown Court, but also some where most do not, such as guilty pleas on summary or intermediate charges. There are also situations where individuals and groups struggle politically to achieve legal definitions and remedies backed by the power of the state (and vice-versa), such as Legal Aid for tribunal representation; but these we cannot count as 'legal' until such campaigns have been successful. There are also areas where the official definition alters in the opposite direction, for example the removal of Legal Aid for representation in undefended divorce cases in 1976.

As has been hinted, a key difficulty is: who decides who has a need in what situation? When is a need 'legal'? Can a legal need also be some other kind of need? What happens when a legal need exists but legal solutions do not; does it cease to be a legal need? Why is it that needs become defined as legal, which were not previously so and vice-versa?

An uncritical approach to such issues was apparent in much of the research that accompanied the emergence of the 'Access to Law' movement in the early 1960s. A typical example concerned the city of Baltimore in the USA. (Derby 1966, 328, 334-5) The researcher found that in the Municipal Court (a petty sessional criminal jurisdiction with power to order custodial sentences up to 3 years and handling 55,000 cases a year) proceedings tended to be 'perfunctory' and 97% of defendants were unrepresented. They were inarticulate and did not understand the potential value of a lawyer's mitigation. Traffic offences were handled with even more perfunctoriness. These finding were not surprising in their day and no comment is made on them here.

Derby comments that there was virtual unanimity amongst welfare and voluntary organisations on the existence of legal need in this population. However he adds that they differed in defining the scope and nature of that need. (*Ibid* 330) It is of course precisely that scope and nature which causes the problem of definition, and notably this was not confronted. Such research into legal need originated in the USA after the passage of the Economic Opportunities Act in 1964. The focus and mode of such research has changed little since then.

In his overview of legal need research, the Swedish sociologist Bleiklie analysed four strands in such surveys. (Bleiklie 1983, 55)
a)   General descriptions of the underprivileged, showing social bias in the distribution of services, including underconsumption of legal services. (An example would be the recent 'discovery' of rural legal need in Britain.
b)   The relationship between social policy and administrative practice shows up shortcomings in delivery systems. (Prominent examples in Britain are the wide variations in applications for and refusals of Legal Aid, of Bail, and gaps in the Duty Solicitor system).

c)   Interdisciplinary projects intended to improve the
implementation of services provided for the poor.   In
Britain an example was the former Home Office funded
Community Development Projects.
d)   Studies   which   concentrate   on   the   relationship
between bureaucracy or professional, and client.   Some of
the studies of law centres and duty solicitors verge on
this approach, but better examples are Sherr (1986) or
Danet's   studies   of   solicitors   interviewing   clients.
(1984, 248)
     It is Bleiklie's conclusions I wish to stress, that all
four types are uninformed by theoretical perspectives.
     Virtually all of these studies are predicated on a
notion of legal need, which is frequently disclosed, but
almost never developed.   There is a real risk in such a
void   since   'the   concept   of   need   is   thought   to   be
fundamental   to   the   study   of   social   administration',
(Clayton 1983, 213) the risk being that other criteria
will be used such as merit, or market power, or ascribed
status.
     To be fair, legal need research is only an extreme
example.   The concept of need is used extensively in the
public services but 'the notion of need has received
scant and unsystematic theoretical treatment.   All too
often however the strategy is to note the problems of
definition and usage but continue nevertheless regardless
of them'.   (G. Smith 1980, 41)   There is recognition,
particularly by academics, of the problematic nature of
legal need, but no way through the ensuring thicket has
emerged, or even been proposed.   It is suggested that a
major reason for this is the nature of the discussion
itself.   Discussion of legal need is affected by the
general form of legal analysis as a segregated and
introverted discipline, typified by 'Jurisprudence' as
contrasted with 'philosophy of law'.
     These findings will now be supported by examples from
prominent works on legal problems, and legal need.   In
the case of Zander it is regrettable that criticism
should appear to be personal; this results solely from
his remarkable pioneer role in this field in Britain.   In
his excellent book surveying 'Legal Services for the
Community'   three   pages   are   devoted   to   'Problems   of
Definition' in introducing a chapter on 'The Need for
Legal Services'.   In those pages half a footnote cites,
without discussion, Bradshaw's leading work on need
analysis in social policy.   (1978, 273-6)
     Another example is the leading student textbook on 'The
Modern English Legal System' which commences with a
chapter   entitled   'Problems   about   Problems'   and   two
sections on 'What is a Problem?' and 'When is a Problem
Legal?';   these cover four pages in a text of 759 pages.
The discussion is somewhat broader: Bradshaw is not
mentioned but the relativist approach of Morris, Cooper
and Byles (1974) is, as well as the Adamsdown Community
Trust analysis.   It would be wrong to criticise a text

for modesty; however it is fair to say that it concludes
with a series of questions, none of which are confronted,
and finally an abdication:

> "How can a general proposition of need be formulated
> when there are so many personal variables? Should
> any such proposition even be attempted"? (Smith and
> Bailey 1984, 319-20)

Similarly leading American researchers in this area:
(Marks 1977, 191)

> "We need to abandon our quest to define legal
> needs."

and in Australia: (Cass and Western 1980, 4, 18)

> "A legal problem, like pornography, defies exact
> analysis and the debate ... has been little informed
> by the use of any measure or attempt at
> conceptualisation of the problem or for that matter
> any awareness of the desirability for consistency in
> the use of terms".

In two instances academics have reviewed the situation
critically, with awareness of the broader debates on
other disciplines. Thus Campbell: (1982, Ch 9)

> "There has been constant reference to unmet legal
> need since the 1960s yet its meaning remains unclear
> and seriously problematic ... for over a decade
> reports on empirical research ... have exhibited
> indelible attachment to arguments about unmet legal
> need even though the phrase has remained
> pathologically ambiguous ..."

also Twining: (1980, 558, 561-6)

> "There is inadequate conceptualisation which is
> reflected in the confusion and controversy
> surrounding such terms as 'legal services', 'unmet
> needs' and 'access'. There is a dearth of funded
> research and serious analysis into basic problems;
> the provision of legal services still await the kind
> of sustained consideration by economists and social
> administrators that is accorded to other services."

This short tradition of research and writing, which
abstains from theoretical discussion and its impact on
research, has consequences. Such work is positively
characterised by two features. First, need is equated
with absence, as if a lack of food in a house equated
automatically with hunger. Second, the theoretical
vacuum is filled by 'normative' definition, that is by
the professional providers of these services.

Bleiklie concludes that the providers are the group to attend to, as their ability to regulate demand

> "may primarily be regarded as a question of how clientele is defined."

More cynically but relevant, because it brings out the problem of power, are the directors of the Harvard Law School Clinical Program: (Bellow and Kettleson 1978, 337-8)

> "As Humpty Dumpty said to Alice:
> 'When I use a word it means just what I choose it to mean - neither more nor less.'
> 'The question is', said Alice, 'whether you can make words mean so many different things'.
> 'The question is', said Humpty Dumpty, 'who is to be master, that is all.'

Or, as Shakespeare put it in Lear:

> "Oh, reason not the need ..." and "the act of our necessities is strange ..." (II 4,266, III 3,70)

In O'Malley's comment on the development and status of sociology of law in Australia, he shows that the eight 'law and poverty' investigations by the Australian Government Commission of Inquiry into Poverty during the Whitlam Premiership were totally dominated by lawyer authors,

> "despite the manifestly sociological nature of the issues raised and the research involved." (O'Malley 1984, 91-5)

These reports led to a massive boost in the legal aid funding and the publication of the Australian Legal Service Bulletin,

> "which has from its inception acted as a central organ for reformist legal workers. It has cemented a further domination of the field of analysis of law by an engaged, reformist and overwhelmingly atheororetical problematic.   It has also unintentionally reinfored the field's domination by lawyers."

In addition the Victoria and New South Wales Law Foundations were stimulated into research on their legal professions:

"It is certainly the case that this work largely
reproduced the lawyer dominated empiricism of the
previous decade."

In general O'Malley comments there were

"few signs of having been affected by the
theoretical turmoil of British criminology and
sociology of law,"

a comment apposite as much to British legal needs
research.

As a result policy altered and institutions were
established, with little or no evaluation of those
responses. (Campbell 1976, 206; Partington 1982 Ch 5)
An example is the federal Australian Legal Aid Office,
which was wound up in 1981, but even prior thereto

"the activities of that agency, in terms of the type
of clients it served, the nature of their problems
and the results remain largely a mystery". (Gardner
1981 Ch 6)

Equally the significance of the virtually simultaneous
discovery of unmet legal need throughout the western
developed countries is unlikely to have been a
coincidence. If we were to examine the emergence of that
concept we should consider whether it related to distinct
groups of legal occupations, and with distinct interests
and values. (Abel 1982 Ch 1) These points should not be
overstated; as was remarked previously, acknowledged
abdication may be a mask of modesty, though it has not
been accompanied by calls on 'outsiders' to fill the
theoretical, research, or social policy vacuum.
Occasionally insecurity does surface, as leading
Australian researchers put it: (Cass and Western *op cit*
15-16)

"In the final analysis, an individual has a 'legal
problem' only if and when he sees that he has one.
It is the individual's perception of self and
relationship to the community and law that
determines when a problem is called a legal
problem."

The weakness in this approach is that it places the self
and its problem at the periphery rather than at the
centre, 'in the final analysis'. There is also a problem
in using Demand as a measure of legal need. Demand can
be positively measured, but non-demand may well be
thwarted or inactive demand, which is only discoverable
by attitude testing for 'felt' need, with all the
difficulties of assessing subjective attitudes.

It follows that it is important to review the type of
research on which the legal access movement was based,

because the relative simplicity of its approach eliminates 'the dilemma of setting priorities - to meet an ambiguously defined and elusive concept of legal need'. (Meeker, Dombrink and Schumann 1985, 225) Since it is at the level of officialdom, in State institutions that such priorities are set it is relevant to examine official attitudes to this central concept of need. Whilst one can never be certain what interests or values coalesce into such official statements, they are nevertheless valuable in the absence of more detailed historical information. One such statement is the Evidence of the Lord Chancellor's Advisory Committee on Legal Aid to the Royal Commission on Legal Services.

It is stated that the concept of legal need

> "is a useful, and indeed an inevitable concept, but it is necessary to bear in mind the subjective character of 'need' in this context. We do not believe that there is a precise degree of unmet need which can be established by scientific inquiry ... and it is important to distinguish between the need and demand for legal services. Nevertheless, when all abatements are made we are in no doubt that there is an unmet need for legal services." (HC 172, 1978, Apx 1.2)

However, five years later this confusing assertion was replaced by calls for much more specific research, in particular on the interdependence between the courts, police, prisons, probation service and the criminal legal aid system as research assessing criminal legal aid was 'virtually non-existent'. (34th Report HC 151, 1983-4, 495-8)

A final point is provided indirectly by the Deputy Head of the Home Office Research and Planning Unit, who suggests that there will continue to be particular limitations and skews in officially directed and funded research. (Tarling 1988, 112)

Against these changed positions in official approaches to legal research two mitigations can be put forward. First, although new legal need research is

> "essential, indeed it has hardly begun. Such discussion is enormously demanding and has not been systematically attempted". (Thayer 1973, 145)

Second, researchers who confront existing orthodoxy take a risk because their work can be interpreted as an hostile act and

> "no good evaluation ever goes unpunished" (Rossi and Williams 1972, 32) since "many evaluators have paid a heavy price for their naive failures to recognise the political nature of evaluation and that they

operate in a basically alien and inhospitable environment". (McClintock 1981 Ch 5)

As has been said a rash of studies of this area occurred after 1964, first in the USA, then, influenced by the former, in Britain and elsewhere. In the early studies there was a strong tendency to use lawyers' definitions. This was hardly surprising since they were mainly conducted by lawyers.

Some of the problems of such 'normative' research can be exemplified by Fogelson and Freeman's study published in 1968. (ed Wheeler Ch 9)

These researchers used a panel of lawyers to 'code' 83 cases from three agencies. Each agency had a different orientation; one was protective, one was family centred and the other was psycho-analytic. The records were limited and were themselves the product of social workers' perceptions. The coding method was to isolate 'legal' issues and 'legal' disputes. They found a median of three legal incidents per case. As they put it: 'the lawyer finds legal content everywhere', or as another writer put it 'buying a loaf of bread qualifies under this kind of definition'. (Griffiths 1977, 260, 269) A major Dutch study, by contrast, found an average of 2.6 legal incidents per _life_ in the reports of the subjects interviewed; 15% reported none and 5% reported more than six. (Schuyt _et al_ 1976) It is easy to criticise a study such as the one Fogelson and Freeman made, for instance there was no control on the legal panel. Nevertheless the study is interesting, even surprising. For example the panel admitted to disagreements in over 20% of the codings, and they found 7.2% of the cases with no legal content at all, ranging from 3.4% of the Protective cases to 15% of the Psychoanalytic cases. Yet it was the Psychoanalytic agency which they most closely associated with property disputes (41.1%), typical and traditional lawyer's territory.

Another American study published a year later openly faces these difficulties. Christensen argued that there are two axes along which the issue can be viewed: (Christensen 1970 Ch 1)

> "One method would be for the bar alone to determine what is good for the public and to decide what the public should have. The other would be to rely solely upon the public's evaluation of what services require a lawyer's special abilities."

He also recognised the dangers of lawyers' self interest in such 'normative' definition: 'coloration from the fact that lawyers see things through lawyer's eyes'. Christensen found the concept 'need' unacceptable, as too subjective and too contingent upon who is doing the evaluating, for what purposes and under what conditions. He preferred, as do economists, the notion of demand

because it is not subjective and abstract, nor what
lawyers think people should have, 'but rather the action
people may be expected to take ... to obtain laywers'
services ...' From that perspective he noted that demand
may vary according to the nature and number of
alternative solutions, and that persons of different
means may have different 'legal' problems.

That was an advance, though it must be said that some
of these points were likely to emerge once one started to
look at legal services from a class perspective as
Christensen implicitly does. However he did not go
further and consider the politics of demand and their
relationship to need definition, nor the problem of
selection from alternative methods of resolving problems.

Such research also occurred in Britain. The watershed
work was a study of problems in three run-down London
boroughs. The authors decided which of their
respondents' problems were legal and when they were
unmet. (Zander, Abel-Smith and Brooke 1973) They found
masses of 'unmet legal need', ranging from 40% to 90% for
different problems.

The only exception was house purchase. In the case of
buying a house there was no unmet legal need. Due to the
solicitors' monopoly it was, at that time, virtually
impossible to buy a house without employing a solicitor.
(Joseph 1976)

In the same year a series of critical essays on the
topic of legal need were published which made some of the
points illustrated so far, and some additional ones;
(Morris, White and Lewis 1973) for example, legal
solutions can be a cause of problems; lawyers'
definitions of need can lead to the conclusion that it is
the rich and the powerful who have most unmet legal
needs. Another class aspect they noted was that the
middle-class attitudes of lawyers and typical clients may
be very different from those of working class people,
being preventive rather than curative. In addition, it
was clear that the empirical investigators of unmet legal
need were using negative criteria such as inability to
pay for legal services or failure to benefit from
traditional legal skills. Their findings would have been
very different if they had used positive criteria, such
as the thwarting of active seekers of legal help -
'expressed' needs or demands by the poor for legal aid,
congenial tribunals and so forth. The investigators had
used checklists based on the past use of lawyers. This
implies that people should use lawyers and ignores the
cultural and psychological aspects that make up the habit
of not using a lawyer or even cultural patterns of law
avoidence. It also ignores the reality of lawyer
avoidance by those presumed to use lawyers most.
(MacAulay 1966) The studies also assume that lawyers are
homogeneous and that there can be no conflict between
them and their clients' interests. (Blumberg 1967,
Casper 1972)

This failure to notice the difficulties inherent in discussing or surveying need mean that working definitions of need risk bearing no relation to the lives of the very people whose needs are being surveyed. An example is from the classic London study mentioned above. The authors' checklist excluded all complaints about goods where the faults appeared more than one month after purchase, and also excluded all tenants' problems where there was no formal agreement with the lessor. One does not have to be an expert on the lower levels of working class life in London to realise the size of such exclusions from lists of 'need' to be measured. (Phillips 1979)

Another approach is to make judgments ('normative') in advance about which 'target' groups are likely to be in need or at risk and then test their attitudes and behaviour. The tendency however is to assume that there will be such need without testing it. Instead, effort is devoted to finding areas with concentrations of target groups, especially where their characteristics overlap. An example from Australia is Cass and Western's 'Who Needs Legal Services?'. They established five social characteristics and six personal characteristics, some of which were present in the area to a considerable extent, such as low personal and family income (48.1% and 23.6%), low socio-economic status (29.9%) and pensioners (21.8%). The total was 171.4% which certainly indicated a concentration of these groups, but the assumption of legal need was never tested and the possibility of varieties of legal need never considered.

This survey again illustrates the risk of 'the sophistication of the measurement technique which quite outstrips the quality of any underpinning analysis of substantive issues and implication'. (Schwartzkoff 1981 Ch 8)

Sometimes there has been awareness of the richness of the problem but the attempts to grapple with it have been confused. An example is Downes, Hopkins and Rees discussing need in the context of the report of the Royal Commission on Legal Services: (1981, 121, 124)

> "By which criteria should we judge adequacy? Those of the usual solicitor's client of today? Those of the solicitor himself? Or by some criteria which reflect the real need for legal services in the community? We argue that only criteria of this third category can be used as a basis for criticism."

The criterion selected by them was 'real need' and they added that this must be exclusive. But no distinction was made between 'need' and 'real need' and no criterion set up for 'reality'. No further discussion elucidated the matter. From the general drift of the essay one could infer a criterion of need, but even that is not clear or consistent. This inference would be from their reference to the Report of the Scottish Royal Commission on Legal Services which gave particular attention to the consumer rather than the professional. From that perspective need criteria might include two of Bradshaw's criteria - to be discussed later - attitudinal 'felt' and behavioural 'expressed' need, but no analysis of Bradshaw or the Scottish Royal Commission's approach occurred. (Paterson 1980, 321)

The Scottish Royal Commission's report is unusual because it openly recognised the plurality of solutions available to a person with a problem. For example, not all work done by lawyers can be called 'legal' in the narrow, technical sense, and equally not all legal services are provided by lawyers. (Cmnd 7846-I 1980, 2-1, 7-8) The Scottish Royal Commission did not go on to analyse how choices between perceived alternatives might be made. However, it did overtly decide against 'normative' definitions:

> "So it is not much use defining problems as legal according to a researcher's idea of what a solution should be." (*Ibid* 2-7)

Another problem concerns the focus of a study of need. As an example one can consider a classic study of British research into legal need in criminal justice on representation and acquittal rates in magistrates' courts. (Zander 1969, 632) It appeared that the acquittal rate for those represented was two and a half times greater than those appearing in person, at 10% against 4%. However, those percentages refer to acquittal rates of all such defendants. If one examines the acquittal rate in relation not to gross, but tried defendants pleading Not Guilty, the acquittal rate is the same for both groups, at 20%. The gross acquittal rate differs because the Not Guilty pleas differ for each group. It is 50% for those represented and 20% for those appearing in person. This is the source of the two and a half times differential.

Finally, the distinction between preventative and curative law should be repeated. If one were to make a judgment that prevention is as valuable as cure, and therefore needs for legal 'cures' to crises should be given equal consideration, there would be significant differences in the populations affected. Thus middle class persons might have large needs for preventative law such as company formation, trusts and wills and less need for curative law. For working class persons the position would often be the reverse. (Parry J 1914)

2 Competing Professional Definitions of Need

An obvious method of foreclosing on issues of relativity in defining need is by achieving an official or state definition of the situation which excludes alternative or competing accounts. Such definitions are rare; section 21 of the Powers of Criminal Courts Act 1973 is an example; the former Judges' Rules relating to accompaniment for juveniles and the mentally disabled during police interview were further examples.

'Normative' accounts of need by professionals often enlarge the area of definition, but in doing so they may well encroach onto the territory of other professionals, who by their own criteria are defining the need differently. Occasionally such definition will be rejected by the person in 'need'. Campbell gives the example of a 17 year old male remanded on multiple murder charges. Both the normative and commonsense definitions would be that he has a legal need. However, as a member of the 'Provisional I.R.A.', he might well reject all legal advice and representation as part of his refusal to recognise the court itself, which would be redefined as a political rather than legal institution.

Phillips states that 'problems are differently classified by people who deal with them'. (*op cit,* 29) Phillips was primarily concerned with the competing normative definitions of lawyers and that of social workers, the latter group evincing some hostility towards the former and who have many non-legal techniques for dealing with problems which a lawyer might treat as legal, for example a family under Notice to Quit might be referred to the Local Authority Housing Department. (*Ibid* 36)

Phillips gives as an example a case of possible non-accidental burning of a child, with conflicting explanations by the parents and a dispute between two Social Services Departments. Eventually the area team decided to take Care proceedings.

"Once the case had reached this stage the social worker effectively lost control of it. The solicitor began to point out all the difficulties: conflicting evidence, witnesses travelling 90 miles, an excellent defence solicitor...."

The lawyer's approach based on 'Rights' was emotionless compared to that of the social workers, for example he talked of rules of evidence that would exclude matters known to the social worker. These two occupations interpreted the same situation with different language and purposes. In this context Campbell argues:(1974, 13)

"Legal training however also teaches 'legalistic' skills which may lead well-intentioned reformers to turn social problems into 'legal needs' for which the solution is mistakenly believed to be found only in legal strategies."

In support one can consider the first solicitor of the North Kensington Law Centre: (Kandler 1974, 67)

"For many years I did a lot of divorce work and I am quite convinced that 60%, and sometimes 99%, of my time on cases was in fact doing social work ... it isn't even legal advice, this advice could be provided by social workers..."

The British sociologists Morris, Cooper and Byles (*op cit*, 301-3, 318) went further by stressing the relativism of need and its overlapping nature; a legal need may simultaneously be some other variety of need, and in particular that an individual need may also be a collective one, and changes fundamentally so defined. A well-known example is the provision of legal advocacy for confined mental patients. (Himelfarb and Lazar 1981, 17-21)

Usually such relativity consists of overlaps in clients' choices, but occcasionally overt competition may occur. An example is recorded from Lancashire where in 1979 the Law Society's legal services committee produced a leaflet on 'Legal Aid and Services for Accident Victims' for display in doctors' surgeries. The Oldham Health Authority and five out of nine family practitioner committees refused to give permission for such display on the ground that it would encourage 'compensationitis'. (Harper 1980)

In this country an example of difficulty over the appropriate form of legal need is in the juvenile court where "children are represented with increasing frequency almost always on legal aid". Hilgendorf asserts that the specialist solicitors in this field retain a responsibility to decide what is in the child's best interests. (1983, 60, 67) She then argues that:

> Those who argue that lawyers exceed their professional authority when they decide what is in the best interests of the child are clearly correct. There is nothing in a lawyer's training or knowledge base, the foundation of their professional authority, which fits them to make such a decision."

To continue from another source: (Phillips *op cit*, 29, 36, 40)

> "A common complaint was about defending solicitors in criminal proceedings who used Social Enquiry Reports, drawn up by the social worker, as the basis of a plea in mitigation. The solicitor was making money out of the social worker's knowledge and hard work. Solicitors were seen as arrogant."

Another example of contradictory purposes and definitions occurred in the Wandsworth Legal Resources Project's attempt to set up a legal service for convicted custodial defendants. There was hostility to the scheme. The Prison Governor saw it as a source of complaints against the regime. The Treasury and Home Office opposed it because of its cost and risk of fruitless appeals. The project organisers saw it as primarily concerned with the family relations of prisoners, in particular tenancy, mortgages and hire-purchase, social security and matrimonial law. The first two views predominated and the scheme did not go beyond the pilot stage.[1]

It is not surprising that in view of the admitted relativities in defining legal need in criminal justice that some authorities have been content to attempt no definition at all, apart from stating the problem. (Wilkins 1975, 5-6) This is a tenable position, provided that no attempt at prescription is made, but that never seems to occur.

The discussion so far has suggested that the foundations upon which a legal ideology of need is built are precarious.

One example is from the USA and demonstrates both the differences between the lay public and professionals, and simultaneously the differences within professionals themselves. Boyum referring to unpublished materials from Sykes' Denver, Colorado survey demonstrates that for criminal matters, where the responding citizens perceived legal need, a quarter of the attorney panel disagreed; and where the citizens did not perceive a legal need, half the panel agreed. (1983, T5) Hence there is no consensus as to what should count as need in the legal process.

A particularly striking example of these differences on need was provided by the Australian Law Reform Commission.[2] Magistrates and Judges were asked their opinions on the desirability of making legal representation available to defendants. Three situations were proposed: for mitigation; where a custodial sentence was contemplated; and an open-ended question on 'other' situations:

Representation not necessary

Mitigation		Custodial Sentence	
Magistrates		Magistrates	
Tasmania	72.7%	Queensland	34.7%
Victoria	45.8%	Tasmania	27.3%
Australia	35.1%	Australia	22.0%
Judges		Judges	
Australia	13.9%	Australia	12.7%

'Other' situations		'Other' of those saying not necessary:	
Magistrates		Australia - Magistrates and Judges:	
Tasmania	66.0%		
Australia	31.1%	All situations	75.7%
Judges		Legal issues/	
Australia	13.8%	defence	81.7%
		Bail	90.1%

It appears therefore that about 10% of professional judges and 20% of lay magistrates in Australia rejected totally any conception of legal need, and, at least with the latter group, there were striking regional variations in this rejection. This rejection would certainly have been in equally striking contrast to the expanding definitions of legal practitioners at that time.

It is not surprising that gaps can occur between definition by and action by the 'legal' problem solver. The National Association of Citizens' Advice Bureaux (NACABX) gave evidence to the Royal Commission on Legal Services, based on a two week survey of the Bureaux, in 1977. They received 112,362 inquiries and stated that 35.7% of them contained a legal component. However, their Annual Report later stated that over half of these were handled by the Bureaux workers themselves without referral for legal advice. As will be discussed below, one of the few objective ways of settling a definition is existentially, rather than essentially, by seeing who actually resolves a problem by what means. From an essentialist standpoint there were 35.7% legal problems, but from an existential standpoint it may have been around 17%.[3]

The same point emerges more starkly in the 1978 Annual Report of the North Kensington CAB, which was one of the first in Britain to appoint a full-time salaried 'resource lawyer' to advise and educate staff and undertake representation and referral. The report stated:

> "The real debate is no longer 'Is there any unmet need for legal services?' The question today is, 'How are legal and other services to develop to meet the need for legal services?'"

But then it continued:

> "In very many cases, despite the apparently legal nature of the problem, there is no need at all for the qualified lawyer to be involved."

Basically, what this section has attempted to demonstrate is that the difficulties of analysis associated with need generally are replicated in a particular 'adjectival' need, legal need.

Footnotes

1. Editorial 133 NLJ 2/9/1983; Sir H. Benson <u>The Times</u> 17/2/1982.

2. Report No 15 'The Sentencing of Federal Offenders' Canberra (1980) Aus. Govt. Publishing Service, Apdx B, T5A, 5B, 380. Interstate comparison of professional judges is not possible because the numbers are too small.

3. See NLJ 19/1/1978 and 21/9/1978.

3 Clients and the Pragmatics of Legal Need

Gilbert Smith's Case Studies Re-analysed

The British sociologist Smith's book 'Social Need' is addressed to the practice of need. He argues that the theoretical use of the concept has been muddled or absent. He does not deny that ideas of need are important, but he shows that need is constructed in practice, in which ideas of what it may or might be, are but a part, and that the role of the decider, the timing of the decision and the context of the decision are usually more determinative.

There are no indexed references to legal need or legal institutions in his work, but it transpires that legal institutions and personnel are far from absent.

His interest in need originated in the major reorganisation of social work in the 1960s. The Ingelby and Kilbrandon Reports on Children and Young Persons, the White Paper 'Social Work and the Community' and the Seebohm Report (1960 Cmnd 1190, 1964 Cmnd 2303, 1966 Cmnd 3065) on Local Authority and Allied Personal Social Services (1968 Cmnd 3703) all derived from the perception of the juvenile offender as a social problem. In both England, Wales and Scotland these documents led to the creation of an unified social work service (except for adult Probation) in criminal justice.

These Reports tend to view need as an objective, measurable and universal phenomenon. The model on which such need is calculated is a medical one. This is ironic because it is in medicine that most research has been done and clarification achieved, showing that simple medical need is largely an illusion; it is in practice as much an evaluative moral concept as an objective one.

One use of the concept 'need' in these Reports was the conflation of social problems with social need. This use is relevant to criminal justice. The general tendency of the Reports was to elide need with criminal delinquency: delinquency was an objective indicator, a proof of need. Indeed delinquency may itself be a matter of social construction, of selection and processing from amongst those 'in need' with those of other particular characteristics, which are morally evaluated as being delinquent and in need of social control. There is a well known literature on this aspect of policing. (Cicourel 1968)

Even if we leave these issues to one side, there remains a further logical problem. If 'juvenile delinquency' is redefined as 'need' (with 'treatment' by social workers under the DHSS) then how is it that adult crime is any different in essence? (Kilbrandon *op cit* para 246)

Smith argued that 'need' is a construct of a given situation. In this construct a significant role must be played by the relevant organisation members' own subjective ideas about the matter in question. It is not simply a property of an individual but the product of a rather complex pattern of interaction between client and professional/s. (Smith *op cit* Ch 1)

Smith shows that although Reports, such as Seebohm, used 'need' as a central assumption and organising concept, they were never able to define precisely what it meant. He traces six senses in which it is used.

(1)   as an existing administrative category, either of existing or of proposed services;
(2)   as an implicit conception of current social work practice;
(3)   as the client's conception of his or her or their own need or needs; (Bradshaw: 'felt' or 'expressed' need)
(4)   as an assumed consensus as to what counted as criteria for an institutional response by the 'community';
(5)   as 'true' need, as a matter for 'expert' diagnosis and prescription; (Bradshaw 'normative' need)
(6)   through the conflation of social problems with social need.

Again, when considering response to need, the individual is frequently envisaged as the first line problem solver. But if the individual as delinquent is deemed to be in need, how can the delinquent in need, as author of this social problem, be its solution?

Smith concluded:

> "What would count as a more appropriate set of
> categories was not clearly indicated. The concept
> of need was not defined." (*Ibid* 36)

It would be wrong to concentrate on these governmental
inquiries, despite their importance for institutional
development. The idea of need is used extensively in the
public services but "the notion of need has received
scant and unsystematic theoretical treatment. All too
often however the strategy is to note the problems of
definition and usage but continue nevertheless regardless
of them. (*Ibid* 41)

Smith counters from a phenomenological and
ethnomethodological perspective that need is a socially
constructed reality; it is practically managed and
accomplished through organisations and routines which are
'situated' and, which in turn focus, in a given context,
within given constraints, on what is presented in a given
form.

The case studies Smith produces certainly bear out both
his criticism and his theory. There is reason to think
that such matters as the variation in eligibility for
Legal Aid from area to area, and crime to crime, are best
explained by studying actual practice as prescribed by
Smith.

Smith comments elsewhere that there are two overt
approaches to need in institutions. One is centred on
the management of caseload; the other is applicant
centred. In practice the establishment of need involves
a chain of related decisions in which earlier ones weight
later ones. They are highly routine and constraints of
time and hierarchy predominate. Definitions of case or
client are largely constructed by documents and the form
of the documents themselves may well structure that
identity. These three aspects - process, routine and
documentation - reduce the opportunity for applicant
influence drastically. (*Ibid* 75-80) It can actually
happen that within the relevant institution to die 'at
the wrong place or time' is not to die. (Sudnow 1967)
He concludes pessimistically with Zald that partly
because most clients' status is low relative to experts',
they do not normally buy the service they actually
receive - genuine alternatives seldom exist and are
rarely perceived to be available. (Zald 1965)

Smith pays particular attention to the linkage or
referral process, between prospective clients and the
welfare insitutions. This classification is an important
initial constituent of client need. (*Op cit* Ch 6, 129)
In practice classification often falls to untrained
receptionists.

In court referral cases narrated by Smith what is most
striking are the consistent non-legal classifications
used. I am not here arguing that a legal response was

necessarily appropriate, but in some of the cases a legal response could not be considered marginal, such as eviction for rent arrears, or probate on three bereavements. This closure by the actors and by Smith is interesting as it suggests that once a definition has been made it forecloses other options. (*Ibid* 125-137) A reverse example is appropriate. In one of the Court referral cases which involved a Social Enquiry Report regarding two unpaid fines, the Court's documentary classification of the problem or need as 'financial' apparently had the effect of foreclosing any discussion or action on the needs of the children of the defaulter by the Social Services Department. (*Ibid* 142)

Smith's Case Studies

Smith concludes with five extended case studies, of which I shall ignore one as it was incomplete, though it supports the points to be made.

I   Mrs W, whose husband was unemployed complained that their electricity bill was too high.
     There was a question about the tariff rate. No further action was decided.

II   Mr D, was, without authority, occupant of a sub-let council flat. His wife was due to have a baby, so he applied unsuccessfully for acceleration on the Housing List.
     No further action was decided.

Comments: Both of these cases could hypothetically have been classified as 'legal' - for the Law Centre in the first case and for Legal Aid in the second. A 'normative' legal perspective would have made such classification. Relevant to such non-classification might be that no such request came from those with the problem (Felt/Expressed/Need), also that legal definitions were generally outside the experience and socialisation of those working at the Social Services Department. More concretely the Department was accustomed to being the receiver of problems defined as non-legal by its legal referral agency, the local criminal court.
    There is another possibility however, which emerges in cases III and V.

III Mrs B had a complicated set of relationships involving 'husband', 'partner' and children. There was a conflict over Social Security special entitlements. There was also an expressed need for representation at the Supplementary Benefit Appeals Tribunal regarding 'cohabitation' disentitlement, and there was an issue over transitional rights pending appeal. However it was the solicitor who

had referred her. She was recorded as saying: "My
solicitor doesn't know all that much about the rules
and regulations at Social Security and Welfare. He
said that I should come here and find out about it
to see what will happen to it."
It was recorded that: "her solicitor is unable to
enforce a decree of maintenance". After interview
and case conference it was decided to allocate the
matter to a social worker.

V   Miss G. A married woman was separated from her
husband. Her personal property remained in their
jointly owned flat. Access was denied by her
husband who demanded £150 for entry. She had sought
Variation of an Access Order regarding their
children because of the melancholia, anal fixation
and generally disturbing behaviour of the husband
during the children's visits. She was referred by
the Citizens' Advice Bureau.
Mrs G commented: "The judge didn't even read what I
said ... In the legal system they're not interested
in persons. They're only interested in rules. I've
been sentenced all along and I've not done anything
wrong. The courts are supposed to pass judgment but
in fact they pass sentence ..."
"Yes, but the law is not interested in people. ...
The Sheriff did not like the welfare to be involved.
When I was contacting the RSPCC he asked what the
RSPCC had to do with it ..." (*Ibid* 171-9)

It should be stressed that Smith, consistent with his
theoretical standpoint, makes no comment on the
appropriateness of particular definitions. He does
however return to this case to raise further
administrative questions which may shed some light on the
question of definition.
Mrs G was coded as 'not known' when she clearly was due
to an earlier filed inquiry regarding a nursery place for
her daughter. It was her infant daughter who was coded
as referral agent: (Miss G). Despite the clearly
presented problems of the £150 and court intervention,
the file focus was on the <u>daughter</u> alone. Again the area
allocation was based without prevarication on her current
flat, rather than the presenting problem - the former
joint residence with her husband. As her daughter was
deemed the principal client, the case was treated as a
continuing one from the previous issue of a nursery
place. However a new social worker, who had no
involvement with the past application and did not know
them, was assigned to the case on the basis of current
territorial allocation. (*Ibid* 185-9)
Since the allocation proceedings are highly routine, to
meet administrative demands in finite time, allocation is
limited to existing need categories. These tended to be
'non-legal' because of the Court and lawyers' delegation

to the Social Services Department as in-referrers from their own insitutions. Once a problem fits an existing fact category, search beyond the immediacy of the presenting problem tends to cease ('foreclosure'). Coding involves, for the same reason of administration pressure ('satisficing' rather than 'maximising') the 'first available' rather than 'ultimate best'. Decisions may often be taken or determined before the official allocation phase. All these routines are heavily dependent on documentary material which is given special credibility status ('factisation') and displaces undocumented material; incidentally this weakens the position of the client in the process of definition. One may also interject that from the experience of the client, to code and allocate in any way that might suggest legal action, was considered inappropriate from the start:

Smith concludes from this case:

> "Not only is 'Need' here a professionally and specifically situated construct but also that it is in substantial part an administrative constraint <u>used</u> for distinct management and organisational purposes." (*Ibid* 190)

The value of ethnomethodological work such as Smith's is that it encourages caution. It appears that even when one rigorously applies taxonomic classificatory devices of need (such as Bradshaw's), the actual practice of officials in institutions may disrupt or subvert such definitions. This makes it all the more important to attempt to develop a bedrock definition of what is <u>not</u> need.

4 What Clients Do

Need as Cost/Benefit Process

It can be argued that an exclusively normative (expert or professionally defined) conception of need risks devaluing the potential client, to the extent that problems become divorced from those with them. Normative conceptions of need also risk splitting response from problem, whereas the two are, for the person with the problem, intimately connected. Certain aspects must now be clarified.

First, a problem is not recognised as such until it is perceived as a resolvable issue; until then it remains a background condition of existence, such as the inevitability of ageing and mortality. The recognition of the phenomenon as a resolvable issue necessarily raises the issue of acquiescence or activity. This logically precedes the issue of mode (though often not in practice; at the level of practice there is a close connection between the two). Different writers stress either 'intertia', such as Curran, (1980, 13) or 'autonomy', such as Kay's finding that 61% of tribunal appellants had a clear preference for representing themselves. (1984, 51) It is usual for a choice to be made between these two states. The issue of mode subdivides into segments; whether to resolve by oneself or through the intervention of others. (Renshon 1974 Ch 16) If the latter is chosen, there may be the further question of variety of mode. (Vidmar 1980) At the most primitive levels there are a series of decisions to be taken including primitve cost/benefit appreciations, which come to characterise the whole business of defining need. What experts tend to underplay is that all these processes will go on independently of and prior to involvement with agencies of any kind.

There are a number of studies of legal need and legal use which exemplify or even highlight the cost/benefit function. Curran sees three factors in the process. First the type of problem itself, and second, the intensity of disruption involved. This will of course have different effects for different groups and individuals; she found for example that 66% of white tenants 'lumped' when faced with an eviction notice compared to 17% of black tenants, and attributed this to the much tighter housing market that blacks had access to. (Curran *op cit* 15) Third she provided evidence that the probable effectiveness of the lawyer in achieving the desired outcome, at a cost reasonably related to the potential benefit, was a factor. (*Ibid* 13)

On economic cost one American study found there was a fairly consistent tendency for surviving spouses to consult lawyers more as the size of the estate of the deceased increased:

$5000: 15% - $9999: 30% - $24,999: 54% - $50,000+: 64% (*Ibid*)

'Costs' should be broadly construed and include waiting time, (Ashworth 1984, 57) 'fuss' and the effect on wages. (Thamesdown Law Centre 1984, 34.2) But it is becoming clear that these factors are secondary to the issue of autonomy, an important psychological component of that, being self-confidence. (Matthews and Weiss 1967, 231-5) A further, often unconsidered, factor is whether the remedy sought will in reality work effectively. (Marks *op cit* 918, Reifner 1980, 38)

Another important and complicating feature in the cost/benefit transaction is whether there are viable alternatives:

> "Need judgment is based on acceptance of relative valuations of the welfare consequences of alternative intervention in relation to their costs." (Culyer, Lavers and Williams 1971)

and at the level of practice:

> "Although the cost/benefit nature of the need judgment has long been recognised, need studies conducted in the social sciences rarely take into account a wide enough range of factors necessary for a sound cost/benefit judgment ... The studies of need ... rarely probe the alternative streams of welfare consequences that follow from the

application of different services. For instance few
of them investigate the consequences for shortfalls
in subjective well-being of receiving different
packages of services. Indeed they assume that there
is no choice to be made between alternative ways of
achieving a desired set of welfare consequences.
(*Ibid* 41) Those who have designed Need indicators
have neglected the implicit cost/benefit nature of
the need judgment as much as those who have designed
the Need studies." (*Ibid* 143, Attfield and Dell
1989 Ch 3, secs 4, 6, Ch 4)

If no alternative is relevant and action has been decided
on, there is only one such transaction: to act oneself or
through an agent. But if there are alternatives, for
each positive response which yields a net benefit, the
quantum and relativity of net benefits of other responses
will have to be weighted, however crudely or primitively.
(Cass and Western *op cit*, Mayhew and Reiss 1969, 309,
Marks *op cit* 918, Grossmont and Sarat 1981, 124, 136-7;
L. Friedman 1971, 189, L. Nader 1979, 998)

It has become clear that the negative weights in the
scale can be considerable. Pauline Morris and her
colleagues asked why none of their 112 interviewees had
appealed from adverse social security decisions. The
prospect of a successful appeal hardly figures in their
replies which stressed the negative aspects of the
experience of going before tribunal. (Morris, Cooper and
Byles *op cit* 301-4)

In one study Menkel-Meadows stated that the use of
professionals generally involves clients losing control
over the decisions necessary to resolving problems.
(1983, 237) An earlier study by Hosticka tested this
contention through observations of 50 meetings between
indigent clients and federally funded legal services
attorneys, in two programmes, over 9 months. Hosticka
used two measures: interruptions and types of utterance
in relation to topic control and 'field control' -
control of the situation. The differences between
lawyers and clients were striking:

	Client %	Lawyer %
Question	7.0	57.0
Leading Question	0.1	21.3
Self-Explanation	2.4	10.5
Interruptions	3.9	10.4
Changing Topic	20.1	1.1
Continuation of Topic		
initiated by self	6.0	0.9
Answers	61.1	1.3

There was little variance between attorneys. (1979, 599
T1, T2)

A few writers have drawn radical conclusions from a consideration of the cost/benefit analysis of legal need. Not only do they tend to minimalise definitions, they attack normative definitions of legal need: (Rosenberg 1981, 294, 300)

> "We (lawyers) think happiness is a thing called Certiorari. Clients think in more substantive terms of friction, effort, trouble, costs, time. The pain of loss in a courtroom battle is not anaesthetised by one's recollection of the purity or elaborateness of the process."

Buckle and Buckle-Thomas made an ethnographic study of 'trouble' handling by the inhabitants of 'Johnson Square, East Waterford' against three models of the client. Model I is the 'Rational Client' maximising benefits whilst limiting costs. Model II is the 'Misguided Client', who is acting on imperfect information. Model III is the 'Lost Client' who is consistently thwarted and constrained - largely by making the cost/benefit calculations inaccurately - so that the cost of use is significantly in excess of the value of using the services.
  The study showed that self-help was clearly the first choice, then networks of close neighbours, followed by 'the City' - municipal institutions including the police. Finally came a mix of local notables, the City Council politicians, then 'the Law'. They concluded that the inhabitants were nearer Model I and II and did not fit Model III. The exceptions were the young as 'outsiders' and old as 'dependent'. There were other variables affecting demand, in particular the type of problem. (1980, 1982, Ch 5)
  Griffiths also writing from a cost/benefit perspective is scathing: (1980 Ch 3, 31)

> "If those who investigate legal needs are not content to accept the idea that need is always relative to a price and therefore to accept the assessment of individuals of their need as reflected in their behaviour as consumers of legal services, they are equally unwilling to accept their subjects' subjective experiences of need unrelated to price."

He continues that even if one ignores the subjective aspect of experienced need and applies cost/benefit to need as an objective condition, the benefit ratios are either weak or dubious. He describes normative panel assessments as 'guesses' and their notion of need as an 'idealised' version of middle class consumption patterns - usually lawyers'. He concludes:

"In short the 'objective' conception of need leads either to the absurd idea that needs can be thought about wholly independently of the costs of satisfying them or to a substitute of the observer's ideas about the benefit of legal services for the ideas reflected in the actual behaviour of actual consumers." (*Ibid* 32)

Self-Representation in Criminal Justice as a Cost/Benefit Process

So far no attempt has been made to isolate factors that may contribute to defendants not becoming clients. These can include psychological and cultural predispositions but also process related matters, typically plea, offence and possible sentence. However they rarely present themselves as discrete matters in this way, and particular factors can cause tension in opposite directions.

In the field of criminal justice the Toronto study brings out the defendant's perspective: (Ericson and Baranek 1982, 76):

"One of the few relatively autonomous decisions available to the accused concerns the acquisition of a lawyer."
The potential benefits include specialist 'recipe' knowledge and access to other crime control agents to negotiate.
The costs included the financial burden for private representation and loss of control over decision-making."

This research also showed that the cost/benefit analysis by defendants in general led them to favour self-representation[1] for plea and trial, but not for sentencing. (*Ibid* 79-80 T3.1) They consciously recognised that once an attorney took on their case they lost control of it and accepted that as part of the decision to seek representation.

Economic cost is often envisaged, after ignorance, as the major reason for failure to take up legal services. Neither of these reasons deserves the prominence they are given, even though they are real factors. (Cass and Sackville 1975) Gregory's Home Office survey placed cost third, at 22% of responses (1975); the Sheffield survey placed it second, at 21% and the Toronto survey placed it third, along with other related reasons. (Ericson and Baranek *op cit* 76)

One American study of poor, employed, unionised blacks tested attitudes to lawyer use for a particular offence, drunk driving, in relation to the financial cost of such service. Four questions were put to the respondents:

	%	ex 15 situations
A) Only a lawyer can help	53	7th
B) A lawyer would be most help	22	11th
C) Someone else would be most help	5	12th
D) A lawyer would be no help	20	6th

By counting (A + B) - (C + D) or A - D one can calculate the general sample's attitudes, without reference to particular sub-categories (the respondents were fairly homogeneous), thus:

$$(53 + 22) - (5 + 20) = 75 - 25: + 50\%$$
or $\qquad$ 53 - 20 $\qquad$: + 33%

This can be compared with the response to the other fifteen problems:
(A+B)-(C+D): Range +84 (Credit) to -58 (Lost Wallet):+26%
or A - D : Range +69 (Credit) to -61 (Lost Wallet):+ 9%

Clearly, for this group, in the situation of Arrest for that offence, one would expect at least a third to use an attorney at some stage. (Marks *et al* 1974 Ch 6) At this point economic cost was relevant, and in this study before a free legal service plan was introduced, the cost was deterrent of use. The mean criminal matter fee was $239: the range on the fifteen problems was $36 - $239. The percentage of those unable to pay for criminal legal advice was 40%; the overall range was 10% - 40%. The source of payment was cash in 84% of bills and the mean fee for those unable to pay was $417. It is clear that in that context positive attitudes to lawyer use had been previously offset by economic cost. (*Ibid* T5.11 and 6.4)
One reason for dispensing with legal representation is the additional time that it takes up. Not only are defendants often aware of this but, for example in Feeley's New Haven study, court officials such as prosecutors may ensure that they are made aware, and that it is seen as a disadvantage. (Feeley 1979, 82) In Derby's Baltimore survey defendants who were interested in legal representation almost always waived their rights when informed that there would be a 48 hour remand in custody whilst this was arranged. (*Ibid* 328, 338) Feeley estimated that the average number of court appearances for defendants with attorneys in his New Haven sample was 4.7, and cost $43.43. For defendants without attorneys, with 2.1 average appearances, their lost income per case was $19.77. The average fine was $28. (*Ibid* 23-40)

The relevance of time is further illustrated by a study of 29 courts in New South Wales:

	Median days to disposition	% less than 1 week
In Person	5	74
Legal Aid	12	41
Private Solicitor	26	27
Barrister	64	1

(Cashman 1982 Ch 8)

This point is made very strongly by Hann in his systems analysis of criminal justice in Toronto, Canada. Total appearances per case averaged:

	Liquor	Average All	Drugs
In Person	1.42	1.94	3.47
Represented	2.20	3.66	4.68

(Hann 1973 T7.8)

Days from first to last appearance, median:

	Liquor	Average All	Traffic Code
In Person	0	10	32
Represented	1	46	98

(*Ibid* T2.9)

He concluded:

"Throughout this report we have had trouble trying to disprove the hypothesis that having legal representation *per se* does not affect the costs and benefits to be expected by the accused during and after the court process - except for the statistically significant effect legal representation has in increasing the delays in court." (*Ibid* 428)

Another example closely connected to plea and charge, but where information, advice and 'guesstimates' are all relevant, is the possible type and level of penalty that may be awarded. If this is perceived as less onerous or severe, appearance in person is more likely. (Ericson and Baranek *op cit* 89) In Messier's Quebec study it was found that for Guilty pleaders, legal need arose in relation to the financial consequences of conviction, including the cost of a lawyer to satisfy that need. (Messier 1975, 53)

Also relevant but impressionistic is Burney's observation that in every court that she observed, where defendants appeared in person, pleading Guilty to speeding charges, they received reduced fines. (1979, 176)

There is some evidence that those who have been represented previously will repeat the experience, and *vice versa.* A major study of Sheffield found that 55% of those appearing in person had been represented previously, against 69% of those represented in their current prosecution. (Bottoms and McClean 1976, T6-8, 150-1, 160) However the Toronto survey found that 28% of those appearing in person would be represented in future if the costs were not too high; 8% of the represented would appear in person in future because the outcome achieved was minimal compared to the effort and cost. (Ericson and Baranek *op cit* 92) Here the attitudes - in distinction to the expressed behaviour of the Sheffield defendants - shows a cost/benefit approach.

At a more general level Ericson and Baranek, echoing their respondents, argue that a major, perhaps the major, reason for not resorting to legal representation and which links all the matters mentioned above, is that the benefits of representation are not perceived as significant, or are outweighed by the costs. (*Ibid* 79-80) Feeley makes similar observations in his study of criminal justice in New Haven. An example of rather sophisticated cost/benefit method were the New Haven defendants' responses to pre-trial diversion. Pre-trial 'diversion' is a widely used method of keeping unconvicted 'guilty' defendants out of courts; it typically involved compulsory counselling and job placement over several months. It is seen officially as a 'soft option'. Nevertheless, only 2.3% of those eligible in Feeley's sample (19 from 800) participated. Using a control group to test defendants' views that Diversion was not a soft option, it was found that between 20% - 33% of them obtained *Nolle Prosequis* or Dismissal of the charges on the record; most received a small fine, between $10 - $20. None went to prison. In short, the defendants had more accurately perceived the net costs of Diversion relative to these other possibilities, than the official version. (*Ibid* 233; also Curran *op cit* Ch 1, 19)

A number of cost/benefit examples are given in the Toronto study. In one case the lawyer was considering obtaining a psychological assessment of the defendant. The defendant thought that if he was represented in this way the judge might think that he could afford a heavier fine, and that this would be more likely if the judge was angered by the lawyer 'going overboard' with the psychological mitigation. Representation was rejected by this defendant. In all, 16% of respondents overtly rejected representation on the grounds that any concessions gained would be outweighed by delay, costs and other disadvantages. Fitzgerald's finding that Victoria lawyers sometimes advised their clients to appear in person, underlines this point. Practically all the examples quoted are explicitly cost/benefit in perspective. An example:

"... the fine for this is approximately so much. It would cost you all of that to get a barrister to go and look after you and you'll probably still be fined. I think you might just as well go out, and if you've done it, tell the magistrate you are sorry, and take your medicine and save legal costs."
(J. Fitzgerald 1977, 31-2, Wood 1967, 80)

The Australian Commission of Inquiry also found a group of disqualified drivers, 80% of whom were unrepresented; they were also younger, less skilled and less educated than the population of the areas surveyed. They accepted the fairness of this penalty and that legal representation would have been of no value to them in balancing its costs against this outcome. (Cass and Sackville *op cit* 54-5)

To conclude: clients, including criminal defendants, typically operate a cost/benefit evaluation of their total situation, using whatever information and sources are available, in deciding whether to seek legal representation. It is this process which colours their attitude to legal need. Its methods may be crude, but conceptually it may be more sophisticated than the rather simplistic views of the professionals they encounter.

Footnote

1.   R. V. Ericson and P. M. Baranek *op cit* 79-80 and
T3.1.   J. Gregory's study of the Venue decision on
Intermediate Offences in Britain 'Crown Court or
Magistrates' HMSO (1975) Cmnd 6323 shows quite
complex balancing by defendants, particularly
recidivists.

5 The Contribution of Other Disciplines

Contemporary Philosophy

(1) Need, Want, Merit; Three Elisions

Need is not a concept with a well-established lineage back to Plato:

> 'Philosophic and social science dictionaries, encyclopedias and indexes yield almost no reference to the concept of need, which seems to have been absent from the writings of the classical political thinkers as well.... (The modern interest) appears to be a real philosophical innovation.' (Springborg 1981, 5)

Two reasons for this can be suggested. The first is linguistic. If the term is absent or has not been developed then one should not expect analysis of it. The use of the word as a noun in English is modern. A second possibility is connected with the nature of the concept itself. In societies whose stage of general development, especially technological, was low and in which lack was more or less contiguous with existence, and therefore satisfaction hardly worth debate, it would verge on the absurd to develop such a concept. On the other hand where there is such potential for satisfaction, which is apparently thwarted, one might well expect such discussion. (Xenos 1989)

The Stoics and Epicureans were concerned over the issue
of false desire or wants, and their debate was revived by
Marx in the mid nineteenth century. His example was the
'false consciousness' of the English working classes'
tendency to drink themselves into oblivion in gin shops.
(Marx 1959, 116-122) The example is striking but is easy
to criticise. The first issue is whether gin was wanted
or needed. Need is partially predicated on absence and
is concerned with means for filling that lack. That was
patently not the case with gin at a penny a pint. Gin
itself was a means and the need it could fulfil was
oblivion or unconsciousness, rather than Marx's 'false
consciousness'. The example is important also for its
extrinsic, 'normative' view that people may not know what
they need, which carries with it the germ of
authoritarian control, over which Marx remained
ambivalent. The problem of autonomously or
heteronomously defined needs is of great importance
ethically and for social policy.

This study is concerned with a particular variety -
legal - of a general type of need - 'adjectival'. There
are other types of need such as functional need which is
a prerequisite for achieving some function, such as
manual dexterity for a surgeon. 'Adjectival' need is
merely jargon for those varieties of needs which can be
resolved by specialist occupational agencies. (Miller
1979, 126)

Needs are also related to wants and merit. There
are overlaps between the three concepts, which can be
employed to rhetorical, but misleading advantage.
(Feinberg 1970, 273; Hospers 1961 Ch 9) For example, one
can put forward want as need in order to intensify the
strength of an illegitimate claim for something, and one
may intensify the claim further by claiming that one
merits a response. The opposite tactic is also possible
and equally unreliable. A want is intentional whereas a
need involves a condition or disadvantaged status
requiring some remedial response. (Wiggins 1987, 6)
Again undeserving people - those without ascribed merit -
may have needs but there is no mechanistic connection
between their desert status and their need. Merit might
be relevant in deciding how to respond or in terms of
arranging rationing or priorities, but it could never
affect need status as such.

Want is the simplest of these concepts since it is
self-reflecting and merges the subject with the object
desired solely at the level of description: 'I want a
lemon sorbet and a coffee'. Merit usually refers to some
other as well as self and again merges the subjective and
objective, but at the level of prescription: I ought to
be valued therefore I ought to be responded to.

Need is the most complex of these three concepts. As
with want and merit it merges the subjective and
objective, and like merit it is not solely self
reflecting but encompasses a responding other. However,

in addition it merges the descriptive and prescriptive:
'I am hungry therefore I should be fed'. It is less bald
than 'I want food' and less brash than 'I am a gastronome
therefore I should be served quails' eggs'; here a merit
criterion is superimposed on what may be need as hunger,
but as an addition. This addition may be relevant to
response but not to need status, that is recognition of
need. Recognition of need status does create a claim but
does not necessarily entail a right to a response. (Watt
1982, 541)

The distinction between need and merit should be
underlined especially in the field of criminal justice.
If we confuse or elide need and merit, we become
embroiled in problems of moral evaluation and teleology.
(Lucas 1972, 237, Nathan 1977, 35-6) An example is an
alleged arsonist with previous convictions who seeks
Legal Aid for his legal defence. Such a defendant would
certainly have the cards stacked against his application
if his past and future moral status were relevant
considerations. Need is in that limited sense an amoral
concept in the context of criminal justice. (Springborg
op cit 261, Barry 1965, White 1974, 159)

The relation between need and want is less problematic;
needs are frequently expressed as wants, but not every
want expresses a need. Thus, if someone has a disease
for which there is at that time no medical solution known
they cannot then need, say, a kidney machine or insulin
or antibiotics, but one can want a cure, an abstraction;
and one might also need care which can be expressed as
wants of particular kinds. Once a cure has been invented
one may then need and express a want for a kidney machine
and so on, because one can then direct one's motivation
toward such concrete manifestations of that abstract aim.
(Soper 1981, 15, 21)

(2) Need: An Essentially Contestable Concept

I have attempted so far to suggest that need, unlike the
related concepts of want and merit combines the
subjective and objective with the descriptive and
prescriptive. (Nielsen 1977, 142-6, MacIntyre 1973, 1-9,
Galtung 1980, ix, Doyal and Gough 1984, 6) Further layers
of complexity must be revealed now.

Two perspectives in philosophy dominate the discussion
of need. The universalist perspective has its roots in
Aristotle's Metaphysics, though Aristotle used the
language of 'want' or 'desire'. Since this perspective
is concerned with human survival requirements it tends
towards minimal definitions. In extreme form this
approach can evaporate all practical meaning from need,
where it limits itself to the pre-conditions for human
existence: what we must have to be. Such a perspective
is close to limiting itself to functional need.

In a less extreme version, need is defined as being
those requirements for the avoidance of stated harms,

such as malnutrition, suffocation, illness and so on:
what we cannot do without. (Anscombe 1958, Mallman and
Marcus 1977 Ch 6, Bay 1968, 242) Whatever version of
universalism applies it will be stated in objective
measurable terms and will be intended to cover all humans
at any time.

The other perspective is relativist. It recognises
that different epochs and situations have produced
different environmental conditions and cultural relations
with that environment, so needs must alter with
particular historical conditions. It follows that a
check-list, a *priori*, definition of need is difficult,
even impossible. (Roy 1977 Ch 7, Wiggins *op cit* para 1)
One problem with the universalist approach is reduced by
this abstention; it is the risk of paternalist, normative
evaluation of others' need by the 'expert'. (Heller 1977
Ch 8, Wiggins *op cit* 319, 25) Instead the focus is on
the individual's own definition of need. In one version,
the assessment is of 'felt' verbally expressed attitudes.
This may be so wide and so variegated that again, 'need'
is devalued. Another more rigorous version attends to
need 'expressed' by behaviour, such as active steps to
avoid 'harm'; (Rist 1977 Ch 10, Wiggins *op cit* para 8)
in this version subjective opinion may combine with
objective behaviour. This school differs primarily from
the universalists in accepting the subjectivity of need.
Since this tends towards wide, maximal, definition,
because so much can be defined as need at different
moments in different cultures, much of what the
relativists (historical subjectivists) call need will be
dismissed as 'desire' or 'want' or even 'luxury' by
universalist-objectivists. Universalists argue that
wants and desires change over time but needs do not.
For example, to say that one needs a car, or even a Mini,
is to confuse a particular possible satisfier with a
need, the need in question being an abstraction: such as
transport, destination or mobility. Incidentally this
example is useful because it demonstrates that
'objective' need and its satisfaction is inseparable from
other 'subjective' wants or needs, such as status o
style. (Mallman *op cit* Ch 2, Galtung *op cit* Ch 3,
Mallman and Marcus *op cit* Ch 6, Masini 1980, Ch 9)

It is also being recognised that the universalist
versus historicist and objective *versus* subjective
distinction is a false dichotomy. (MacPherson 1977 Ch 2)
A more fruitful approach is said to lie in considering
the interrelations between these two poles, and in
particular which varieties of need are interacting. This
requires analysis of the influences on need perception
and their integration into a general social context,
which must include the pragmatics and politics of needs.
We need to know who decides what is a need, on behalf of
whom and with what justification or rationales:

'Very little is yet known about the politics of need
and the scope of this issue. A framework to cover
the wealth of related problems is still missing.'
(Galtung and Lederer 1977 Ch 15)

This is important because the nature of the concept of
need, as a bridge between perception and action, risks
conflating the intellectual with the political. Whilst
this ambiguity and essential contestability is a problem
for pure analysis, it is valuable in politics because a
'need' claim's compelling power lies in its apparent
bridging of the gap between 'is' and 'ought'. This
suggestiveness dissolves the conceptual difficulty and
can appear facilitative in the separate terrain of
political argument. (Condren 1977 Ch 14, Fitzgerald
op cit Ch 11) Pragmatically that may be good rhetoric
but philosophically it is a strategem of bad faith.
(Nielsen 1963, 170) It also raises another issue: the
relationship between needs (if we can define them) and
rights. (Watt op cit)
Recently this failure to recognise the ambivalent
relationship between wants and needs and the objective
and subjective aspects of need has begun to be
questioned. As Leiss puts it:

'In short, all the most important issues arise, just
in that nebulous zone where the so-called
'objective' and 'subjective' dimensions meet.'
(Leiss 1976, 62)

From this perspective the issue is not wants or needs,
both of which might state an abstraction such as 'food',
but the specificity of needs, such as: what kind of
response, (protein/carbohydrate), in what forms
(meat/fish/soya beans), with what qualities
(raw/cooked/fresh/canned), in what context (self
service/soupkitchen/restaurant/queue/voucher). In
addition one cannot separate one perceived need from
other perceived needs, for example, if the responses are
insufficient to satisfy both of two needs, then one need
might revert to a 'want' subjectively. Needs stand in
relation to other phenomena and are contingent on that
relationship. This suggests that 'need' involves a
subjective decision - a process - and is not merely a
passive condition.
These distinctions are important not only for theory
but for social policy. The false divorce between needs
and wants and the equation of need solely with absence or
lack, tends to produce a conception of need as requiring
a solely quantitative solution, to an objective
measurable problem, (Springborg op cit 200) and also
risks a de-individualised conception of persons in need.
(Pretecaille and Terrail 1985, 3) Such a response will
marginalise qualitative aspects.

Such divisions between needs and wants and the
subjective and objective reflect a dichotomy operated
consistently from the time of the Stoics concerning true
and false desires. (Springborg *op cit* 245-7) It occurs
in a variety of forms. Typical of them are:
viscerogenic/psychogenic needs; natural/socialised
needs'; immediate/derived needs; physical/symbolic needs;
true/false needs; basic/discretionary needs; lower/higher
needs; necessities/luxuries. (A. Smith 1978, 488)

The problem with these dichotomies is that the
oppositions are too extreme. In the pragmatics of need
such splits rarely occur. If we take the trite
viscerogenic example of food, it can be shown that the
greater the 'need' the more intense the symbolic activity
around it. The classical anthropological study of
responses to hunger, the 'need' for food, in societies at
the most elementary state of technological development -
is Levi-Strauss' 'The Raw and the Cooked'. (Levi-Stauss
1970, Lee 1959, 154-161) This study, and many others,
is, to stress the point by metaphor, replete, bloated
with examples of acculturation and complex symbolic
activity over food including its exclusion: temporal or
personal, sexual or locational. In contemporary society
it is argued that the psychological condition of anorexia
manages conditioned anxiety over the inside/outside,
physical/spiritual boundaries of the person by
simultaneous abstention from, and obsession about the
means of satisfying hunger; (Orbach 1986) in extreme
cases the want or need for food eventually succumbs to
the greater priority for other satisfactions. (Klineberg
1980 Ch 1, Soper *op cit*) On such evidence as this the
anthropologist Lee would go so far as to reject the
'biological' needs of the objectivist-universalist school
as the infra-structure for all activity, because the
distinction between 'primary' and 'secondary' needs is so
blurred. (Lee *op cit* 70-7)

It should be added that these biological or
viscerogenic needs are not specifically human but when
discussed in relation to animals, 'need' concepts are not
always used. Instead they are described functionally as
preconditional for life, in terms of the negative
consequences of anticipated failure to satisfy such
'need'. The notion of consequentiality will be central
to the empirical method of this work, and will be
developed further below.

Even if one starts from a full acceptance of these
dichotomies and then calibrates an hierarchy of needs
from the viscerogenic upwards, (Maslow 1943, 370; 1948,
433; 1968) one has to face the conclusion that the
highest level need - what Maslow calls 'self
actualisation' - can in general only be satisfied through
the activation or development of lower level viscerogenic
needs. (Veblen 1912, Springborg *op cit* 185) The
fulfilment of such ranked needs reveals a circularity in
the practices of response. This point can be illustrated

by the much-cited evidence from Sahlins' study of Kalahari Bushmen. (Sahlins 1974) The Bushmen recognised the benefits that modern medicine could bring to their health 'needs'. In response to this perceived value of some medicine, like vaccination, a clinic was established by a charitable foundation. However, this response to need imposed a cost on another level of the Bushman need structure, hunger. This need was not attended to by the foundation. Bushmen gather in order to satisfy that need in their environment; also nomadic gathering is their 'response' to their need of 'self-actualisation' *qua* Bushman. (Maslow *op cit*, De Charmes 1968, Renshon 1974, Fitzgerald *op cit*) Given those three simultaneous 'lower' and 'higher' needs, the constraints imposed by the settled existence required by the medical centre resulted in the centre being completely ignored. Illness continued to be perceived as simply part of life about which little could be done and was not defined by the Bushmen as a need/problem since no appropriate response was available.

To sum up, to divide need into separate biological and cultural compartments is to make a false dichotomy - with practical consequences, such as rigid standardisation through 'aggregative thinking' about individuals' needs. Needs occur as the products of interactions, often between various histories, contexts and desires. It should now be clear that the experience of need is inherently a dialectical activity in which cost-benefit transactions of some kind, not necessarily articulated, occur. (Leiss *op cit*, Springborg *op cit*) Every state of need has simultaneously a symbolic and material aspect. Impulses are mediated or transformed by cultural forms into need, conscious expressions of desires seeking an external response. These in turn may become set into patterns transmitted from one group or generation to another. These processes break down any simple interaction between the drives of behaviourist psychology and the means for gratifying them since it becomes over time impossible to consider the first outside the context of the second. Thus need is a multi-dimensional relationship, a dialectic between means and end, between individual and society. In the light of the foregoing one can also restate need as "expression" as much as "consumption". This is not a novel idea but its policy implications are usually not noticed. The idea originated with Veblen's 'Theory of the Leisure Class' in which he postulated *homo distinctus* who expresses himself through the medium of 'conspicuous consumption'.

Much of the difficulty and confusion attending discussion of need arises from conflation of the recognition of need with those responses to it. The confusion arises because, as we have seen, individuals rarely have a need solo: there is competition, choice in one's own needs and costs and benefits to be weighed in assessing priorities. Beyond that society has its own methods for evaluating needs in terms of response. Often a bi-product of a decision not to respond involves the rhetorical device of redefining a need as a want. That I argue is not conceptually proper: whether a need exists or not is a separate and prior question to questions of response. Although I agree with much of Wiggins' discussion, cited above, he does tend to conflate the recognition of, and response to need. (*Op cit* 16, 23, 27)

In summary need is a complex concept. It impinges on want; it contains the subjective and objective; it is necessarily descriptive and prescriptive, linking internal demand and external response; and it is a function of expression as much as consumption, simultaneously combining the material with the symbolic. These are the hallmarks of an essentially contestable concept.

6 The Contribution of Other Disciplines: Social Administration

Bradshaw's Taxonomy of Adjectival Need

A Method for Classifying the Problem

Before one can attempt to analyse legal need as a particular variety of adjectival need, further consideration of adjectival need is necessary. This is because the taxonomy of need introduced by Bradshaw assists clarification of the essentially contestable concept of need. (Bradshaw 1972)

Needs are negatively perceived situations where solutions are perceived as being possible; needs are recognised as being of a particular type, by reference to the perceived relevant mode of response. This example of the general set of elisions discussed above links the need situation and end-in-view by the means envisaged. The means become the defining 'adjectival' term of the need situation. Thus, if one was to define one's need solely or primarily in terms of a translator in a courtroom situation, one could be said to have an 'interpretative' need rather than 'advocacy' need.[1]

As has been said earlier, one perspective on need stresses the role of the expert in defining needs and attempts to do so universally and objectively. The other perspective stresses the centrality of the individual subject to the defining process and is sceptical of generalised definitions. Bradshaw constructed a taxonomy of need which employs both perspectives. Resort to his taxonomy is easy and certainly enables one to clarify arguments about adjectival need.

Supply Side

'Normative' need is that defined by an expert as a desirable standard such as a minimum diet, vitamin intake or maximum dosage for a given category of patient. In law, s.21 of the Powers of Criminal Courts Act 1973, providing that magistrates must offer representation to a defendant if they are considering imposing a first time custodial sentence, is a response to a particular 'normatively' defined need. Bradshaw makes some comments on this variety of need. It may not, he says, correspond with other definitions; it may be tainted by paternalism; there may be conflicting expert standards[2] and values may enter into the definition which would reduce its stability. The word 'expert' should not be accepted blindly in any event.[3]

Demand Side

'Felt' need is quite simply 'want' and such 'want' may well be influenced by the limitations of perception, for example whether or which services are available; and by psychological and ideological factors such as pride or fear or greed. Thus, if a probation officer is willing to speak for a defendant after conviction and before the magistrates pass sentence, the defendant might decide that the lawyer is unnecessary for these circumstances. Or, on an 'intermediate' charge, when there is a choice of venue between Magistrates and Crown Court, a defendant who wants to plead guilty might choose the Crown Court because he prefers its atmosphere: a solemn judge, the empanelled jury and the bewigged barrister instead of a suited solicitor.

'Expressed' need is 'felt' need translated into action, or economic demand. Unlike the previous example, a defendant might be persuaded that feelings over a particular Court's ambience are not sufficient grounds for making such a choice; that one ought also to consider the conviction rate differences between the Courts, and their different sentencing powers. If the defendant then switched the choice to the Magistrates, that would be 'expressed' need. Frequently, the 'expressed' need is taken as synonymous with 'real' or 'objective' need. Caution is necessary in going that far. One reason for hesitation is that a lack of action may itself be 'objective' and 'expressive', even when it is combined with 'felt' need. This is rather a basic point in the argument. It is being suggested that decisions and actions are not necessarily simple reactive responses, but may involve conscious or unconscious weighing up and balancing of sometimes conflicting paths of action, as with cost/benefit analysis.

There is a fourth category in Bradshaw's taxonomy 'Comparative' need, which focuses on those with and without responses to their need. We will return to this to develop it further below

Applying Bradshaw's Taxonomy to Legal Need

I shall now exemplify and discuss each of the axes of Bradshaw's taxonomy in relation to the issue of legal need, commencing with the two Demand side axes, Felt and Expressed need. Then the supply side axis of Normative need is considered with an additional category, Imputed need, which will be explained at that time.

Demand Side: Felt Legal Need

Felt needs are usually elicited by questionnaires (with their attendant problems). The subjectivity of Felt Need responses must be restressed here: they may be wrong-headed but remain the felt need of the individual respondent.

A criticism of legal need studies has been that they study historic or existing services and do not leave open the possibility of new options. In this connection, the image of the service which is relevant to satisfaction of need is important, and the questionnaire may not elicit this. Again there is a risk of foreclosing choice where, in the perception of the person interviewed, a choice for A implies the exclusion of B - indeed whether a choice is offered at all, with or without price tags. Finally the borderline between felt and expressed need may be crossed by the administration of a questionnaire, which can be interpreted as a surrogate opportunity for market expression.

Some general findings from research on 'felt' legal need are now presented, before reference to the focus of this book: criminal justice.

(i) Effects of Previous Experience

Attitudes do not always arise in an intuitive way, but may be shaped by previous experience. The categories of 'Repeat Player' - such as recidivist in criminal justice - and 'One-Shot Player', - such as 'No Previous Record' in criminal justice - are relevant here, as are 'Winner' and 'Loser'. An example from dental medicine was found through the administration of a questionnaire to those expressing need by voluntarily attending the waiting room of a dental hospital. The Repeat Player regulars were less frightened and more optimistic about their expected treatment. The One-Shot Players were more anxious and estimated that they would need more treatment and expected more criticism from the dentist. One can see that these attitudes might deter patients and that an unpleasant Cost/Benefit transaction may occur between felt pain and psychological anxiety before need is expressed as demand. (Kent 1985, 259) One can also speculate that from those who have not visited a lawyer's office previously there might be similar anxiety and over-estimation of the problems to be dealt with, and costs.

Another, perhaps predictable, factor in felt need for future transactions comes from Reifner's study of tenants in Berlin. (1980,46) He found that of those who had successfully sued their landlords, two-thirds had a positive attitude to the legal system, whereas two-thirds of those who lost their cases has a negative attitude.

(ii) Effects of Attitudes to Lawyers

A Yale Law Journal project used 28 attitude questions to test the hypothesis that persons with more positive attitudes towards lawyers are more likely to use lawyers. This showed that personality traits, ethics and helpfulness of lawyers made no statistically significant difference in lawyer use. Positive attitudes towards appropriate occasions for lawyer use and negative attitudes towards judges and trials were significant in promoting lawyer use. However the entire equation, although significant at the .05 level, explained only 1% of the variation in lawyer use. (Yale Project 1976)

Morris and her co-workers interviewed 112 people in two London boroughs and isolated a number of psychological dispositions, prejudicial images and ideological constraints, all of which affected feelings about legal solutions and problems. (Morris *et al op cit*, 301, 311-6) These include their contradictory images of solicitors' competence. On the one hand they were seen in the abstract as being effective people with broad competence. However at the level of concrete practice they were seen as working in a very narrow field. They also had strong differential perceptions for different kinds of lawyers. One of the concrete practices for which lawyers were seen as valuable was for when one was 'in trouble'; in such cases one needed a 'proper lawyer'. What a proper lawyer is becomes clear by contrasting their perception of Legal Aid lawyers, who were assumed to be different and were described as 'rubbish lawyers'. These attitudes meshed with strongly held class attitudes to law and justice in the respondents; both were what one could afford.

(iii) Psychological Aspects

There are psychological barriers to expressing demand for legal services. Morris found that those interviewed tended to want immediate results from professionals and not to want delayed gratification. This was combined with a tendency to delay intervention until a crisis had broken. In these circumstances there is a risk that help will be forthcoming too late and be inadequate. This gives rise to a cycle of resentment and powerlessness.

The need for representation is connected with personal confidence and ability to articulate in public with strangers. A Yale Law Faculty Project was able to test this in relation to purchases of 'D-I-Y' kits for uncontested divorce. The researchers asked those who had purchased the kits but not proceeded to court why they had not done so; 30.6% said that they lacked the confidence to proceed without professional assistance. (Yale Project *op cit*, 104 T.0)

Felt Need Features in Criminal Justice

In the past there has been a consistent tendency to ignore or underplay the views of defendants in research on legal need. The defendants' views are, of course, only one set of perspectives in the criminal justice system, but it is only recently that serious attention has been given to them.[4] Once a system of response to purported need is established, and defendants fail to take up or refuse what is provided, their perceptions become too important to ignore.

(i) Ignorance

Prior to the problem of legal need is legal consciousness. There is some evidence that defendants who have basic ignorance of law and legal institutions - such as the difference between a criminal charge and a civil action - are unlikely to have developed views on any subsequent issues such as representation. For example, a survey in Wales, on the County Courts, established that 55% of respondents thought that the County Court, with its exclusive civil jurisdiction, was the appropriate venue for shoplifting trials, and 34% thought it was for parking offences. (National-Welsh Consumer Councils 1979 T33) The Ontario Joint Committee on Legal Aid received information that some defendants did not apply although they knew of the existence of Legal Aid, because they believed that a previous conviction disentitled them. This was not based on survey evidence, but if that was the case it was a variety of ignorance - and a reason for not applying. (Ontario Joint Committee 1965, 20)

(ii) Defendants' Attitudes to Legal Representation

Criminal charges certainly are matters which people tend to describe as legal. In general the courtroom is seen as a place where legal representation is normal, and this includes criminal courts. The poor and defendants have a 'highly traditional' view of this. However, there are important qualifications to be added to this generalisation. For example, in Messier's study in Quebec, attorneys were seen by the poor as inappropriate to juvenile justice, and in general as a final resort. (Messier *op cit*)

One factor is personal morality in relation to the morality of the criminal law. For example, Messier found a very low perception of social security fraud as a legal problem amongst his poor respondents (16.7%). Similarly, where the crime is associated with a particular group, as with juvenile drug taking, public definition of the problem as legal may be reduced (17%). (*Ibid* 73 T4.1) In both these instances a further factor may contribute: low exposure to the problems in question, (*Ibid* T1) though in general criminal defence matters were most readily granted a legal dimension of all the problems considered. (*Ibid* 52) Messier's study is valuable for isolating those items in criminal cases which defendants perceive as involving legal needs. They divide, unsurprisingly, around plea, which will be considered later.

Conclusions on Felt Need

The difficulties inherent in all attempts to elicit and survey attitudes are present in surveys of legal problem solving. They occur at two levels: method and interpretation. Illustrative examples have been presented, as have the main findings of surveys on attitudes to legal services for problem solving.

From these some concluding remarks are now drawn. First, there has been a consistent tendency to oversimplify the questioning, in particular of the priority and costs, both material and symbolic, of seeking and receiving legal services. Second, one has to consider specific problems' in relation to these general findings; here the example of criminal defendants is pertinent, as it has features which by the nature of the process differentiate their need issues from others. Finally, the major study of Meeker and colleagues in California suggests that the ground of attitude research is so unstable that one should at least turn one's attention to objectively expressed demand for legal services. (Meeker *et al op cit*)

Demand Side: Expressed Need

This category of Bradshaw is the equivalent of economic demand: of observable, existential acts to meet a need by a particular means. Superficially this is an attractive measure for both met and thwarted need. A recent example is the statement by the Chief Executive of the Pharmaceutical Services Negotiating Committee that it is now common for medical patients, with multiple prescriptions, to ask chemists which is the most important item and then to drop the other items because of the prescription charges which may exceed the retail cost of some items. (The Times 1/3/1988) Typical of such measures are waiting or transfer lists and times.

Expressed need measures operate on a whole range of assumptions, which are frequently given no weight. The Scottish Royal Commission on Legal Services noticed that legal need would fluctuate with the degree of formalisation of relationships and the volume and complexity of such relationships. (RCLS (Scotland) 1980 I 2.3 - 2.6)

The result is a tendency to omit those who do not act at all, and to omit collective demand, politically expressed, often for new services. In this context it is significant that there have been no such campaigns for novel legal services by lay persons in Britain.

Active participation in the process appears to increase demand. An unusual, possibly unique, campaign to democratise Legal Aid by large-scale participation of possible clients in the organisation and setting of priorities occurred in the state of Hawaii between 1974-1976. The effect of the campaign was to transform Legal Aid from being a 'divorce-mill' in the main island's capital for 4,000 a year out of an estimated eligible population of 180,000, to one covering much broader legal topics such as social security, public health and housing for the out-islands and their rural populations. This resulted in the voting of a 30% increase in funds by the state legislature. (Fuller 1977, 40)

Again, if the original response was unsatisfactory, later felt need may be unexpressed or taken to a different service; there may be a relationship between the response to expressed need and future expressed need.

Expressed Need in Criminal Justice

In some instances it is possible to determine need by observing behaviour. This is an infrequent method, and is usually a bi-product on some other focus of interest.

Before Criminal Legal Aid became generally available, subject to financial testing, offers of assistance were made by the Courts where defendants lacked representation. The last year that figures were published showing the refusal of such offers was 1968. At that time the rates were:

Committal - murder	0
Assizes	0
Committal - other	6.8%
Examining Magistrates	16.3%
Quarter Sessions	18.5%
Magistrates	19.2%

(Cmnd 4098 (1968) TXV11, 227)

Clearly there is some degree of correlation between venue and acceptance of assistance. In the lower courts expressed legal need was around 80%; in the Assizes it was 100%.

In a few contemporary situations, legal assistance is offered or available proactively, typically in the Duty Solicitor schemes. A study in Cardiff over a 3 year period found a refusal rate - expressed non-need - at between 22.3%-23.4% per annum. (Thomas and Smith 1978, 324 T1, T2) Similarly convicted offenders, considered for their first experience of custody, must be offered legal assistance under the Powers of Criminal Courts Acts 1973; one study of 293 young offenders found that 2% refused such offers, and a further 3% had accepted, but not taken up such offers. The latter group is yet another example of the difficulty of assuming any direct link between felt and expressed need. A further example of proactive legal service is in s.30(7) of the Criminal Appeals Act 1974 regarding advice on appeal on conviction. In one study 45% of those wishing to appeal had received no drafting assistance. In terms of 'normative' definition that must constitute 45% unmet legal need, but it is not possible to go beyond that maximum in terms of felt or expressed need because we have no information on the opinions or actions of these would-be appellants; such a deduction might have been possible if we know how many failed to maintain their appeal. (Bottoms and McClean op cit 183-7)

A Lord Chancellor's Department survey examined 3,000 cases relating to 5 offences in 59 magistrates' courts. The pattern for appearance in person for these offences was:

Drugs offences	73%
Shoplifting	63%
Average	59%
Crim. Damage; Supp. Ben. Fraud	58%
Multiple charges	47%
Assaults on the police	25%

(LCD 10/1983 T10)

We shall return to this kind of evidence, but it shows that there is some link between offence charged and representation. At the same time the Committee on Legal Aid under the then Lord Chief Justice, noted that 63% of refusals of Criminal Legal Aid were on the grounds of adequate means of the defendant. However the Committee also noticed that of those so refused, only 34% appeared at their trial with privately retained lawyers. (Cmnd 2934 (1966) para 42) In Bradshavian terms we can interpret this as a maximum of two-thirds of those refused may have been both feeling and expressing legal need, which was not met. We can only say a maximum, because we do not know what other matters may have entered into their behaviour and any choice they made.

Presumably the single dimension of finance would have been central to this particular group.

Supply Side 'Normative Legal Need'

Normative need usually involves the application of a published standard. Experts often use different standards, and it may be difficult to choose between them. For example one might assess the harm that occurs if the need is not satisfied, whereas another might assess the characteristics of those in receipt of whatever need is provided for, and assess the purported benefit over the previous situation. There are also non-'objective' pressures on experts' definitions including demand, organisational requirements and political climate. For example Clayton found a variation in standard in four studies between 1965 and 1976 from one which considered 5% of the elderly to be in need of a service to one which found 27%. (Clayton 1983, 213)

Contemporary writers tend to be sceptical of normative need definition by experts or professionals:

> "When we inquire about need we are adopting an extrinsic perspective on the human actor...naively he or she does not know about needs...." (M. Smith 1977, 131)

Wallace argues that there are acute epistemological problems in normative definitions of others' needs. He objects to the fact/value separation usually asserted by experts, because they are often inter-linked, in that the field within which the relevant factual phenomenon emerges is itself a matter of choice, in which motivation plays an important role. He repeats that definition is extrinsic and adds that:

> "defining a problem as legal is a political judgment, especially when expert (normative) and client (felt) differ". (Wallace 1981 Ch 4, 71)

He continues by suggesting that the expert may re-define the felt needs of the client and therefore the type of action to be taken.

Two Problems of Normative Legal Need

(i) Normative Definition and Official Definition

The Baltimore example cited previously as a typical example of this type of research, is typical in another respect in that it is prescriptive. On every item mentioned there were detailed prescriptions. This raises the important issue of the link between normative and official definition of need because, it is when the normative and official marry that the problems mentioned above cease to be academic.

There is irony in Zander's statement that:

"The concept of unmet legal need is in fact a very elusive one, difficult to define and difficult to quantify. Whereas ten years ago it might still have been controversial, it is now officially accepted that there is an unmet need for legal services." (Zander 1976; 1978, 280)

He is referring here to the recognition given to the concept by the Lord Chancellor's Legal Aid Advisory Committee. (23rd Report 1973, 36) What Zander does not do however - and this is a matter of historical record rather than an attack on modesty - is mention the dominant, almost exclusive, role that he played in the achievement of official recognition. Such recognition included his quantitative, and programmatic approach. Professional hegemony was particularly marked in the Royal Commission on Legal Services of England and Wales, in which Zander was again acknowledged to have made almost the sole impact on need evaluation. (Elliott 1980, 1-12) Luckham commented (1980, 543-5):

"critics have argued that it is precisely because the profession has appropriated a field of knowledge by reference to which it can define clients' needs and control the market for their services that law has been mystified and clients exploited.

...The Commission's failure to discuss alternative views on the profession to its own does not even serve the interests of those who would have liked a reasoned defence of professionally organised and controlled legal services...

...No more than mentions in passing the fact that members of the profession have played a large part in political life (2.25). The economic functions of the profession are also inadequately treated (2.19)...

...cooperation with other specialists is noted on the whole with apprehension..." (Garth 1981, Ch 2; Stephens 1985, 77-82, Huber 1976, 768)

To link the official definition of need with the non-objective and non-neutral imperatives, that can underlie normative definition of need, I shall cite an over-dramatic example. The point is solely to show what can, rather than what must occur, and that it did link occupational problems and state politics in the official redefinition of legal need and professional services.

Between 1923 and 1930 the number of attorneys in Germany increased by 35% without any equivalent increase in legal services. There was a separate legal advice association, similar to NACABx. The Council of the German Bar Association negotiated with the legal advice association for participation in their centres. The National Socialist party had representatives on the Bar Council and were able to promote directives for legal advice, incorporating the notion of 'Legal Welfare' which was part of the aims of the legal advice association for participating in their centres. 'Legal Welfare' had a meaning which was distinguishable from 'advocacy'. With advocacy the Bar represented one party, whereas with 'welfare' the interest of the state was paramount; the client's interests (seine Rechte) were subordinate to those of the state (das Recht). This alteration in the definition of general legal services was an essential moment in the move for the National Socialist takeover of the legal system and the subjugation of the independent bar. (Reifner *op cit* 238-9, Willig 1976, 1)

Ironically, since first finding this material and reporting it, the NACABx has for the first time become concerned for its independence in relation to its dependence on public funds and the possibility of allocation of particular categories of problems to it by the Legal Aid Board constituted by the Legal Aid Act 1988.

To sum up, one of the main risks of a normative definition is that it may impose values alien to the client population and imputes needs which may not exist in felt or expressed form. (Soper 1981, 5-6) Mayer comments:

"the basically empirical claim that 'the people' levelled and free of restraints do not really know what is best for them. This is a claim which weighs heavily against the impressive intellectual credentials of democracy, and it has served as a viable instrument of political elites through history who have justified their rulership on the presumption of offering enlightened conceptions of human needs." (1974, 197)

(ii)   Imputed Need

The term 'imputed' need originated in Illich's classic polemic against professions. (Illich 1977, 22) It is treated separately from normative need to make it clear that although the risk of imputed need is present in normative definition, normative definitions are not in themselves imputative. (Runciman 1966 Chs 8-11) Imputed need is in Bradshaw's terminology more than the presence of normative need and absence of felt and expressed need; it involves the manipulation or coercion of evidence or opinion to fit the needs of the expert.

The only empirical study of need creation - for odorised and deodorised commodities - explicitly rejected all typification of need including normative and imputed varieties, despite the study providing strong evidence of the latter. (Springborg *op cit* 9, 199, 213) Leiss took the view that all wants and needs are historically and culturally determined. The difficulty with this truism is its over-abstraction and the playing down of the variety of forms of need production; it also risks dehumanising consumers. Like Illich he underestimates the degree of avoidance, resistance and counter-manipulation from consumers, (Leiss *op cit*) and that despite extremely sophisticated market research, advertising and consumer preparation, the majority of novel products fail, (Springborg *op cit* 216) largely because passive reception is not sufficient to create a market; a degree of positive psychological commitment is essential and far more difficult to promote. (Runciman 1966 Soper *op cit* 68-9, 210) An example of the necessary interplay between donor and donee was Sahlins' case-study of the rejection a static medical clinic provided for Kalahari Bushmen. This was considered earlier as the dialectical element in need.

The value of the imputed need argument is as a corrective to arrogance and paternalism by social workers, who may not even be aware that their view of the world and range of methods have as many limitations as any others and that they may be enforcing alien values on the needy as a condition of giving help.

Springborg points out the risk of theorists and administrators setting themselves up as judges of what people 'really' need. (*op cit* 251), and Illich and his colleagues argued that imputed need is typical today. Professions are seen by him as a new kind of cartel, creating, adjudicating and implementing need; from learned adviser they have mutated into a crusading and commandeering philanthropist who impose solutions on the recalcitrant client; lawyers are specifically included in the castigation. (Illich *op cit* 15-20) Satisfaction becomes a learned response which 'drowns out any desire for alternatives'. (*Ibid* 23) In time definitions of need extend from the positive to the negative, on what is not needed and in extreme cases clients are subjected to imperative need whereby they must be certificated to help themselves, as with midwifery in the USA. (*Ibid* 35-6)

McKnight continues the attack and specifically relates it to professional overproduction, for example 40% of Judicare lawyers were newly graduated lawyers. He does however exempt the professionals from charges of hypocrisy or conspiracy because he attributes the professionalisation of need to an ideology of need in which "the client is less a person in need than a person who is needed" and from whom need must be manufactured. (McKnight 1977, 73-4)

He argues, with some justification, that crime and the prison population has increased correlatively with the increase in police, public defenders and prisons, so that the services can be seen to be counter productive. (*Ibid* 75-7)

The most important consequence of normative definition is that the expert can and often does redefine the nature of the client's problems.

Another consequence is the tendency to transform the individual's problem into a depersonalised 'case'. This is not without its beneficial aspects from the professional standpoint, but it often does enter in the cost/benefit scales when the client is deciding to treat the problem adjectivally as a legal one, with a legal solution. These tendencies are not merely sociological interpretations of the professional role since the case-law itself holds that counsel have 'unlimited ostensible authority' in relation to the conduct of the case, which he might settle, compromise or conduct in any manner that seem fit to him. The only limitations are on introduction of matters totally extraneous to the original subject matter or if the client had expressly placed limits on that authority. (In re Debtors No 78 of 1980 Ch D Walton J The Times 11/5/1986)

The difficulty with the somewhat denunciatory style of Illich and his colleagues is that their polemic is not strongly grounded in empirical evidence, at least as regards the legal profession. There is such evidence available, though little from the United Kingdom. Most of it is from the USA. It is significant that a former Director of the Legal Services Corporation has not chosen to dispute the following:

"a full employment bill for lawyers, to cope with the overflow from law schools...the most extreme paternalism of the American welfare state, denying the poor what they explicitly lack - money - in favour of the goods or services the government thinks they should have. There is much validity in the libertarian argument that this approach denies the poor both the freedom to decide their own needs and the responsibility, essential to individual independence and self-reliance, to accept the consequences of such decisions...given freedom of choice demand would be much higher for food, shelter, clothing, even entertainment than for legal services." (Chapman 1977, 9-14)

The Director of the Harvard Legal Clinic Program has made similar comments:

> "It is not client demand ... We have observed many instances in which they virtually control the client's choices and are quite unaware that they are doing so...." (Bellow and Kettleson 1978, 337, 341, Bellow 1977, 119)

Black and Garth in the USA and Geerts in Holland call imputed need, 'mobilised' need and associate it with the proactive 'outreach' mode of legal services. In their view the danger is that need is assumed on the say-so of the expert and may ignore such evidence as there is. (Black 1973, 125, Garth *op cit* 4, 221 Geerts 1980, Ch 16) Flew goes further and writes of the "enforcement of the appropriate means of satisfaction"; he argues that the onus of proof be on the expert. (Flew 1977, 213-6) Abel sees the causes partly in professional self-interest and political domination, (Abel 1975, 5, 36-7) and Breger, in the day to day routine and consequent stereotyping inherent in high volume, saturated public legal services. (Breger 1982, 338-341)

One case study does exemplify imputed need. It concerned only one transaction and examines it in detail, using ethnomethodological techniques of 'conversational analysis'. The transaction involved an older orthodox Israeli man and a young woman lawyer working under the Israel Legal Aid Scheme. (Bogoch and Danet 1984, 248) The stages which occurred were as follows:

1. Due to a procedural defect the applicant's claim was classified administratively as 'National Insurance'.
2. Client, when interviewed by Legal Aid attorney, insisted that his case was 'Civil Assault'.
3. The Legal Aid lawyer did not accept this, preferring the pre-existing paperwork definition, 'National Insurance'.
4. She pressured the applicant into signing the Legal Aid application for 'National Insurance'.

The researchers used four measures to demonstrate the coerciveness of the attorney's control of the applicant and, the strategy of translating the claim into one of the routine categories handled with Legal Aid:

Interruptions of	Lawyer	Client		
Total	9%	14%		
Mid-utterance		77%		
End-utterance	70%		(*Ibid*	T1)
Conversational moves by	(Total 85 N82 N)		(*Ibid*	T2)
Opening	53.3	7.3		
Non-support: challenge	24.7	12.2		
Support				
(Maintain/contribute)	4.7	64.6		

Type of Directive by	(	80 N	8 N)
Request for action/		17.5	0
confirmation/classification		16.2	87.5 *Ibid T3)*
Discourse, forms of	(N:15)		
Recommendation		33	
Imperative		27	
Performative		13	
Questions-existence		13	
Coerciveness of request	N	79	9)
Negative Yes/No		11	0
Positive Yes/No		63	22
Wh-Question		20	0
Wh-echoic question		5	78

The researchers comment that the general mode of the client interview was modelled on the lawyer's training in courtroom cross-examination. (*Ibid* 268-70)

A debate on the lawyer's role and relationship with the client, concerned with issues such as these, occurred in the USA during 1976-1978. The initiator put forward the model of 'Lawyer as Friend'. This was defined as a person who will use all methods, not actively prohibited, to advance the client's cause and damage his opponents. It was however, stated to be a non-reciprocal relationship. (Fried 1976, 1060, 1074)

This was attacked mainly on the grounds of mistaken choice of metaphor. The polemical alternative was:

"A lawyer is a person who...treats other people the way bureaucrats treat all people - as non-people. Most lawyers are free-lance bureaucrats. (Dauer and Leff 1977, 573, Fried *op cit* 584)

Neither of these contributions descended from the level of idealism to empiricism or even much analysis. This was provided in another form by Simon. (1978, 29) Simon discussed four role metaphors for the lawyer. The last of them was 'friend'. He also took the view that Fried had intended a different meaning for his analogy, but was nevertheless scathing of the role-metaphor since it assumes a degree of personal relationship which is missing in the professional model. He wrote that if that sort of analogy was intended, the correct version would be 'prostitute' because:

"Fried celebrates the frankly exploitative alliances of convenience between desperate, selfish little men. Fried explicitly strives to infuse with pathos and dignity the financial problems of the tax chiseler and the disagreeable dowager....Fried's clients have almost no individuality, summated by friendship with a finance company." (*Ibid* 108)

Simon argues that a better analogy for what Fried had in mind was 'Champion', or lawyer as 'Hired Gun', which recognises the non-reciprocal nature of the relationship. This he develops at length, stressing the backing for his model in procedural rules and the dependence of the client in the courtroom situation:

> "in the area of the criminal law, lawyers and laymen have recognised increasingly the extent to which the lawyer dominates the client in conducting his defence..." (*Ibid* 39-60, 154)

The other models discussed are 'Para-Bureaucrat', which is seen as relevant to plea-bargaining (*Ibid* 61-89); and 'Acolyte', which is seen as relevant to cosmetic defences at jury trials. (*Ibid* 90-105)

An onslaught on the new legal welfarists by Brakel enables one to make this point more provocatively. (1974, Ch 9) He explicitly challenged the paternalistic rhetoric of some of the leading advocates of legal 'welfarism',[5] masquerading under the guise of a professional obligation to serve all who are in need, and working to priorities made for, not by, the poor. What he was attacking was the removal of choice from poor legal clients:

> "the problem is that so many lawyer-referral advocates do not know and do not care to know about the clients' needs or preferences."

Brakel's critique is important, but one should consider the conditions under which it appeared. The welfarists were arguing, and at one stage appeared to be succeeding in establishing a specialised Law Centre movement, which was intended to remove much work - typically social security, housing and consumer matters - from the mainstream sector of the profession, the private attorneys. Brakel's work is an effective ideological counter-attack, but it is limited to the question of choice **between** varieties of legal professionals. The client's dependence is assumed to be constant. Indeed a group of researchers had already noted that paternalist problem solving harmonises with the general relations of administrators and the state to citizens. (Carlin, Howard and Messinger 1965, 12, Carlin 1967)

As Partington has generalised:

> "It has been frequently pointed out that the concept of 'unmet legal need for legal services' is as much the product of lawyers arguing that they should be paid for doing more or different types of work, than the result of any objective analysis of consumer demand, actual or potential." (1982, 131)

He noticed also that the proposals for legal services for unmet need, proposed by the profession to the Royal Commission, were not costed and would if implemented be so expensive that no government would authorise it. Campbell concluded:

> "'need' operates to camouflage imperatives under an empirical guise", and "since 'need' is heavily ambiguous, empirical research and grounded theory is unlikely to be constructed." (1980 Ch 9, 201, 235)

Finally, it must be noted that there are internally generated limits on the production and distribution of expertise.

Imputed Need in Criminal Justice

A distinction has been made between normative need as professionally and externally defined, and imputed need, where such definitions are imposed or projected onto clients. In economic terms the supply side overrides the demand side in such instances. For example, in Holland the Criminal and Criminal Procedure Codes of 1890 made representation compulsory in criminal cases. (Griffiths 1977, 260) In such circumstances, where alternative paths are denied to the defendant, it becomes difficult to talk of meeting need, where that notion overlaps with an imposed obligation.

It is important not to overstate the case here, but equally it is clear that imputed need occurs in criminal justice. One form of imputed need can arise in bargaining or negotiation on behalf of a defendant which does not give the defendant's case proper weight, or equally fails to take risks that the defendant is willing to take. Both the Sheffield and Birmingham studies in England, and the Toronto study in Canada (Bottoms and McClean *op cit* 160, Baldwin and McConville 1977, 61-80) provide a number of examples of defendants apparently being 'sold down the river' through coerced guilty pleas. (Inns [1975] 60 Cr App R 231)

The other example is the public reconstruction of defendants' personalities, usually for short-term tactical advantage, but which may be immensely damaging to the defendant as a person, and who frequently has not participated in the decision to denigrate or reduce himself or herself.

One study of juvenile justice in Britain attends to this issue. The study was limited to 20 school truancy cases in Sheffield. The researchers noted that 'considerable pains were taken at times to ensure that families had legal representation - even though this could lead to quite lengthy delays, and where it could be argued that no responsibility for the delay rested with the family'. (Pratt and Grimshaw 1984, 257-9) It transpired that the effect of representation was to limit

family and defendant participation to giving a commitment
that 'things were back to normal' and that the truant
shared the same norms as the magistrates. The tendency
was to label them as weak, deprived people, who could not
cope without public intervention. Whether this reflected
the reality of their lives was very doubtful, as the
Court would, through the legal representatives, limit as
far as possible 'dreaded performances' (*Ibid* fn 22, 273)
when a family might break out of the established
discursive framework and attempt to give their own
account of the case.

An example of the public reconstruction of the client
occurs in Susan Edwards' 'Women on Trial':

> "I would ask you to look with some compassion at
> this case. It is a matter for you to decide - but
> if you look at the practicalities of the matter,
> would you sleep with this woman? What sort of
> prospect has she as a prostitute?"

> She was convicted and fined. (1984, 68)

Ericson and Baranek generalise from their major study of
criminal practice in Toronto:

> "The accused is made to feel not only that he does
> not understand the system, but also that he is
> incapable of understanding it ... A prevailing view
> is that it is necessary for the lawyer to make the
> key decisions (e.g. election; plea) ... lawyers with
> this approach place the onus on the accused to
> comprehend rather than attempting to make themselves
> comprehensible."

These authors suggest that the cause of this tendency
lies in

> "the halo effect of his professional status: what he
> says is treated with respect ... what the accused
> says is treated as suspect." (*Op cit*, 83, 96)

Wood puts it slight differently: (1967, 250)

> "The client of the criminal lawyer is typically an
> unreliable or dishonest person. Consequently, the
> status difference between attorney and client is
> disparate, taxing to the limit even the
> professionally defined relationship which is
> designed to ameliorate the problem ... lawyer and
> client can never appear as equal, as readily happens
> in the practice of business law."

Cranston adds a further factor from British experience regarding coercive advice to plead guilty: (1985, 64)

"for example, in magistrates' courts there may well be links between the police and regular lawyers - the police may well acquiesce in their requests for remands, or about the timing of cases, facilitate their access to the cells, and put business their way, provided that they in turn are not obstructive and 'straighten out messy cases' beforehand, such as ones with a 'confused plea'.

General Conclusions on Bradshaw's Need Types

'Felt' need puts the person with the apparent need at the centre. Some interesting information of a phenomenological nature can be found in such studies. However the problems of eliciting attitudes and interpreting subjective opinions are immense. The findings can be contradictory, so much so that it is impossible to draw policy conclusions from them.

'Expressed' need. The relationship with felt need is complex both chronologically backwards and forwards. More importantly there is remarkably little empirical evidence of expressed need as thwarted demand.

'Normative' need. Most research on legal need has been conducted by professionals who see themselves as part of the solutions to legal need; they therefore place themselves inside the problem which is not theirs. Such research has its own problems, for example experts may differ and the standards set up may be artificial; frequently their policy prescriptions do not follow from their findings. In addition to these problems of description and prescription, the pragmatics of response to the described need and prescribed action are sometimes at variance with both; in any event as the division of specialism in legal topics and amongst professionals increases so the difficulties of matching the two increases.

A strong form of normative need is imputed, or imposed, need where the professional definition of the situation is enforced on the client. This is a risk in all normative accounts by experts of clients.

Footnotes

1. See The Independent 4/10/1989. Trial in sign
   language at Cardiff Crown Court of Timothy Robson,
   accused of murdering Suzanne Greenhill, both deaf-
   mutes.

2. For an example of need tested by 'normative' expert
   criteria against subjective 'felt' need, see
   M. Zander, 'The Unused Rent Acts' New Society
   12/9/1966, 366.

3. An example of the difficulties in defining expertise
   has been in relation to investment advice. A survey
   has shown the shakiness of the purported expertise,
   and the Department of Trade introduced a licensing
   system: 'Money Which?' 18/9/1982 and L. Bourke, The
   Times 18/9/1982.

4. Such as J. D. Casper, 'Criminal Justice, the
   Defendant's Perspective' in the U.S.A.; A. E.
   Bottoms and J. D. McClean, 'Defendants in the
   Criminal Process' in England, and R. V. Ericson and
   P. M. Baranek, 'The Ordering of Justice' in Canada.

5. Such as D. F. Christensen, 'Lawyers for People of
   Moderate Means'; J. Carlin Law and Society Review
   (1966) 9, 25; E. Cahn and J. Cahn 73 Yale Law
   Journal 1317 (1964). See also Introduction to B. A.
   Curran, Integrated Report, OEO Contract No 4047,
   Final of 6 Reports to Assess the Need for Legal
   Services by the Poor, ABF, 31/12/1969 and Guideline
   3 of the US Office of Economic Opportunity
   Guidelines for Legal Services Programs, 5.

7 Towards a Negative Definition of Need

Developing Bradshaw's 'Comparative Need'

Almost nothing has been written about this axis of Bradshaw's taxonomy of adjectival need. Comparative need with Bradshaw, describes those with and without a particular object or service, as 'Haves' and 'Have-Nots'. The value of such description is that one may discover shared features as much as differences. The classic example of such comparative description in legal services is Galanter's 'Why the Haves Come Out Ahead'. (1975, 95) He demonstrates that although wealth and education are important features in access and success in legal proceedings, a cross-cutting category is more important, namely 'Repeat-Player' versus 'One-Shot-Player', the former having the advantages.

Unlike Bradshaw, Galanter pays some attention to outcomes. (*Ibid* 101, 114) Bradshaw's category then is one of pre-entry comparison, of those with and without a particular service. However there is no reason why comparison should not also be post-entry, that is of the condition of those with and without the service at any later point of time. An illustration from criminal justice: let us say that 10% of defendants before magistrates on charges of committing 'Intermediate' offences and maintaining pleas of Not Guilty lack legal representation (or equally it could be a lack of barrister representation). We can apply a pre-entry comparative evaluation and state that there is 10% unmet legal need in that group. If we find that the average of convictions is 70% on such charges before magistrates and that 25% of such convictions result in custodial sentences averaging 3 months, we might, applying a post-entry evaluation, find that the average was the same for both groups and conclude that there was no unmet legal need. We might add, borrowing a medical metaphor, that to assert such need from that criterion is to confuse cure with care. To continue this example we can also raise some problems with it. First, we are dealing with groups and therefore averages; need may be more properly discussed in individual terms. Second, one must in all these questions of method be sensitive to particularity. It might be difficult to specify fully such issues but there is no theoretical difficulty with refining the issues; for example one could examine need for different varieties of representative, or one could narrow down to particular offences and particular types of defendant and one could focus on smaller groups of court, or even a particular bench.

Examples of such research are difficult to find. One such is by this writer and compares outcomes at Plea, Verdict and Sentence between the two major private insurance schemes for Road Traffic offenders. (Robertshaw 1987, 671) A pre-entry comparison would only have investigated those who joined each organisation's scheme, compared to those members who did not, and possibly motorists generally. Such research is best envisaged as a type of supply orientated market research rather than as a consideration of needs.

A further illustration from that research shows the possible value of post-entry comparison:

Organisation B	London Counsel	London Solicitors
Not Guilty Plea:		
(All offences)	66.4%	38.9%
(Careless dr.)	60.7%	31.3%
(*Ibid* 675)		
Acquittal:		
(All offences)	47.7%	55.6%
(5 major offences)	48.9%	54.3%
(Other offences)	30.7%	21.4%
Fine <u>Av</u>.	£51	£48

Clayton points out that comparative method does at least escape the problem of relativist method, discussed elsewhere. With relativist method the major difficulty is deciding on a meaningful reference point or reference group. It is for example of little value comparing the needs of the defendants discussed above with corporations charged with tax evasion. (Clayton *Op cit* 224)

Clayton also points out that to use Bradshaw's method in practice is not easy. First it may not be possible to acquire information relevant to each type of need. Second the difficulties pertaining to each type may each create its own distortion. Cumulatively these, combined with the incursion of value judgments in using them may have a multiplying effect at each stage. She does not however, as has been said, disavow either the approach or methods as such.

The Relevance of Consequentialism in Philosophy

Bradshaw never developed his concept of Comparative need. It involved mapping the characteristics of those who lack a defined service against those in receipt of it. Presumably the objective would then be to alter those characteristics or to overcome them so that those without the service would be enabled to receive it. It does - like all the early unmet legal need studies - assume that something is absent from those that lack the service, apart from the service itself. This I have defined above as 'pre-entry' comparative need.

However there is philosophical argument that post-entry comparative need is the appropriate criterion for need. By 'post-entry' is meant that at some defined point or points where the service is terminated it can be evaluated by whatever criteria are appropriate against those not in receipt of it. I now submit that if those in receipt of the service are not significantly better off than those without them, there can be no need. Further, that the radical test for an adjectival need is that if a service does not meet this criterion of outcome ('consequential' need) then even client 'felt' and 'expressed' need is vitiated, at least regarding the 'cure' analogy.

A policy issue flows from this. The extent to which a response to a purported unmet need fails to meet the ex-post consequential comparative test, is the extent to which the service is wrongly charactertised as a public welfare service and to that extent is a public subsidy to a profession or occupation.

This is perhaps a strong claim, particularly as it can be seen to reimport 'objective' tests into a debate whence it might be thought to have been banished. But it is more modest than that since it is not so much 'objective' expert-labelled need that is being raised as the introduction of basic scientific method through falsification of an hypothesis: that is testing negatively for non-need.

It sounds as if this is uncongenial to at least one philosopher, Soper, when she writes:

"To scientise need is to remove ourselves as political agents from matters that concern us."(1981, 13)

In reply one can point to the preceding paragraphs, which hardly removes us from the political arena. In fact it is doubtful that Soper had any intention to disavow control groups, blind testing, and so on. My interpretation of her 'scientise' is as pejorative for 'normative'. In any event another statement of Soper supports the approach taken here:

"Tests for need claims must be by the adequacy of justification propounded for them including explanation of their own concepts and demolition of alternatives." (*Ibid* 12)

To find allies does not prove that one's cause is right, but there are philosophers who appear to take a similar view of comparative need as this writer.

White for example, says that a test for need is whether it relates, and how, to the relevant End-state and whether there is such an End-State. (White 1974, 159, 162) A number of philosophers, such as Miller argue towards a consequentialist definition of need, as that which is necessary to avoid harm. (Miller *op cit* 130-9, Doyal and Gough *op cit* 6, 11, Bay *op cit*, 242, Meyer 1974, 197, 204-210) It has to be said that there are difficulties about 'harm' avoidance, because it certainly it not a problem free concept. It is of direct relevance that Miller's principal example is of an arsonist and that his discussion centres on the need to avoid fire-raising in relation to harming that individual's 'life-project'. Fortunately, at the lower level of adjectival need for services much simpler criteria are apposite, which avoid the problems of moral teleology in a decision to commit arson. In effect all that is being said, again, is that 'merit' criteria are out of place in adjectival need recognition. It is also clear from Miller's discussion that such lower level amoral 'harm'-avoidance is within the terms of an adjectival need. Thus if a person without a particular service arrives at the same point as a person with that service, and the person without the service is by the criteria relevant to that point, not worse off than the person with the service, then whatever that person felt or expressed as a demand and even if a relevant expert agreed that the service should be provided, nevertheless the purported need is unreal; since there is no effective response to that need it fails as that 'adjectival' response.

Further support for this position comes from Galtung and Lederer (*Op cit* Ch 3, T3.2, 3.4; Ch 11 T11.1) and explicitly from the economist Williams who states that where the efficacy to treatment (response) is Zero or negative, need evaporates. This conception of need is limited to its productive effect and from this perspective need is a factual, not an evaluative matter. (Williams 1974 Ch 4, 61-8) One can take this much further. 'Zero/Negative' could be an extremely simple matter, such as more or less than £50 per week maintenance or £1,000 damages for 10 broken ribs, but price and gains can be as complex as one wishes. Further one may perform all these operations on all the adjectival responses available. Williams concluded that a service provided which does not meet these criteria can be characterised as 'care' but not as 'cure'.

One must however bear in mind that empiricist method relies on statistical comparison. Other limitations are the degree of actual comparability and the risk of omitting a relevant feature from analysis, for example one might consider that a study of driving offenders which did not examine where possible, males and females, or the young and the old, or motor cyclists and car drivers separately, would be weakened, even flawed. Clearly it is frequently impossible to cover all relevant variables, in which case good research method acknowledges such limitations openly.

There is however a more radical philosophical criticism to be made of empiricist comparison, which must be considered here. It is that one can never compare A+ with A- except under artificial and therefore drastically non-empirical conditions. Thus one may argue that unless one can show that a particular real individual would have had such and such an outcome with legal representation and another one without it, one is reduced to statistical generalisations with all their attendant imperfections. It would be impossible to do this because one would have to perform the two tests at the same time with the same persons. If alternatives are performed serially then they would not be the same persons and secondly and, more important, part of not being the same persons would be precisely their knowledge of and reaction to the earlier situation. In addition the empirical weakness of this approach will have emerged in the earlier sections of this work. It is that it is not possible for A+ to be A- since A+ would not be A+ if he was A-, this is because, for example, becoming a represented client or unrepresented defendant appearing in person involves a history, a process and a decision in each instance, so A would not be A at that instance if he had taken a different course. The only way out of this problem philosophically would be by resort to meta-empiricism by the use of clones or identical twins with identical histories. Given these insurmountable difficulties the openly exposed limitations of conventional empiricist method are the best available solution to the problem.

Zander has suggested an alternative experiment, the random assignment of cases with and without legal representation. (1976, 904) This would certainly be of great interest, but it does not surmount the problems alluded to here since it abstracts the contingency of representation from its other connections and risks making chance the independent variable.

As it happens these issues have been considered recently as a point of law, as an issue for authoritative closure, in the important case of Robinson in the Privy Council. The majority (3-2) took the view which has been taken here. This decision will be considered in greater depth in the context of legal need in criminal justice below. ([1985] 2 All ER 594; Robertshaw 1987, 338)

The Example of Medicine and Medical Economics

If one assumes that there is only one species of adjectival need in relation to a particular problem, such as medical need, from the demand perspective need exists where the ill person says that he needs medical services and in particular when he demands it by behaviour of some sort. However, the demand may not receive any response and the demand may then cease; the need does not therefore cease to exist, so demand is an ineffective measure. The same is the case where no cure exists at all, for example for dysentery before the discover of sulphur drugs. If one switches to, as does the economist Williams, supply perspective, the need does evaporate since one is not evaluating need by demand. More importantly if a service does exist, is demanded and supplied but no positive alteration in condition occurs, then one can deduce that the adjectival need was mistaken. One may still have a first order abstract need, for example for a cure, but one cannot need the cure because that was not provided. One had confused cure with care, or diagnosis and use with satisfaction. From this perspective proof of need is a factual matter linking the need-problem to the instrument of response and measuring the consequences.

Using such a consequential-comparative test for need might also allow one to reconcile the apparently different standpoints, according to Klein, of administrators and politicians to the provision of public services. Klein suggests that politicians are concerned with the visible demonstration effect of such provision, whilst administrators are concerned with cost-effectiveness. (Klein 1977, 88) These are not inherently contradictory requirements; politicians might have less interest in cost than administrators but effectiveness and demonstration affect are clearly reconcilable through consequential testing.

The limitation of this argument is precisely that it is ex post. It must therefore be qualified in two respects. First, it is necessarily probabilistic if applied pre-entry, and second, to have any probabilistic significance it would have to be tested over time on a group, presumably with a control.

Typical of such studies are medical investigations of deficiency, which include broader issues than physical deprivation - such as overcrowding, low income and interrelations of a variety of negative factors. The decision of the British Medical Association's annual conference in 1985 to mount a national study of the effects of poverty on health falls in this tradition.

A more developed scientific method combines consequential study with relativism by comparing the effects of need on those without an item or service or condition of life, with those with them. Surprising results can be obtained. For example, the well known, and still topical, finding that the amount of heart disease in U.S. conscripts during the Korean War could only be found in the oldest North Korean prisoners of war; this produced the paradox that the Americans had a need to eat less in order to survive.

A recent American example involved a study of 562 patients referred to hospital specialists by their general pracitioners. Of them 4.1% did not take up the appointment, and of them 64% suffered 'no major consequences' and 4.3% died. (Connelly and Campbell 1987, 1829)

Another simple example would be the statement of a diagnosed diabetic saying:

"I want sugar but I need insulin."[1]

This statement indicates both an understanding of need in terms of comparative consequence, and an understanding of the difference between want and need.

Another simple but striking example is provided by Doyal and Gough: the need for life support maintenance machines for victims of serious accidents. Their criterion for life is both viscerogenic and psychogenic since their human ontology recognises both consciousness and activity in the world. (*Op cit* 6, 16) If, by neurological testing, there is no possibility of future conscious activity as a person, then they argue, no harm can flow from deprivation of the machine. It follows that there is no objective nor subjective need for this support, even if others desire it, so it should be switched off. It must be added that different problems arise where there is competition for such scarce resources between those defined as needy by this criterion.

Greenberg reminds us of how this kind of 'hard nosed' approach can promote both efficiency and justice by only meeting need where it can do precisely that, exclusively. He refers to 'triage' in the First World War, whereby treatment was eventually provided only for those wounded who could probably be saved by treatment and not for those for whom recovery was improbable. This has spread to other areas of medical need where there are scarce resources; under the Calabresi-Bobbitt test the less-ill

are given priority over the more-ill, for dialysis access
on the criterion that they will be active longest i.e.
their relative benefits are cumulatively greater than
those of the more ill, and the costs deferred rather than
sunk. (Greenberg 1981 Ch 13 s.33)
   Skillen adds a polemical example: (1984, 6)

> "Earlier this year, a World at One interviewer was
> barbecueing a Liverpool Social Services official
> over the fact that a mentally handicapped child had
> been sexually assaulted by her foster-father, a man
> already known to be under police suspicion of a
> similar offence.   In response to the interviewer's
> attack...the squirming official finally made the
> point, not only that this was 'in other respects an
> excellent foster-parent but that in any case it is
> exceedingly difficult to find families who will take
> on fostering of handicapped people'.   These remarks
> were pounced on by the spokesman...as a feeble
> excuse.   But the truth is that a high proportion of
> mentally handicapped people in this country
> presently live, out of sight and out of mind, in
> conditions which make life in such a family home,
> with its perversion, a relative blessing."

Whether from the Demand side, with its emphasis on
expressed need, or from the Supply side, with its
emphasis on responses to such expressed need, a concern
with evaluation is apparent in medical economics, and far
more developed than for legal services.   Where the
response has no net positive consequences then economists
would say that there can be no adjectival need for that
response.

The Development of Evaluation of Legal Services

Evaluation of legal services has arrived late.   It
certainly has relevance to a negative definition of need.
   The historical roots of legal need research lie half
buried in the American realist movement exemplified by
Karl Llewellyn's injunction to 'study what lawyers do'.
(1930, 12) However the fervour of the Legal Needs
movement of the 1960s and early 1970s assumed that what
lawyers do would do good to those who were newly provided
with routes of access to them.   A typical English
pronouncement of the time was that so many thousands or
percentage of unrepresented defendants were gaoled by
magistrates and that this was a glaring example of unmet
legal need.   It may have been; it has to be mitigated
that such uncritical assumptions are part of a tradition,
which it would be churlish to belittle in terms of its
concern and energy, but it is a tradition with unexamined
limitations.   As far back as 1926 Gurney-Champion was
scandalised that poor people enmeshed with the law had to

receive charity from altruistic lawyers. (1926, Pref., Ch 9) He argued that this was too much of a lottery and that it is a primary duty of government to ensure equality in the administration of justice. He later discussed ideas such as Legal Aid, as part of a welfare state, and Public Defenders in the U.S.A. However he assumed throughout that the poor will use and will gain from such representation, and did not consider that potential gains could be offset by disadvantages.

Evaluative studies of representation of various kinds did occur in the USA from as early as 1969, but they were sporadic and did not become or aspire to become a normal means of examining the new initiatives of the legal services movement. The earliest such study that I have found evaluated an 'outreach' programme of private practitioners through a centralised office. It concluded:

> "The Houston Law Forum has failed positively to affect either the psychological condition of the individuals it has served or the social structure of the communities in which the clients live." (1969, 939 IX 1170)

Similarly in 1971 an evaluation of the Office of Economic Opportunities Legal Services Program produced detailed evidence, already discussed, that clients' wishes played a very minor role in case preparation and handling. (Finman 1971, 1001-84)

An Australian study prefigures the preoccupations of much contemporary research into legal services, in terms of cost and administrative overheads. Sackville found that administrative costs of Law Society Legal Aid schemes ranged from 9.1% in Tasmania to 32.3% of expenditure in New South Wales and that contributions by clients yielded nothing in Victoria and Western Australia but 36.2% of income in South Australia. (Sackville 1975 T5.16, 5.18)

An interesting example of comparative evaluation of the 'attrition process' in Holland was provided by Schuyt and his colleagues, which suggests that the 'cure' analogy in outcome analysis is not the only relevant matter for study, and 'care' aspects may be at least as important.

Discontinued Contacts:

Welfare Agency	29.2%
Client paid Lawyer	25.2%
Labour Union	22.4
Law shop	19.0
Legal Aid lawyer	15.6
Citizen's Advice Bureau	5.7

(Schuyt *et al* 1977 95)

There is one Australian study which combines comparative evaluation with 'normative' judgment in the shape of peer-review of other lawyers' work.

Thus Lawyers' views of the quality of Legal Aid work done by

	Barristers	Solicitors
At least some...is worse	-38.2%	-22.3%
Better service to L.A. Clients	+ 5.8	+ 2.0
	-32.4	-20.3

(J. Fitzgerald 1977 T5.1)

Lawyers' ratings of voluntary legal services:

Positive accomplishment only	+67.3
Nothing worthwhile accomplished	-15.3
	+52.0

(*Ibid* T5.2)

and Barristers' opinions of the Public Solicitor's office:

	Who had had no PSO briefs	Who had had PSO briefs
Worse than private practice	-36.4%	-63.6%

(*Ibid* T5.3)

These are interesting findings, particularly the latter, but they would have been more reliable if cross-referenced with clients' opinions.

In the field of social work such studies have existed on a large scale since 1970. The main factor influencing client satisfaction is any material outcome; two contributory factors are low expectations of the client receiving benefit and unexpected non-material benefits. Unsought non-material advice and assistance cause dissatisfaction when not coupled with material benefits. (Mayer and Timms 1970 Chs 8, 9)

In legal services the Director of the American Bar Foundation national survey and others have concluded that the decision to involve a lawyer relates primarily to the intensity of the issue or problem but, in addition, the probable effectiveness of the lawyer in achieving the desired object or outcome at a cost reasonably related to the potential benefit is the other major factor. (Curran *op cit* 13-15, Reifner *op cit* ch 4, 38, Marks 1976, 913, 918)

It was not until 1979 that critical analysis of legal representation as need response occurred:

"We generally assume that legal representation confers an advantage on a client in dealing with the world and that the lack of such representation works for the client's disadvantage. This common sense assumption can draw some support for the willingness

of private institutions and individuals to spend
billions of dollars a year to purchase legal
representation. Unfortunately we lack good
empirical data on the benefit actually conferred by
having a lawyer.

I have provisionally assumed a homology between
antecedent advantage and having a lawyer and
antecedent disadvantage and lacking one. But a
central theme of this paper is to make that
assumption problematic...." (Abel 1979, 5, 9)

Two commentators on the Royal Commission on Legal
Services in England and Wales moved towards a similar
position:

"the absence of independent criteria for the
evaluation of professional services obscures the
most socially significant issues. Are there popular
standards of justice...against which the performance
of the legal system can be compared?

What is the difference between lay and professional
justice and how can such a difference be justified?
(Luckham *op cit*, 543)

We are still in a state of remarkable ignorance
about how a solicitor spends his day and about his
relationship with his clients and what exactly he
does for them. True we have a new phrase unmet
need." (Cottrell 1980, 549)

From about 1980 such questions have crystalised in a
general concern with 'Evaluation'. This links with the
permeation of management accounting philosophy and
techniques to all areas of public expenditure and
especially those with a welfare function. Legal welfare
has to justify itself for the first time as cost-
effective, though that does echo the original
'consumerist' rhetoric of the Legal Services movement.
(Armstrong and Graycar 1981 ch 7, 72)
    Thus a Dutch writer in surveying the history of the
movement shows the lack of interest in substantive
outcomes, even ignoring them for the formal satisfaction
of 'equality of arms' (Geerts 1980, 220-3, Cappelletti
and Gordley 1972, 347) and noted its first criticism by
Ralf Nader in 1976. (1976, 247)
    A German writer also comments that legal need is not an
end in itself - though the meeting of legal need can be
an end in itself for those who are paid and promoted to
do so. This was recognised by Capelletti and Garth,
leading figures internationally in the legal services
movement, in 1981. They agreed that the 'first wave' of
the Access to Law movement emphasised procedure and
'outreach' in a broad way. They then argued that there

have been second and third waves, the last concerned with results and monitoring organisation and costs. (Cappelletti and Garth 1981, x-xix) However, at the same time Garth was cautioning:

> "There is and will continue to be, little Legal Service Corporation scrutiny of the actual performance of programs." (1981, 65)

Also in 1981 an Australian group published a book on 'Research and Delivery of Legal Services'. The first chapter of which was 'Thinking about Evaluation'. The author considered both objectives and methods and specifically referred to testing control groups against untreated groups with factorial design, and assessing outcomes. (Hanks 1981, 25) Later he states:

> "I cannot see why we should accept that services being delivered are intrinsically beneficial to the consumer of the service: that is a proposition which needs to be tested...look at the impact...Accordingly a quasi-experimental study. (for example the results achieved by legally aided persons with those achieved by unrepresented and privately represented persons) is a vital part of evaluating the effectiveness of the service... must weigh a substantial variety of individual and social Benefits and Costs for each programme..." (*Ibid* 31)

Problems of method in such evaluation are considered by American contributors to the same book. For example court judgments do not always determine the final outcome; failed negotiations need to be investigated carefully because one cannot assume that they are, for example, the attorney's 'fault'; professionals do other things for clients beyond winning or losing cases for them. (Fiocco *et al* 1981 ch 10, 132)

It is still exotic to find any attempt at evaluation of successful representation.[2]

It now appears that the pressure for such work originated in the USA, from the General Accounting Office of Congress and as a result the Director of the Harvard University Legal Services Program started his Delivery System study. (Cooper 1983, 86)

His general conclusions were sanguine:

> "What is most significant about the new legal services programme is the degree of continuity it shares with its predecessors."

He cited as "recurring practices" routine, standardised work, lack of research or investigation, the domination of the lawyer-client interaction and 'highly questionable settlements'. (Bellow 1977, 1981) Worse, "even in offices with relatively low caseloads, the same routine service appears". Cooper describes evaluation as

"the major issue of coming years." (1983, 247)

The value-for-money interest of the Treasury in Britain has permeated the Lord Chancellor's Advisory Committee. Whilst one may ask whether the real purpose of the Treasury is a crude cost-cutting exercise, this does not mean that a policy of evaluation is without value.

Currently controversy exists over the proposal by the National Consumer Council that Legal Aid Board investigators should pose as clients of franchised firms of solicitors as a means of evaluation of their performance. (The Lawyer, 10/4/1990, 24/4/1990)

Conclusion

In this chapter I have discussed four disparate disciplines and methods. I suggest that they comprise the strands of a unified perspective on need analysis. Those strands: social administration, social philosophy, medical economics and the recent emergence of evaluation of legal services, focus on the consequences of absence. If no 'harm' flows from that absence, or if the posited substitute gives no additional relief or positive benefit, then that species of adjectival need does not exist.

Footnotes

1. Nevitt, who is highly critical of 'needologists' such as Townsend, correctly points out that to expand the definition of need without considering its supply side, financial, implications is dangerous. However she makes the opposite error of contracting need to fit an equally problematic level of financial response. Responding to need clearly involves finance, alternatives and priorities, but need itself is an independent status. See D. Nevitt Ch 8 in H. Heisler ed. 'Foundations of Social Administration' MacMillan (1977) 116-7. The same difficulty can occur in medical economics: J. E. Spek in M. H. Hauser ed. 'The Economics of Medical Care' Allen and Unwin (1972).

2. An example is of 4 methods used by successful drink-driving defence attorneys in the DWI Journal, cited NLJ 6/7/1990, 955.

8 Testing for the Absence of Need

Comparative - Consequential Evaluation: Testing Outcomes

In the discussion so far 'harm' is envisaged as a net condition of costs and benefits. This 'harm' may be extremely difficult to calculate; these costs and benefits are not solely material and objective, but also symbolic and subjective, which intensifies the difficulty. One small advantage of the harm criterion is that in the field of legal need, the structure and ethos of the adversarial system insists on a morally neutral approach to any matters - such as the Justice model of maximised information - outside the narrow objectives of the client's crude, short-term interests in relation to each stage of the relevant process from plea to sentence. (Bellow and Kettleson *op cit*, 337)

One danger should be pointed out. Testing negatively for non-need does not thereby produce a positive descriptive residue. (Lederer 1980, 1, Brown and Madge 1982, 16) It merely reduces the area of doubt. All the problems relating to definition of need which have been discussed above remain, but there may be less to dispute over.

I have suggested that comparative-consequential definition of legal need has not happened, but should have. Although that is a useful generalisation, and not misleading, it has to be admitted that examples of such method do exist. They are thin on the ground, and in the field of criminal justice will be considered later.

Most of the examples are interstitial and not the main
focus of the research from which they are abstracted.

However a few examples are presented here to
demonstrate their existence, interest and difficulties.

Abel-Smith, Zander and Brooke noticed for example that
tenants threatened with eviction by their landlords
quitted more often when without legal advice than when so
advised (72%   52%); also that those with legal advice
after an accident received compensation more than those
without advice (66%   12%) and received more compensation
(18% £50 -; 82% £50-). (*Op cit* 167-178) These findings
may reflect different populations: those with strong
cases against their landlorda may be more likely to seek
professional help than those with weak cases.   Also the
quantum of claim in the cost/benefit decision to sue for
compensation may account for those with minor injuries
negotiating on their own account.   In the case of
compensation for injury the claimants were asked to
evaluate their compensation as

	'About Right' %	Too Low/None-wrong	% Net
Advised	42	42 + 12 : 54	-12
No Advice	3	14 + 49 : 63	-60

In net terms both groups have a negative evaluation. The
difference is that the advised are less negative, at -
12%, against the unadvised, at -60%. Whether this is an
advertisement for legal services is moot.   It may be
helpful to add that there was another evaluation, which
suggests that the groups are not fully comparable:

No Compensation - about right %

(<i>Ibid</i> 176)</div>

Advised	4
No Advice	34

However it must again be stressed that even this kind of
analysis did not occur in the original study, and that
these comparisons were almost unique in a large study.

Evaluation studies of Legal Aid or Law Centre practice
in comparison with private practitioners have also
appeared.   There is one British study evaluating a
private firm of solicitors and a law centre in 'unfair
dismissal' practice.   (Domberger and Sherr 1980)   A
weakness in the study was that the files were selected by
the solicitors.   (*Ibid* 13)   On balance, clients were
somewhat more satisfied with the outcomes of the private
firms, but had a relatively positive experience of case
handling in both types.   (*Ibid* T5, 6) It is also likely
that the private firm was atypical, both in its
specialism and handling of clients and much nearer the
law centre model than traditional practice, so the
comparison may have been more apparent than real.

In the important area of undefended divorce there is one large study in Britain. The researchers concluded:

"In terms of outcome there is no evidence that solicitors made the slightest difference. Their presence therefore must be seen in terms of emotional support to parents." (Davis *et al* 1983, 121 T3)

Finally, in the USA, Bellow has evaluated the 'Test-Case Strategy'of the law centre movement. Despite a few spectacular victories

"a number were lost and a great many accomplished little more than affording publicity for lawyers...some that 'lawyerised' the issues they raised in ways that undercut potential grass roots political organisation, and many more, which although successful were never effectively enforced. Similarly, much legislation fostered by the programs has not prevented new patterns of domination from arising...e.g. higher rents passing on the costs of new improvements." (Bellow *op cit*, 106-7, Huber 1976, 754, 761, Prosser 1983, Brill 1973, 38, 43-9)

Comparing Outcomes as Consequences

Four Limitations and Twelve Refinements

Four limitations of this approach should be canvassed. They are not insurmountable, but they raise considerable problems, necessitating large samples and complex statistics, or completely different types of method. They are:
(i)   Throughout, the emphasis has been and will remain on visible criminal justice outcomes as indicators of need. The analogy in all these instances is with medical 'cure'. There is a risk that such an emphasis could have a distorting effect. Qualitative method and research might show, for example, that care has been undervalued in relation to 'cure' outcomes - the research already cited does not at present support such speculation.
(ii)   It has been assumed and will continue to be operationalised that there is a simple dichotomy between appearance in person and representation. That misses an important intermediate possibility: that legal advice is given, accepted and acted upon in some instances by persons who represent themselves in court.
(iii) Court processes involve a large proportion of unofficial outcomes. In some instances these may be more or less open and testable, such as plea-bargaining in Federal Courts in the USA. However in Britain such openness is rare and illegal if judicially controlled. In this context the introduction of s.48 of the Criminal

Law Act 1977, allowing for pre-trial review in Magistrates Courts must have an effect of skewing which cases get to open court.

(iv) One methodological issue of negative testing for adjectival, legal, need must be considered now. It is the issue of specificity. It derives from the philosophical discussion of need, and is butressed by the concept of adjectival need itself, as a particular variety of need, whose adjectival definition arises from selection from possible alternatives. This problem is the degree to which comparison should and can be particularised. The first issue involves the desirability of maximising the variables considered and maximising similarity of all compared variables except that of representation. But additionally the focus of comparison should be narrowed and intensified maximally. This gives rise to sampling problems, because if one is to achieve both desiderata, the risk is that the cells to be compared will rapidly become too small. Thus if one compares 1000 defendants with and without lawyers matched by age, gender, ethnicity and so on, but taken from 100 courts, the focus will be far too blurred for satisfactory interpretation; if one limits focus to one court, one could only make conclusions about that court. One therefore has to risk compromise in sampling, for example by including or excluding certain offences.

These considerations arose from reading comparative work by social administrators on the efficacy of tribunal representation and is now presented as a methodological model for comparative consequential evaluation.

The primary source of the model is work by Bell in which she was said to have demonstrated the following propositions: (Bell 1975)

In welfare tribunal appeals,
Those who do not attend, are least successful;   (5%)
Those who do attend (with a friend)
are more successful;   (30%)
Those who attend with a lay representative
are more successful;   (40%)
Those who attend with a professional
are most successful;   (50%)

It should be made clear at the outset that qualifications were entered early, and later work by Bell herself, has produced the refinements mentioned here.

There are 12 such refinements.

1.   It is risky generalising from one body to another.
2.   It is risky generalising from one body to another of the same type.
3.   It is risky generalising from one body's members to others.

4. Representation is not homogeneous - either of 'friends' or varieties of professional. Earlier I gave an example of the relative combativeness and effectiveness of counsel and solicitors provided by the same motorists' organisation.
5. There is a constant tendency to generalise from insignificant samples, instead of excising them.
6. Topics of appeal are not homogeneous (5 also applies).
7. The relationship between representation and self-representation can be problematic.
8. Testing material outcomes involves an assumption that that is what is important.
9. Initial outcomes, such as negotiations or 'supercessions' may not surface.
10. Representation may be too bland a variable - intensity, and experience may also be relevant (see also 4).
11. Psychological attributes of the client have an important bearing on both representation and outcome.
12. Acceptance as a client may be as important as the decision to become one.

It is of course virtually impossible to comply with all these criteria and retain above minimum cell size for each variable in each body sampled. However what is being stressed is the need to be modest in drawing conclusions from such research. It also raises an issue which will be examined in greater detail in later as 'inverted' legal need, whether decision makers are more important than advocates.

Conclusion

In this chapter I have developed a method from a number of disciplines and activities. The assumptions of this method (comparative consequentialism) is that adjectival need, such as legal need, cannot be measured positively, but that one may be able to show negatively where it does not exist. Some preliminary considerations regarding the operation of this method have been put forward.

The hypothesis to be tested by falsification is the 'cure' assumption of the legal services movement:

'The outcomes at the various stages of the criminal process after charge are more favourable to the legally represented than for the self-representing.'

This is both a general hypothesis, falsifiable by any test, but more importantly any number of subsidiary particularistic hypotheses, some of which will be tested below.

9 Legal Need in Criminal Justice

Normative Perspectives

(1) (a) Due Process and The Rule of Law

The dominant justification for recognising need in defendants in criminal process lies in what is known as Rule of Law theory in Britain or Due Process constitutional requirements in the U.S.A. These ideas are most openly expressed in the leading American cases.

The premise upon which all intervention, private or public on behalf of defendants in the criminal process is founded, is that the defendant's burden and risk is increased with the absence of legal representation. The case, which paved the way for all the developments of the Warren Court in the 1960s was the 'Scottsboro' Boys' case of 1932, <u>Powell</u> v <u>Alabama</u> ((1932) 287 US 45, 68-9) where Sutherland J, concurring said:

> "He has no skill in the science of law....He requires the guiding hand of counsel at every step...."

A leading American writer commenting on the best known of the Warren Court decisions, <u>Gideon</u> v <u>Wainwright</u> ((1963) 372 US 335) which allowed for the public provision of legal representation for indigent defendants, wrote:

"The social significance of this opinion lies in its
unequivocal assertion of the importance of
lawyers... the confidence of lawyers in their
critical importance to society rings with an
assuredness...lawyers are not 'luxuries but
necessities' and that truth is 'obvious'". (McDonald
1983 Ch 1, 17)

If that assumption is accepted then a certain urgency
follows to provide research as to the scale of the
problem to be met.   Such research will, given the
premise, concentrate on quantification and location of
the problem so that resources can be marshalled and
channelled to the appropriate venues.   The most important
of these was the US National Defender survey in 1973.
This estimated that 65% of indigent felony defendants and
47% of indigent misdemeanour defendants lacked counsel;
the range was from 0-90% in different localities.   In
individual terms it was estimated that several hundred
capital defendants went to trial without legal
representation, as well as about 600,000 felony, 2
million misdemeanour, and 1.7 million juvenile
defendants, (Albert-Goldberg and Hartman 1983 Ch 3, 79)
in all some 4 million persons each year.
  In the UK the same had already occurred in one of the
earliest, 1967, examples of 'legal need' in popular
writing, which advocated the response of establishing a
system of Public Defenders, as in the USA:

"Of the 1,400,000 people tried in the year (1965),
only 13,500 were represented by a lawyer on legal
aid: less than 1% of the total, and only 6.5% of
those charged with indictable offences..." (191 New
Society 1967, 25)

A variety of inter-related beliefs are said to be served
by intervention, in response to such need. They include:

i.   a belief that the law enforcement process is subject
       to human error and that evidence can be unreliable
       unless effectively tested.
ii.   that the principle of legality requires that an
       accused shall have a proper opportunity to question
       the legality at every stage of his prosecution.
iii.   the presumption of innocence until positively proven
       guilty.
iv.   that guilt is a matter of legal as well as factual
       decision.
v.   that any social disadvantages of the accused should
       not hinder the defence.
vi.   that those liable to hatred because of the
       accusation against them, or simply who they are,
       especially merit legal representation.
vii.   the 'Rule of Law' as a major constitutional
       principle requires equal access to representation

(including the redistribution of legal resources, both individually and geographically when necessary).

viii 'Fairness' or 'Due Process' require intervention especially in criminal justice because of the possible drastic consequences for the accused.

ix. the individual indigent is, regardless of merit, in an extremely unbalanced conflict with the full resources of the state. Liberal democracy requires a balancing of the scales.

x. payment by the defendant as client may overstretch his resources and lead to a reduction in essential defence efforts.

xi. there is a widespread belief, including judges, that representation has, and should have, a favourable impact for the defendant, so as to buttress the presumption of innocence.

xii. representation maximises concessions in pre-trial conditions, such as bail, and negotiations over charges.

xiii representation maximises the supervision of cases by increasing the likelihood of appeal.

xiv. representation reduces the class-bias in the legal system.

xv. representation increases the efficiency of the police and prosecution process.[1]

The positive scope, and negative limits and restrictions on these ideas are subject to considerable discussion, disagreement and negotiation. A small number of illustrative examples now follow:

i. In some circumstances the type of lawyer may be more important than representation as such, to elicit relevant information and instil confidence. (Milne J (1983) 681, 686)

ii. Representation may be more important pre-trial than later; in general the earlier a lawyer is appointed the more effective the lawyer is, (*Ibid* 687) so emphasis on the trial may be misleading.

iii. Bailed defendants may need as much assistance as remanded defendants, whose needs are usually given priority in response. (Bridges 1982, 12)

iv. Assistance may extend to ancillary matters crucial to effective representation, such as investigation, forensic testing, or interpretation. (Helmes 1982 Justice 1987)

v. If need is equated with probability of severity of outcome, then it may be argued that representation is most needed when such probabilities are strongest. (Derby *op cit* 328)

vii. In the majority of criminal cases defendants plead guilty. There are differences of opinion as to whether representation is appropriate in such cases. (Borrie and Varcoe 1970 pa 116)

One might have thought that these concerns were unnecessary in the light of an apparent recognition of 'need' at the international level:

"All guarantees necessary for his defence." (Article 11 Universal Declaration of Human Rights 1948)

"Legal assistance assured to him in any case where the interests of justice so require, and without payment by him in any such case if he does not have sufficient means to pay for it." (Article 14.3 International Covenant on Civil and Political Rights 1976)

However, the enforcement on ratifying states of Legal Aid by the European Court of Human Rights was not straightforward. Article 6(1) of the Convention simply provides for an entitlement to a '<u>fair hearing</u>'. Both the major cases on this Article involved strained interpretation and dissents. The second case, <u>Airey</u> v <u>Republic of Ireland</u> (9/10/1979 ECHR) did provide for legal aid, building with some difficulty on <u>Golder</u> (UK [1975] 1 EHRR 524) which entitled prisoners to correspond with solicitors with a view to litigation. Whether 'fair hearing' requirements are contiguous with 'need' is not an easy matter.

At one end of the spectrum is an example of 'expressed' legal need, <u>R</u> v <u>Harrison</u> in the Court of Appeal (Criminal Division) 'a very disturbing case'. Harrison had been convicted by a jury of conspiracy to defraud. The conviction was quashed on the grounds that the trial was not fair. Until the pre-trial review he had paid for private representation. He then applied for Legal Aid and was refused several times. At his insistence his application was then referred to the judge, who informed him that he could have legal aid on condition he paid £1,500 into the Crown Court. Since he no longer had any funds he could not meet this condition and the trial went ahead with the defendant, unwillingly, appearing in person. The Court of Appeal did stress that their ruling would have been different if the defendant had not demanded legal representation. (<u>The Times</u> 12/7/1985 Watkins LJ)

This decision can be contrasted with an unsuccessful application rejected by the European Commission of Human Rights, [Application No. 13475 87 v UK <u>Law Soc Gaz</u> 29/9/1989] a civil case regarding alleged medical negligence. The defence was that the applicant's son's deafness was caused by the disease being treated, meningitis, rather than a massive penicillin overdose. The applicant was a litigant in person most of the time. He won at first instance, but lost on appeal. The Health Board defendant had the advantage of expert legal advice from the Medical Protection Society and Health Board Central Office. The basis of the applicant's dismissal does not on the face of it appear to have been on the basis of need but on the basis that full and fair consideration of his case had not been given and that undue consideration had been given to the weighty battery of legal expertise of the defendant.

The leading European Human Rights court case is now Granger v UK [ECHR The Times 29/3/1990], a successful Scottish appeal by a convicted perjurer sentenced to 5 years imprisonment. It is submitted here that the basis of this decision (which is not criticised) is not need based but turns on the language of Articles 6(1) and 6(3)(c) of the European Convention:

(1)   "...entitled to a fair and public hearing.."
(3)   "Everyone charged with a criminal offence has the
         following minimum rights...
(c)   "to defend himself in person, or
         through legal assistance of his own choosing, or
         if he has not sufficient means to pay for legal
         assistance to be given it free when the interests of
         justice so require"

The Court was unanimous on this point, but the factual detail is significant in this case. (Referring to Monnell and Morris judgment 2/3/1987 Series A No 115 p.22 para 56, The Times 3/3/1987)

The applicant had entered an appeal against conviction on four grounds. His counsel advised against appeal but his solicitor did not accept this advice. The defendant was refused Legal Aid for the appeal, conducted by his solicitor. On one of the four grounds the High Court of Justiciary hearing the appeal adjourned, because it decided that it could not determine the point without considering the trial transcript.

It was on this point alone that Granger succeeded. The Court of Human Rights, it is suggested, took - as Article 6 declares - a primarily 'Due Process' and 'Justice' approach to that ground of Granger's appeal.

The judgment refers to "inequality of arms" and that expert legal argument from both sides would be of benefit on a complex issue; further that this approach had been taken by the Scottish courts in later cases. (Larkin v HM Lord Advocate and Williamson v HM Lord Advocate [1988] Sc Crim C. Reps 30 and 56)

If 'need' appears in this judgment it is not an express consideration, but it may be present in "enabling the applicant to make an effective contribution to the proceedings."

We shall examine two other relevant cases later. One, from the majority of the High Court of Australia emphasises administrative considerations, the other from the majority of the Privy Council takes a comparative-consequential approach.

In public policy discussion, argument is normally over the <u>stage</u> at which intervention should occur, or the <u>scope</u> of service to be provided at a given stage. An example of the former is whether to provide pre-trial services to those remanded on bail, or only to those remanded in custody.

An example of dispute over stage comes from New Zealand:

> "Limiting it to those in custody or on police bail...is fine in theory. However in practice the majority of defendants do nothing about consulting a lawyer before their Court day. The reasons...could include apathy, but this is not the point. The point is that defendants still come to court without a lawyer and unless the Duty Solicitor acts they will appear without one...."

The discussion then switches to scope:

> "with the possible exception of defendants charged with offences not carrying possible prison terms and the definite exception of parking offenders...." (Working Party Dept of Justice 1982 paras 2.18, 2.21)

In the UK a response to this kind of discussion has been the establishment of a Duty Solicitor scheme, (under the aegis of the VERA Foundation of New York), at Colchester for defendants remanded on bail.

Given these problems, the general difficulties of need definition remain. One prominent British writer on this topic has noted that need is not static. For example, the need for criminal legal aid can grow with the growth of crime or crime control rates. Equally, the successful meeting of need can stimulate further demand as the consumers may advertise the services received to others with the need. The same writer has recognised that - quite apart from administrative constraints - need is not an absolute concept. For example, the Lord Chancellor's Department and Home Office would make a distinction between Summary and Intermediate offences for Legal Aid in the Magistrates' Courts. (Zander 1978, 292) It was suggested that there should be a stratification of priorities of need; for example Legal Aid, being essential for a defendant confronted with a charge which could result in the death penalty, - unlike the majority of the Privy Council in <u>Robinson</u> - but that legal need is greater where innocence is asserted rather than guilt admitted. I contest all these assertions on the basis that the rational defendant with full information could have good strategic reasons for self-representation on a capital charge, and equally for a mitigating solicitor on an admitted drunk and disorderly charge.

(b)   Criticisms of the Due Process Approach to Legal Need

As the preceding paragraphs illustrate, there is a weak connection between the acceptance of Due Process or Rule of Law theory and its practical application, even at the preliminary level of definition.   A related matter is more fundamental.   The Rule of Law conception of legal need is a formalist one, and therefore tends towards minimal response.   It can therefore be criticised for its cosmetic aspect and lack of focus on inequality in the quality of legal services. (Richards 1979, 1372, 1409-18)

These problems are well known and not the subject of general controversy.   There is however another view of the emergence of an active relationship between Due Process theory and legal need as equal access to representation.   This is broadly an historical and sociological interpretation derived from study of the time of its emergence:

> "Thus on the eve of <u>Powell</u> v <u>Alabama</u> the legal profession was desperately protecting its flanks and seeking to convince the American public once again (as in 1917) that lawyers were not just useful luxuries for the rich, but essential necessities for the entire society.   To be convincing this bold and problematic claim would have to be announced by the most honoured and prestigious legal institution in the land, the US Supreme Court.   Its self-serving consequences would have to be carefully camouflaged behind a cause whose value to society no right-minded American could deny.   It would have to overcome the perennial sentiment against lawyers expressed at that particular epoch by a layman, I.P. Gallison:

> "The preponderating cause of the failure of American justice is the American lawyer...."

The reforms which undoubtedly have occurred can be said by this well-known middle-of-the-road commentator to be:

> "for the sake of the legal profession as much as the ideal of equal justice.   Elite lawyers recognised their vital interest in maintaining a reasonably compensated criminal bar...which frees the elite from *pro bono* work in the polluting atmosphere of the criminal courts." (McDonald *op cit* Ch 1 33-6, Clark and Costret 1983, 1272)

There is another radical, but less cynical, view of the legal access movement, which is that it reinforces professional hegemony.   This has two aspects, the first being that the courtroom - and criminal process - is marked out as reserved territory. The other is that the professional hegemony of the lawyer reduces the defendant's involvement to observer status in their own drama. (Caplan 1977, 93, 103) This particular scathing denouncement of professional 'champions' exempts - without explanation - criminal representation from the general castigation. (*Ibid* 97, 99) However, even moderate observers such as Shapland recognise these dangers, such as the use of language incomprehensible to the defendant, (Rueschmeyer 1969, 17 Shapland 1981, 146) or the use of 'commonsense' which is alien to the defendant. These dangers have been considered under the rubric of 'imputed' need.

It may be concluded that the Rule of Law or Due Process models of legal need as 'fairness' are more profession than defendant centered.

(ii) 'Justice' and Legal Need

The Justice model requires representation for another set of reasons. Here the aim is to maximise information at all points. Representation is assumed to assist that process. (*Ibid* 145-6) Shapland argues this position for the maximising of information in her work on the mitigation process. Unrepresented defendants say little in mitigation, although the content of mitigating statements is similar to that used in giving an account of oneself in everyday life; they do not refer to the prosecution accounts of their behaviour or attitudes; they do not give sentencing suggestions; they do not have the knowledge of sentencing to enable them to do so. Generally, they are 'silent in court'. (Dell 1971) This model of legal need tends to oppose such practices as plea-bargaining which suppress and distort information, particularly that relevant to sentencing. (Baldwin and McConville 1978, 544) There is a continuing tension between the administrative pressures which produce such negotiation, and adjudicated justice. Yet these 'distortions' of the Justice model of adjudication depend upon and reflect the representation of defendants by advocates.

However if we ignore these problems, the point to notice about the justice model of legal need is that it is system orientated. Its purpose is to maximise information, and that may equally lead to gains or losses to the defendants. Representation within this model is neither profession nor defendant centred.

(iii) The Management of Criminal Justice

a) *Externalities as Need*. Strictly speaking the issue to be raised briefly now is more properly considered as Response-to-Need, but since it is concerned with the prevention of harmful consequence it is of relevance. It is rarely discussed, but can be considered to be analogous to a minimalist definition of need, though as will become apparent the motivation is not the same. It derives from the economic concept of 'Externality' and from this perspective need is meaningful in terms of its adverse consequences on society, rather than on the deprived individual. (Leffler 1978, 165)

Such an approach would ground the recognition of and response to individual need solely in terms of its prevention or reduction or channelling into less costly avenues.

An example is appropriate. If persons commit acts which are criminal offences and the consequence of their becoming unrepresented defendants is that they are denied bail, convicted and imprisoned, significantly more or for longer than those with legal representation, then solely in terms of the externalities of the cost of remand, cost of court escorts, cost of prison, cost of social security for dependants and cost of social security for the defendant on release, it will be appropriate to recognise the need of these defendants for advocates and also to respond with Legal Aid provided its cost is significantly less than the other costs. (Robertshaw 1983, 329)

What one can conclude from such an approach - which is not practised in a pure form anywhere - is that it makes plain what may be an important or even predominant factor in definitions of need:-

"Most of the contemporary discussions of indicators is in terms of the policy operators, not the outsiders.." (S.M. Miller et al 1970, 17)

This is acknowledged by Townsend for example:-

"Tough and arbitrary judgments are made at the really critical stages of fixing the level of the poverty line." (Townsend 1974, 21)

Holman has concluded that official measures of need tend, for understandable administrative reasons, to be simple to operate, though this may be inefficient or cause further hardship. (Holman 1978, 22) It has to be interjected however that whilst that statement may be true in some areas it is not normally the case for either civil or criminal Legal Aid, where rampant discretion and local variations have frequently been criticised.

In conclusion some examples are apposite. 'Justice' has recently called for a considerable improvement in the arrangements for witnesses in criminal trials. They are handled so indifferently by court officials, let alone the difficulties of cross-examination, that witnesses frequently do injustice to themselves, the defendant or the court. This can seriously impair the administration of justice with all sorts of knock-on effects. (Justice 1986) The Lord Chancellor's 34th Legal Aid Annual Reports supports this view and stresses the substantial

risk of unnecessary expense through retrials and appeals.
(1984 paras 193-6, 240)

Currently the Advice Services Alliance is arguing that
if Citizens Advice Bureaux, Legal Advice Centres and Law
Centres are cut back further or closed, there will be a
risk of people taking things into their own hands, with
the consequent risk of further riots and damaging public
insecurity and expenditure, and similar views have been
voiced in Parliament. (HC Debs 14/3/1986 D. Clelland MP
and S. Holland MP)

b)   Administrative Imperatives.   There is a less tough-
minded, but related need perspective, which may lack the
precision of externalities - the administrative
perspective.   Here the focus is narrower, being concerned
less with extra-court costs and more with speed and the
achievement of an organised flow of routine cases,
typically Guilty pleas with tariff sentences. (Bottoms
and McClean *op cit* Ch 9)   From this perspective the
control, even choreography, of the defendant is
important.   Negotiation before or around the trial may
become salient.   To achieve this aim of efficiency and to
reduce spontaneous or irrational interruptions in the
flow, legal services are necessary to the system as much
as to judiciary and administrative staff.   This would
remain the case even if in perfect conditions no other
value is relevant, for example to the defendant.   One
should, however, be cautious to dismiss the word 'need'
from this administrative model because there may be
perceived subjective gain to the defendant, which would
not have occurred without such intervention.   This gain
might consist of the feeling of relative well-being
associated with being processed as low-status stigmatised
stranger behind the protective barrier of an high status,
competent, insider.   So if absolutely no outcome gains
are made there may still be need satisfaction, but in
terms of the analogy of 'care' rather than 'cure'.

These two perspectives, economic and administrative,
have however hardly figured in the literature of legal
need.   This literature presupposes that the unrepresented
defendant is itself the problem.   This perspective
assumes the relative incompetence, irresponsibility and
dependence of defendants.   It must be remarked here that
this professional view of the defendant can be defined as
an ideology of interest. (Frankfurt 1971, 5-6, Dworkin
1970, 23-8, Richards *op cit* 1405-9)

The tensions between the Rule of Law approach to legal
need and the administrative perspective are well brought
out in the McInnis case which restricted the legal rights
of those who fail to obtain legal aid.   The defendant was
a defendant in a rape trial, refused Legal Aid the day
before the trial commenced.   He sought an adjournment so
that he could apply to the Federal Legal Aid Commission.
He had made no attempt to raise money for privately
retained repesentation.   He was given half an hour to

read the depositions and the trial then commenced with the defendant unrepresented. He was convicted. The majority of the Court of Criminal Appeal of Western Australia dismissed his appeal, based on procedural irregularity. The majority of the High Court of Australia then refused special leave of appeal on a point of law. The Chief Justice stressed the judicial discretion, for example in relation to the state of the victim, inconvenience to jurors and further pre-trial delay. Murphy J's dissent was based on 'Rule of Law' notions of equal justice for the rich and poor in criminal cases. ((1979) 27 ALR 449, 453)

(iv) The Politics of Criminal Justice and Legal Need

It is frequently forgotten by lawyers and welfarists that legal disputes, especially criminal prosecutions, are not solely forensic exercises. They can be hard fought, even bitter adversarial matches, in which court procedure and dignified ritual have been developed over centuries to mollify and control genuine and severe conflict. The State may not be a neutral, objective observer and director in particular cases, nor in relation to the criminal process in general. Since governments do not wish to lose a significant proportion of cases that are brought in its name, nor to waste revenue on pointless proceedings, we should not be surprised if they may sometimes or in certain types of matter, resist claims to legal welfare that may reduce the opportunities for state success. (Garth 1980, 10)

The earliest conflicts over the nascent legal services movement were not, as frequently happened later, between young attorneys and established legal practice, but between the movement and the state in relation to criminal justice practice. In 1963 Jean Cahn founded Community Progress Inc. in conjunction with the New Haven Bar Association. The CPI's active defence of a young Black accused of raping a White female incurred considerable local hostility. When Professor Cahn refused to withdraw or modify the defence, she was forced to resign and CPI was ended. Similarly, the 'Mobilisation for Youth' in New York City's Lower East side, which provided aggressive and broadly conceived defence for young Blacks, was also rapidly terminated. (Ibid 23-5, Murphy 1971, Cahn and Cahn 1964, 1316, Pious 1972, 418, Masotti and Corsi 1976, 490)

At the national level in the USA the Legal Services Corporation was established in 1967, under the Office of Equal Opportunity to provide a national framework for the provision of publicly funded legal services throughout the U.S.A. Very considerable conflict ensued over the scope of its activities, notably criminal defence, in which a legislative 'night of the long knives' is said to have occurred.

The original limitation repealed in 1974 (42 USC 8 s.299f(b)(2)) prohibited representation except

> "in extraordinary circumstances where...the Director has determined that adequate legal assistance will not be available for the indigent defendant". (Pub L No 90-222 s.222(a)(3) 81 Stat 698, 1967)

Until 1977 the ban included juvenile criminal justice - often defined as non-legal, non-criminal work in the USA. (Pub L No 15-222 s.10, 91 Stat 1619, 1977) In 1980 an exception was reintroduced for defence to charges of a misdemeanour or lesser offence in an Indian Tribal Court.

What does not emerge fully in this account is the implicit criticism by the legal services movement of existing public legal services, in the shape of the Public Defender schemes and Court-assigned lawyers in most of urban USA. There is a widespread belief, shared by the legal services radicals, that the former are at best provided far too late for effectiveness, and the latter are a cheap second-rate underfunded and unassertive alternative to privately retained attorneys for the rich. Speaking for the majority of US Supreme Court Rehnquist J. said:

> "the duty of the State is not to duplicate the legal arsenal that may be privately retained by a criminal defendant...but only to assure the indigent defendant an adequate opportunity to present his claims fairly." (<u>Ross v Moffit</u> (1972) 417 US 600)

The Perceptions of Defendants

An obvious structural feature of the criminal process is that the defendant is an involuntary agent. It is not just that the defendant can be brought compulsorily to court; for all but the rarest of defendants the provision of the lawyer will be reactive, after arrest or charge. Thus, the situation of response is different to the indigent or others who use law preventatively, whether for matters such as Wills or to avoid prosecution for tax evasion or for nefarious trading practices. (Masotti and Corsi *op cit*, 403, 407) If the process operates in the classical manner the defendant is immersed in the procedures regardless of whether culpable. This does somewhat overstate the situation, as there can be some parallels to civil justice, in that defendants may be able to negotiate to some extent; but even when that is legal, it is hardly comparable in scale in Britain, with civil process negotiation, whereby the vast majority of outcomes are settled. This structural feature may have repercussions on those enmeshed with it: if the legal structure is perceived as overwhelming, then the addition of further legal personnel - such as (duty) solicitors and (legal aid) lawyers - may not be perceived from the defendant's perspective as assisting, but rather as adding to the pressure already bearing on the defendant/client. The availability of such legal services may not in such circumstances be regarded as meeting need, but rather as part of the punitive process itself, especially if the defendant wishes to reduce contact with the system to the minimum. This is seriously argued in Feeley's major work, 'The Process is the Punishment'. (cf Ryan 1981, 79) In Britain, Carlen's 'Magistrates' Justice' is similar in tone.

In certain situations, for example the proactive assistance of Duty Solicitors, this may be intensified, rather than diminished. Silverstein, commenting on his US national survey:

> "The fact that they cannot choose their counsel contributes greatly to defendant's distrust of the public defenders and...even the more zealous legal assistance lawyers." (Silverstein 1965, 95)

Two other reasons appear occasionally. Two of the Canadian studies elicited responses that appearance in person might create sympathy in the court. (Ericson and Baranek *op cit* 80, Messier *op cit* T4.1) A component of 'lumping' in the criminal arena can be a defeatist, no-contest psychology combined with an attitude of self-punishment. These attitudes coincide with admitted guilt of the offences concerned, such as being caught red-handed shop-lifting. This finding has implications for the interpretation of those who plead guilty and are unrepresented.

Perceptions or beliefs about the role of lawyers may be relevant. In Australia, Canada and the USA that role is primarily one of negotiator, for which lawyers are valued. The ironic converse is that they may be less valued as advocates. (Ericson and Baranek *op cit* 80-1) In this country the opposite could be the case.

Conclusion

In this chapter the basis of the Rule of Law account of the need for legal representation, specifically for criminal defendants, was put forward and problems relating to the stages and scope of its application were noted.

However there are other accounts of the need for such representation, such as the efficient provision of information for the system under the Justice model, or for maintaining the efficient movement of the system under bureaucratic imperatives. These accounts are not based on defendants' legal need; in addition there are political examples of actual hostility to responding to such alleged needs. Less well known accounts stress the competition between legal professionals and between lawyers and other professionals for enforcement of different modes of client control. In general lawyer hegemony has been maintained with the attendant risk of imputing needs to a passive client. It has also been argued in the USA that public legal services serve to maintain the legitimacy both of an inefficient system and of the services of the profession, to relatively wealthy clients.

Footnote

1. Some of these assertions originate with the writer. Others can be found in many sources of which a selection are: E. C. Bamberger Jr (Director of Legal Services, U.S. Office of Economic Opportunity) 41 Note Dame Lawyer (1976) 847 R. W. Benjamin and T. B. Pedelski 4 Law and Soc. Rev. (1969) 279; J. Griffiths Ch 3 in ed. E. Blankenburg, 'Innovations in the Legal Services' (1980); P. Cashman in J. Basten *et al* eds., 'The Criminal Injustice System' Sydney N.S.W. (1982) 210-222; E. E. Cheatham, 'A Lawyer when Needed' Col. U.P. (1963) Chs 1-3; S. R. Ehrmann 26 Fed. Prob. (1962) 14, 21; L. G. Forer J, 'The Death of the Law', David McKay (1974) N.Y. 210-215; Society of Labour Lawyers, 'Legal Services for All' Fabian Tract No 454 (1979); Legal Aid Act 1974 s.29; M. Davies J, Conference on 'Priorities in Legal Services' I.J.A. Birmingham 7/1974, 1-2.

10 Appearing in Person: Self-Representation in Criminal Justice

The Scale of Self-Representation by Defendants

Superior Courts - England and Wales

Legal Representation is almost universal for trials in the Crown Court today. When the Court was established appearance in person was already very rare:

Indictment Assizes   1970: 1.4%   1971: 1.1%
Indictment Crown Court 1972: 0.7%   1973: 0.7%

By 1982 the rate for indictment had reduced further to 0.4% and had reduced from 14.6% to 2.6% for sentence committals from magistrates. (Calculated from Cmnd 5402 (1972) TXVII(a), Cmnd 5677 (1973) TXIII(a))
      There is some variation between courts. The Cobden Trust survey found a range from 0 at the Central Criminal Court and Warwick Crown Court to 0.5% at Knightsbridge Crown Court. (Levenson 1981) The Sheffield survey had found a rate of 1%. (Bottoms and McClean *op cit* T6.3)
      In a survey of 25 cases before an Assistant Recorder at Dorchester Crown Court over 11 days in January 1988 I found 1 case, 4%, of appearance in person - an appeal against conviction. If one excludes the 7 appearances for plea, the rate increases to 5.6%, but the small sample size of 18 means that no statistical significance can be attached. In a further survey of 35 jury trials

at Cardiff Crown Court in October-December 1990 one
defendant appeared in person on a theft charge: 2.9%.

*Self-Representation in the Magistrates' Courts in England
and Wales*

Self-representation in the magistrates' Courts of England
and Wales on criminal charges is the typical mode of
procedure for defendants; further, since the great
majority of all defendants come before magistrates, it
can be said to be typical for both summary and
intermediate charges.

This central feature is demonstrated by a number of
studies. Dell, for example, in a study of 565 women
imprisoned in Holloway found that at least 69% had been
without legal representation. (Dell 1972, 17-29)

In evidence to the Royal Commission on Legal Services,
the Winson Green Prison Project produced a study of
imprisoned convicted defendants, over a six week period
in 1978 by Birmingham magistrates; of the 174 custodial
sentences 67.2% were unrepresented. This high rate was
despite the existence of a Duty Solicitor scheme and s.21
of the Powers of Criminal Courts Act 1973 whereby those
sentenced to prison for the first time must be offered
legal representation. (LAG Bulletin 7, 1979, 147)

Zander calculated from 1975 Criminal and Legal Aid
Statistics that 44.9% of those appearing on Intermediate
charges (439,191) were unrepresented. (1976, 147) In a
further study of 1978 statistics he calculated that the
percentage had dropped slightly, to perhaps 40%. For
juveniles about three-quarters were unrepresented,
whereas for summary offences it was around 95%. (1980,
375 T3(a)) King surveyed 782 cases, in 76 Magistrates'
Courts, over two days, in 1974. The rate of self-
representation in this study was found to be lower, at
54%, but this study did include committal proceedings on
serious charges which might be tried at the Crown Court;
further, if those charged of motoring offences are
subtracted the self-representation rate rises to 73%.
(1976, 11) Bottoms and McClean in their study of criminal
defendants in Sheffield found that the unrepresented
comprised 72.4% of the magistrates' caseload and 55% of
the total caseload in the city. (Justice 1971, Part I,
para 14)

It is clear that although appearance in person remains
typical, it has reduced due to the impact of Legal Aid
and duty solicitor schemes. Thus in 1962 and 1969 rates
of 99.4% and 95.6% had existed; (Bottoms and McClean *op
cit*) and at magistrates' committal stage for indictable
offences the rates were 90% in 1961 and 31% in 1975.
(Zander 1976, 903)

This broad generalisation needs one refinement in focus
which has already been made. Self-representation is the
routine mode of proceedings on guilty pleas, and they

are, associated, as are certain offences, with the Magistrates' courts.

Self-Representation in Other Common Law Jurisdictions

The next section of this book comprises a comparative survey of the consequences of legal representation and self-representation, including an examination of all the available material from five Common Law jurisdictions. It is appropriate therefore to survey briefly the scale of self-representation in the lower courts, in those countries.

Australia - Lower Criminal Courts

South Australia - One study exists of representation patterns in courts of summary jurisdiction in South Australia. It covered 13 offences and compared Adelaide city, suburban and country courts in 1980.

One offence, drunkenness, involved an almost total lack of legal representation: 93.9% of defendants appeared in person and there were, with this offence alone, no significant differences between the districts.

Two other offences had high rates of appearance in person: disorderly behaviour (69.1%) and offensive language (69.6%).

With only two offences, and then only in Adelaide was appearance in person marginal: unlawful use of a car (0.9%) and driving under the influence of alcohol (7.8%). Three offences had average rates under 25%, the two just mentioned and assaults on the police (20.1%, 24.6%, 21%).

One very clear conclusion can be drawn from this study. If one excludes drunkenness, the average rate for appearance in person reduces from 51% to 40%, but the differentials between city, suburban and country courts become striking: 24.2% 40.1% 33.6%. (Cashman 1981 Ch 12, T11)

New South Wales - There is a body of information on self-representation in this state, covering a decade. In 1972 the rate in all cases in all petty sessional courts in the state was two-thirds. (N.S.W. Bureau of Crime Statistics Report (1972) 11, 4) In the earliest Australian study of legal need, Vinson and Homel analysed these statistics and found that if drunkenness and minor traffic violations were removed, the rate was 68%, and that this correlated significantly with pleading Guilty. (1973, 132)

Cashman studied the impact of extending the Public Solicitor's Office to petty sessional courts from 1974 (Cashman 1982, Ch 8, 196) and the introduction of Duty Solicitor schemes in the Sydney metropolitan area and Newcastle, Gosford and Woollongong in 1976. I am presenting here my own interpretation of those statistics, with conclusions which he does not draw.[1]

The overall rate of appearance in person in 1976 was 53.1%.

The districts were split evenly between those with self-representation rates above and below 50%. The lowest rates were 33.2%, 33.1% and 38%; the highest 75.3%, 68% and 67%. The lowest rate for particular offences was 21.4% for possession of cannabis, and the highest 76.2% for offensive behaviour and 70.8% for unseemly words. (Cashman 1981 *op cit* T6A, B)

Although the average for all offences reduced to 41% the following year the variations increased, with the lowest being 41.6% and the highest being 64.7%.

As has been mentioned, the introduction of new legal services did have an impact, reducing appearance in person by 13.5%. This can be illustrated:

Appearance in Person	7/12/1976 %	7/12/1977 %
Offensive Behaviour	76.4	60.7
Unseemly Words	71.0	62.4
Shop-Lifting	67.6	46.4
Larceny	65.5	37.1:-28.4
Assault Female	60.2	49.8
Common Assault	54.5	48.3
Av	52.2	38.7:-13.5
Use Cannabis	45.7	39.7:- 6.0
Receive Property	39.7	21.3
Possess Cannabis	38.9	28.5
Drink-Drive	37.5	27.0
Break and Enter	35.3	19.0

This can also be illustrated by the number of districts, whose average for appearance in person for the 9 main offences each exceed 50% in these successive years:

Offences	1976 (28)	1977 (28)
9	0	0
7	4	0
6	6	1
5	9	4
4	4 : 23*	4
3	0	4
2	2	7
1	0	4 : 23*
0	0	0

However, Cashman does not observe first, that the districts with averages for offences where defendants appearing in person remained above 50%, far exceeded those with more legal representation; that in 27 of the 28 districts at least one offence remained in this category; that there were some increases in self-representation in 1977; and that the alteration was not maintained after 1978.

Perhaps most significant was the fallback in legal representation after 1978; this was tabulated, but not discussed. It is, therefore, unclear whether this was caused by the resurgence of established patterns of behaviour in particular districts, or for particular offences, or by the focussing of the new legal services on particular matters - for example on Not Guilty pleas, which occur more for some offences than others, or a combination of these, or other, factors. It is clear that the total average rose to 49.1%, near the 1976 level for appearance in person. Ten districts never exceeded 50%; 5 decreased below 50%; 5 dipped beneath 50% and then rose again above that; 7 remained about 50%, and 4 increased their existing rate beyond 50%. (*Ibid* T6E)

As with his study of Victoria's petty sessional courts, Cashman presents evidence on the geographical characteristics of representation. There is a cleavage between metropolitan, metropolitan-suburban and rural areas. In 1976-1978 appearance in person was more widespread in metropolitan areas:

| City | 56.4% | 52.2% | |
| Suburban | 47.4% | 50.1% | (*Ibid* T6F) |

What becomes clear is that the combined volume of caseload of particular offences - notably 'unseemly words' and 'offensive behaviour', combined with their representation patterns produces the overall representation pattern of a district. (Cashman 1982 *op cit* 200) However, it has been demonstrated that the response to the representation decision can be markedly different from district to district and that these patterns may continue over some time, either generally or for particular offences. A further variable of great importance is the plea tendency for each offence, because there is a link between plea and representation, but this was not discussed.

This issue was considered by Symonds in the same volume. (Symonds 1981 Ch 15) His focus of interest is the representation of children in juvenile courts. He found that 20% of children defendants 'slip through the net of legal aid and go unrepresented'. (*Ibid* 237) He also found that the 20% not professionally represented comprise 95% of guilty pleas, similar to the 62% of adults unrepresented who comprise 91.6% of guilty pleas. It is also interesting to note that 27.1% of a sample of 1086 children were legally represented at first appearance, but only 21% at final appearance. (Wood 1982 Ch 14) Since 52.8% admitted the charges and 70.1% did so at final appearance, it suggests that legal advice has a connection with these plea changes and that advice may either be for appearance in person on a guilty plea, or that representation is no longer seen as necessary.

Canada

Two studies have considered the place of defendants without lawyers in Toronto's courts. Hann found an overall rate of appearance in person at 56.5%. (Hann 1973 T4.14) This average was comprised of rates of 66.7% at first appearance, (*Ibid* T4.15) 54.5% at plea, (*Ibid* T4.16) and 52.8% at final appearance. (*Ibid* T4.17) There were wide divergences between offences and some differences at each stage:

First appearance :
    Indecency 45.1% <u>Av</u> 66.7%   Liquor 82.6%
At Plea :
    Drugs   15.9% <u>Av</u> 54.5%   Liquor 70.3%

    Drugs   30.5% <u>Av</u> 56.5%   'Other Prov' Stats 85.9%
Final Appearance:
    Drugs   18.8% <u>Av</u> 52.8%   Fed. & Prov. Stats 78.3%

It appears, therefore, that in general appearance in person is linked to offences perceived as less serious, or having less serious sentence possibilities.

Also in Toronto, Wilkins found an overall rate of appearance in person at 36.3%. (Wilkins 1975 T3.1) Appearance in person correlated with 'minor' charge where election of venue was available; (*Ibid* 56-7) where shorter maximum sentences were available; (*Ibid* T4.2) with public order offences; (*Ibid* T4.7) with Bail and Bail set at a low sum; (*Ibid* T4.14, 4.15) with a total refusal of jury trial where jury trial was available; with immediate trial (*Ibid* T6.8) and with guilty pleas, at 86%.

They were almost all locally resident, with less previous convictions than average (38.6%; 50.8%). They had no distinguishing features with regard to gender, age or race. (*Ibid* T7.12)

In Nova Scotia, a study found that 38% of unrepresented defendants were charged with minor summary offences compared to 23% of those legally represented, and that 37% of the unrepresented were first offenders compared to 23% of those legally represented. (Renner and Warner 1981)

New Zealand

It is possible to calculate the occurrence of appearance in person in New Zealand from the Department of Justice report on 'Access to Law'. The overall rate of appearance in person was 51.8% in the District Courts, (Oxley 1981 Apdx 6 T1.9) but there were considerable differences between districts. These differences are probably accounted for by the various other factors mentioned here, and in addition by eligibility and take-up of Legal Aid.

```
The city range was from            36.5% at Christchurch
                 to                66.4% at Auckland
                 and              73.5% at Wellington;
In suburban areas, the range was
                 from             28.8% at Invercargill
                 to               56.7% at Whangarei;
and in rural districts from           0 at Waipukarau
                 to                 55% at Blenheim.
```

There were differences for the gender of the offender: males appeared in person more than females, (*Ibid* T28) and for age: 19 year olds appeared in person more than other age groups. (*Ibid* T29)

Europeans were split evenly between private representation, legally aided representation and self-representation. The unemployed were split between legally aided representation and self-representation. Pacific Islanders tended to represent themselves and Maoris to rely on Legal Aid. (*Ibid* T30, 32)

In the District Court there were, as one would now expect, differences in the rate of appearance in person for different offences:

```
Sex Offences                  0
Offences against the person   31.5%
Traffic Offences              43.5%
Property Offences             45.4%
Av                            51.9%
Administration of Justice     52.5%
Drug Offences                 58.1%
Public order                  60.9% (Ibid T4 Ch 2)
```

For children and young persons the rate of appearance in person was higher, at 63.7%. Again there were considerable, unexplained, differences from district to district, ranging from 11.1% at Gove, to 100% at New Plymouth and at Waipukarau. (*Ibid* T34, 40)

U.S.A. - Misdemeanours

It is clear that self-representation rates vary from district to district in the USA; for example:

1.7% San Diego, California (Taylor *et al* 1972, 233 T3)
2.3% Denver, Colorado (Taylor *et al* 1973, 9)
8.2% Columbus, Ohio (Ryan 1981, 79 TA.1)
51% New Haven, Connecticut (Feeley *op cit* T2.3)

A Civilian Jurisdiction - France

I have found one study which addresses this topic for one type of hearing: regional Courts of Appeal on sentence for Rennes and Angers. The survey covered 1000 cases for the whole of 1984. Under the Code in France self-representation is possible for both the defendant and the victim 'la partie civile'. The researchers found that this occurred for 32.1% of the cases for defendants and 21.6% of the cases for victims. They do not state the proportion of cases where both parties appeared without legal representation. (Desdevises and Lorvelec 1989)

A Survey of Self-Representation Characteristics

Introduction

In 1982 the National Association of Probation Officers and National Association for the Care and Resettlement of Offenders (NAPO-NACO) together undertook a survey of the sentencing practice of courts, with particular emphasis on the sentencing of ethnic minorities. The survey covered 9 courts in England between February and June 1983. Of these courts 4 were juvenile courts (3 in London, 1 in the North), 3 were Magistrates' courts (1 in London, 1 in the Midlands, 1 in the North) and 2 were Crown Courts (1 in London, 1 in the North). The sample was produced by co-operating probation officers in the various courts and produced 650 cases. The only types of cases excluded concerned alcohol and obstruction of the highway.

The report was later published by the two representatives who had conducted the survey (Crow and Cove 1984). This was solely concerned with the sentencing of ethnic defendants. It was however clear that much other information had been gathered, for example on bail, social enquiry reports (SER) and representation.

I contacted both authors, who were not going to make further use of their material and generously allowed me access to the computer data. In addition they put me in touch with their programmer and member of the research group, the Senior Probation Officer, Peter Harroway. He too was extremely co-operative and I would like to record my thanks to all three, especially Mr Harroway.

It is well known that material produced by research for one purpose does not always lend itself to research for other purposes. That is not the case here, since all that has been done in terms of method has been to rearrange the material with a different focus. However, the writer wishes to stress at the outset that there are limitations with this survey, limitations that were present in the original publications. These limitations must be acknowledged and borne in mind.

The first limitation is that although the sample size is quite large, certainly larger than is normal in British surveys, it is not large enough. This is because the 'cell-size' is sometimes too small for proper statistical analysis, for example the number of cases of each offence or sentence.

Second, the survey does not distinguish between types of courts or individual courts. The courts surveyed did not wish to be identifiable so this was a concession for permission to undertake the recording. In the case of children and young persons, the type of court, Juvenile, can of course be discovered, since the age of defendants has been recorded. One cannot normally ascertain whether the offence has been tried in the Crown Court or magistrates because of the way the offences have been recorded, since each category includes a variety of related crimes; only occasionally therefore can the type of court be identified, for example if the disposition is a committal to the Crown Court for sentence. It follows that one cannot distinguish between the two varieties of legal representation, or for legally aided and private representation.

Third, the plea of the defendants was not recorded. It is well established that plea, and consequent length of trial, is an important factor in sentencing, both practically and also legally because of the 'discount' that must be given. This limitation must also be borne in mind, because plea correlates with representation and venue choices. However, we cannot assume that those appearing in person are pleading guilty, though it is less likely that they are appearing in the Crown Court.[2]

Because of the routine difficulties of obtaining accurate information on every variable in every case it will be rare, and this is typical, for the full sample to occur on each item considered; but the missing information was never on a large scale.

The offences convicted were in order of volume:
Theft (276), Burglary (88), Drugs (43), Criminal Damage (43), Deception (34), Handling (31), 'Other' Motoring (30), Assault (25), Taking and Driving Away (TDA) (24), Brach of the Peace (20), Grievous Bodily Harm (GBH) (17), Offensive Weapon (9), Sex (8), Solicit (7): 650.

Whilst these crimes and their proportions are typical and representative, and therefore valuable for determining other gross correlates - such as representation, bail, sex, age and ethnicity of offender and sentences - it must be appreciated that for many of them little can be deduced from them except by way of impressions. However, one crime, theft (276), is present in sufficient quantity to enable a certain amount of manipulation without the cell sizes becoming too small too rapidly.

The 15 offence categories are themselves in almost all cases amalgamations of particular common law and statutory offences. Thus:

1. *Taking and Driving Away* (TDA) includes allowing oneself to be carried under such circumstances, and attempts.

2. *'Other' Motoring'* includes driving whilst disqualified or without insurance, or with excess alcohol.
3. *Burglary* includes trespass in enclosed premises.
4. *Theft* includes robbery, shoplifting, attempts, theft from the person and from cars.
5. *Handling* (receiving).
6. *Deception* includes DHSS fraud, fraud, forgery, dishonestly obtaining goods.
7. *Drugs* includes both possession and supply.
8. *Assault* includes actual bodily harm and assaulting the police.
9. *Grievous Bodily Harm* (GBH) includes murder and malicious wounding.
10. *Criminal Damage* includes arson.
11. *Breach of the Peace* includes threatening words, obstruction, insulting behaviour, interfering with motor vehicles.
12. *Offensive Weapons* includes firearms offences.
13. *Sexual* includes exposure, brothel keeping, rape, living off immoral earnings.
14. *Soliciting* (prostitution).
15. *Drunk* includes vagrancy and drunk and disorderly.

These classifications used in the original survey do enable representative samples to be built; however they must also be seen as another limitation of the research presented here since each category may include some heterogeneity.

Because of cell size difficiencies, only theft is available for further comparison in relation to outcomes and other variables.

The survey covers a wider range of variables than some of those previously cited: Offence, Gender, Employment status, previous record, Social Enquiry Report, Race, Age and Marital status.

The Survey

(i) Offence and Self-Representation

	Rep'd	In Person	Total	% In Person
Burglary	86	2	88	2.3
Other Motor	24	5	29	17.2
Assault	19	4	23	17.4
TDA	19	4	23	17.4
Drugs	33	7	40	17.5
Deception	27	6	33	18.2
Criminal Damage	33	9	42	21.4
GBH	32	9	41	22.0
Handling	24	7	31	22.6
(Sex	6	2	8	25.0)
Breach of Peace	16	6	22	27.3
(Offensive Weapon	5	2	7	28.6)
Theft	188	75	263	28.6
(Solicit	4	3	7	42.9)
	516	141	675	21.4

Chi^2 30.97 sig. p 0.01 with 13 degrees of freedom.[3]

This demonstrates an apparently wide range of offences ranging from massive legal representation for burglars, at 97.7%, to low legal representation for prostitutes, at 57.1%. However, three of these results are only useful relatively and have no statistical reliability since the sample is far too small, notably prostitution, sex offences and offensive weapons; but thieves do represent themselves more than the average.

(ii) Offence and Gender

We can break the samples down further to consider offence with the gender of the defendant:

T2A Males	Represented	In Person	Total	In Person %
All	442	114	556 (85%)	20.5*
Burglary	85	2	87	2.3
Drugs	28	5	33	15.2
Criminal Damage	26	7	33	21.0
Theft	148	63	221	28.5**
T2B Females				
All	77	21	98 (15%)	21.4*
Theft	40	12	52	23.1**

Here it can be seen that, in general, there are no significant differences from the general situation in TI except that females conform to the general pattern of theft. It follows that appearing in person as a tendency in theft cases is a male phenomenon.

Comparisons between males with and without representation is only possible for the general position and for theft. The difference in representation rates between males and females for all offences is small, but statistically significant (Chi^2 = 5.36 sig. p 0.05 with 1 d.f.). The difference between male and female thieves is highly significant (Chi^2 = 14.84 sig. p < 0.001 with 1 d.f.).

(iii) Representation and Employment Status

T3	Represented	In Person	Total	In Person %
Part Time Work	49	3	52	5.8
Unemployed	288	83	371	22.4
Full Time Work	78	24	102	23.5
Full Time Education	25	14	39	35.9
	440	124	546	Av. 22.0

Chi^2 = 12.54 sig. p < 0.01 with 3 d.f.

Here there are quite striking and statistically significant differences between the two smaller groups, with professional representation being almost universal for those in part-time work and noticeably less common for those in full-time education - despite the assumption that this group is largely eligible for Legal Aid.

It must also be recorded that the number of unemployed is typical forming 65.8% of the total sample for which information was available.[4]

(iv) Previous Record and Representation

There were only two defendants in the entire sample who had no previous convictions. It was, therefore, impossible to compare their representation pattern with the typical recidivist defendants.

It was, however, possible to compare the 'new entrants' with no, or one previous conviction only, with the 'confirmed recidivists' with 9 or more previous convictions. There were 45 of the former and 34 of the latter; no further subdivisions are possible because the absolute numbers are too small:

T4	Represented	In Person
New Entrants	97.8%	2.2%
Confirmed Recidivists	61.8%	38.2%

Chi^2 = 8.89 sig. p < 0.01 with 1 d.f.

It can be seen that the experienced 'Repeat Players' are significantly more likely to take themselves through the system than 'One-Shot-Players' and that both these divergences are significant against the general representation pattern.

(v)   Representation and Social Enquiry Report (SER)

The absolute numbers in the four possible situations were:

T5	Represented	In Person
SER	210	45
No SER	286	90
	496	135
SER	42.3%	33.3%

Chi^2 = 3.2 with 1 d.f. p > 0.05 <u>Not</u> sig.

Thus, although it was not infrequent for those appearing in person to have a Social Enquiry Report, it was more likely, but not at a statistically significant level, for those represented. Whether this forms a significant link with sentence disposition can, with these absolute numbers, be considered below.

With two offences it is possible to test further the relationship between representation and Social Enquiry Report:

Theft   260 cases
Burglary   87 cases

T5A <u>Theft</u>	<u>Represented</u> %		<u>In Person</u> %	
SER	107	57.4	33	44.6
No SER	79	42.5	41	45.4

Chi^2 = 3.06 with 1 d.f. p > 0.05 <u>Not</u> sig.

<u>Burglary</u>				
SER	40	42.1	2	/
No SER	45	47.9	0	/

Chi^2 Invalid - <u>Not</u> sig.

It can be seen that in the main offence of theft there is a shift upwards in the correlation between this offence and Social Enquiry Reports, but the differential between those represented and those appearing in person continues. Again these observations lack statistical significance.

It will be possible below to compare the sentence disposition for those convicted of theft with and without SERs and with and without legal representation.

(vi) Representation and Race

The original survey concentrated on the ethnicity of defendants. This is an imprecise measure but with a reserve of caution it is more useful than no measure at all. The categories used were: White (532), Black (78), Asian (24), and Other (14). The last two categories have been amalgamated here as 'Other' (38). The proportions are White 82.1%, Black 12%, Other 5.9%. It can be seen that unemployment is a far stronger correlate of conviction than ethnicity. The representation patterns were:

T6	Represented	In Person %
White	79.3	20.7
Black	79.5	20.5
Other	71.1	28.9

Chi² = 1.47 p > 0.05 Not sig. with 2 d.f.

It can be seen that 'Others' appear in person more than 'White' and 'Black' groups, but this lacks statistical significance. This is in fact due to the Asian sample who appeared in person in one-third of all cases. The sample is too small to take this finding any further. The sample of Blacks appearing in person, 16, is also too small for further consideration. Below, a category of 'Non-White' will be deployed to allow for comparison with Whites and to maintain cell size for further comparisons.

(vii) Representation and Age

Using the classification of s.70 of the Children and Young Persons (CYPA) Act 1969, the survey yielded 57 defendants aged under 17 years and 142 defendants aged between 17 and 21 years. Another measure used here is 'typical age defendant' 14-33 years: 376 defendants of the total sample of 491 where age was known; and 'stereotypical-age defendants' 16-22 years, 228 defendants; finally, a minimum sample of older defendants was possible, aged 43-68 years, comprising 38:

T7	Represented	%	In Person	%
CYPA 12-17 years	31	54.4	26	45.6
CYPA 17-21 years	109	76.8	33	23.2
16-22	166	72.8	62	27.2
14-33	270	71.2	106	28.2
43-68	29	76.3	9	23.7

Chi² = 10.78 sig. p < 0.05 with 4 d.f.

There is a slight tendency for the 'typical' and 'stereotypical' aged defendants to appear in person, but more noteworthy is the contrast between the two groups covered by the Children and Young Persons Act: juveniles are represented by lawyers less than any other group, whereas young adults are in line with the general pattern and are represented more than the 'typical' defendant.

(viii) Representation and Marital Status

There are three categories here: single, married and other. There were 378 (63%) defendants categorised as single, 149 (24.8%) were married and 73 (11.2%) 'others'.

T8	Represented	%	In Person	%
Married	126	84.6	23	15.4
Other	58	79.5	15	20.5
Single	291	77.0	87	23.0

Chi² = 3.7 p > 0.05 not sig. with 2 d.f.

It can be seen that married persons were more likely to be legally represented than single or other unmarried persons, but no statistical significance can be attached to this observation.

Summary

Appearance in person was not rare, 21.7%.

Representation virtually always occurs where the charge is burglary, 97.7%. It is less frequent for theft, 71.4%, but female thieves are represented at the normal rate, 76.9%. Those in part-time employment are almost always represented, 94.2%, whereas those in full-time education are much less likely to be, 64.1%. New entrants to the criminal justice system are almost always represented, 97.8%, whereas confirmed recidivists are much less likely to be, 61.8%.

In statistical terms race is irrelevant to representation, though there was some evidence that Asians were less likely to be represented. Age on the other hand was very significant. Children and young persons, 12-17 years, were much less likely to be legally represented than all other age groups, 54.4%.

(ix) The Range of Self-Representation

A progression table is now presented. This is constructed solely from those groups which were statistically significant.

	%
'New Entrants'	2.2
Burglary, Burglary-male	2.3
Part-Time Employment	5.8
Drugs-male	15.2
'Other Motor'	17.2
Assault; TDA	17.4
Drugs	17.5
Deception	18.2
All Males	20.5
Criminal Damage-male	21.0
Criminal Damage; All Females; AV	21.4
GBH	22.0
Unemployed	22.4
Handling	22.6
Theft-female	23.1
17-21 years	23.2
43-68 years	23.5
Full-Time Employment	23.7
16-22 years	27.2
Breach of Peace	27.3
14-33 years	28.2
Theft-male	28.5
Full-Time Education	35.9
'Confirmed Recidivists'	38.2
CYPA 12-17 years	45.6

(x) *Conclusion*

As other surveys show, the offence charged can be significant. With three offences there was a marginal but statistically significant variance from the average. Two were above average for self-representation: Breach of the Peace and Theft, and one was below average: male drug offenders. In addition one crime, burglary, was marked by an almost total avoidance of self-representation.

Two groups, who may well have overlapped with the burglars, were 'new entrants' - with no or one previous conviction - and those in part-time employment. These groups represented themselves very rarely.

At the opposite extreme it is clear that the younger the defendant the more likely he or she is to appear without legal representation. This age group obviously overlaps with those in full-time education. Whether that group overlaps with the 'confirmed recidivists' cannot be answered here; the hypothesis is that that is improbable.

It has already been established that ethnicity, marital status and Social Enquiry Reports are irrelevant to representation in this sample.

Footnotes

1. One court is omitted, whose caseload was too small
    for analysis and three offences whose totals were
    less than 900, and therefore considered to be too
    small for analysis in a sample of 28 courts.

2. Similar comments are made on the NAPO survey by
    G. Mair 26 BJ Criminology (1986) 147, 148.

3. i.e. no statistical significance attaches to the
    rates for those offences whose totals are less than
    13: sex offences, offensive weapons, and soliciting.

4. In the 6 courts surveyed by I. Crow and F. Simon
    'Unemployment and Magistrates' Courts' NACRO (1987)
    the lowest rate was 45%, the median 66% and the
    highest 71%, *ibid* T1.

11 Testing Negatively for Non-Need

Comparative-Consequential Need in Criminal Justice

Although the normative definition of legal need for representation in the criminal process undoubtedly remains dominant, doubts about the assumption of effectiveness that underlies such a definition have been expressed before. (Krantz 1976, 93, Luckham 1980, 543, 546) Another type of doubt is more particularistic and concerned with the method to be adopted in testing the assumption of effectiveness; here it is suggested that the range of variables should be wider than outcome and representation, for example offence, previous record and circumstances of the offence could also be considered. (Cranston 1985, 64) The major drawback of this concern is the sampling difficulties that it entails, as it is extremely difficult in practice to obtain sufficient numbers of each variable to yield cell sizes on which statistical significance can be tested. One cannot criticise studies for such omissions, only for not acknowledging them.

Before presenting and discussing the international evidence some preliminary discussion is necessary to justify further this approach and method.

First, there are a number of studies that test effectiveness between different varieties of professional representation. In the USA some larger scale studies using very sophisticated techniques exist, but typically they do not compare those without any of these varieties

of representation. One example is from the US Law
Enforcement Administration Agency in 1975. In their
study of representation by Public Defenders, private
practitioners and law students, they found no
statistically significant variation between the two
qualified groups and the unqualified group on both
verdict and sentence, indeed the unqualified group had a
slightly better acquittal rate. (Evans and Norwood 1975)
Another example by Hermann and his colleagues was the
comparison of public defenders, court-appointed counsel
and private attorneys, on verdict in three major cities.
This survey employed the following variables: original
charge/s, age, gender, ethnicity, prior record, pre-trial
status, trial or plea, and type of trial. The absolute
range of variation for type of counsel was 10%, (Herman,
Single and Boston 1977, T4-3) reducing to 7% if limited
to 'major' charges, (*Ibid* T4-5) and reducing further to
3% after adjustment for the effect of the other
variables: -1%: Court appointed counsel, 0: Public
Defender, +2%: private attorney. (*Ibid* T4-6) This study,
amongst others, demolishes the cherished American myth
that money buys better outcomes.

A further American example tests the effectiveness
of specialist legal lobby groups in criminal appeals
before the Supreme Court. It is entitled: "Friends as
Foes". The two groups are the American Civil Liberties
Union (ACLU) and Americans for Effective Law Enforcement
(AELE). The method the groups used was the Amicus Curiae
brief, and the years studied were 1969-1982. The number
of criminal cases taken by the Court per annum ranged
from 22 (1981) to 42 (1975). (Ivers and O'Connor 1987
161, T1) The average outcome favouring prosecution and
crime control interests was 63.6%; in only two years did
that rate fall below 50%, to 43.7% (1979) and 44.5%
(1974). The rate of Amicus briefs ranged between 25.7%
(1976) to 53.6% (1980) of all criminal law cases before
the Court. (*Ibid* T2) The AELE success rate was 77.1% (of
35 cases) compared to 62.1% ACLU successes (of 66 cases).
(*Ibid* T3, 4) This shows the ACLU achieving a prosecution
level success rate compared to other defence claims, but
still 15% less than AELE; however it is worth noting that
in volume terms ACLU comes out ahead with 41 successes
compared to AELE's 28 successes. A sharply focussed
comparison can be made on Fourth Amendment cases, which
formed the major caseload for both organisations. Here
the AELE success rate was even higher at 85.7% (of 21
cases) compared to ACLU's 69.6% (of 23 cases). It is
clear from these last figures that the key to both
organisations is the selection of cases because they are
transparently not competing directly in the vast majority
of Fourth Amendment cases.

The literature on self-representation assumes, usually
overtly, that this is an undesirable status. The self-
representing person is usually seen as being in a
predicament, and is normally described as "un-

represented". In this way the language used constitutes the person as lacking something and as having a problem to be overcome.

A more sophisticated version is based on an assumed negative relation of self-representation to outcomes of various types, such as plea, conviction, and sentence. I do not want to deny that those representing themselves can and may have severe problems - subsumable under the category of 'care' - nor that their outcomes can be negative, but equally the first view may be no more than a value laden assertion and the second empirically inaccurate. These assertions can comprise a number of errors. The crudest, and more typical, is simply relating self-representation to negative outcomes alone, such as X000 unrepresented defendants per annum are imprisoned. Sometimes comparative need (in Bradshaw's terminology) is asserted by comparing the outcomes of those represented with those appearing in person. This approach will be investigated in depth below. But the simplest error that permeates this entire field is the concentration on defendants. To open the assumptions underlying this topic, I shall concentrate first on the unrepresented prosecutor, and Galanter's distinction between Repeat and One-Shot Players. (Galanter 1975, 95)

Until recently, most prosecutions before Magistrates in England and Wales were conducted by individual police-officers, usually the apprehending constable. (Sanders 1980) The same is true in some other Common Law jurisdictions outside America. (Basten and Disney 1975, 168, 170) In 1967 Zander and Glasser conducted a survey of 60 Not Guilty Pleas at Bow Street Magistrates Court, London. Although the sample size does not allow for any general conclusions to be drawn, the findings highlight the perspective in which this topic is viewed. Indeed, this was part of the first empirical study of representation patterns in Britain, from which virtually all further studies have flowed. Police constables acted as prosecutors in 75.6% of the cases, and defendants represented themselves in 62.8% of the cases. The acquittal rate was 8.5%, which was split evenly between the represented and unrepresented. (Zander and Glasser 1967, Sigler 1974, 642, 648) In 1982 the Home Office estimated that the equivalent of 608 police officers were involved full time in the prosecution of offences. (Jones 1983, 22) The point to elicit here is that no attention was brought to the massive success rate of the prosecutors, nor was any attention given to whether there were differentials between constable-prosecutors and solicitor-prosecutors. On the assumption that the success rate of constable-prosecutors was not significantly different to solicitor-prosecutors, and with the knowledge that such a prosecution success rate is normal before Magistrates, it becomes clear that self-representation may not be the key variable. An alternative variable is that of experience and confidence

- Galanter's Repeat Player - which could be related to outcome. The Royal Commission on Criminal Procedure's Research Study on Prosecuting Solicitors' Departments enables one to calculate the extent of constable-prosecution. All 43 police authorities were surveyed, of which eleven did not have such departments. These tended to be the smaller forces with 15% of total police personnel. Three examples were given from authorities with PSDs. In one rural division constables took 90% of the cases, the balance being complex or legally difficult; in another rural division they took two-thirds of the cases. In one non-metropolitan city with a high caseload, constables prosecuted in 18 of the 22 courts with the highest caseloads, and in the remainder took only motor traffic charges. (Weatheritt 1980, 2.23-26) In the authorities with no PSDs about 6% was farmed out to private solicitors and the balance taken by constables; the 6% were mainly intermediate offences where trial before Magistrates had been selected. (*Ibid* Ch 3) The range of constable-presentation was from 0 to 70% with a median of 43%. (*Ibid* Apdx R Astor 1986, 225, 233)

The Prosecution of Offences Act 1985 came into operation in April 1986 in the former metropolitan counties and in October 1986 in the rest of England and Wales. The statute brought in a separation of powers between the police, as charging authorities, and the Crown Prosecution Service. The police prosecutor is becoming a figure of history, but the points made above about non-professional or semi-professional prosecution cannot be invalidated by this change of institution.

The Sheffield survey also related expectation to outcome. Of those acquitted, half believed that they would have been convicted if unrepresented, and a third of the convicted thought that their sentence would have been heavier if unrepresented (8% thought it would have been lighter). These views could reflect attitudes towards magistrates rather than solicitors, but in any event the survey of the acquitted is also marred by its small sample of 21. (Bottoms and McClean *op cit* 160)

In one study by Zander, defendants convicted at Quarter Sessions or Assizes were asked whether they would recommend a friend to use a laywer in the same situation as themselves. For both junior counsel and solicitors the net recommendations were negative:

	Recommend	Not	Net %
Junior Counsel	37	71	-34
Solicitor	45	81	-36

The reasons for disappointment differed between the two professions. Zander commented that this was in the most obvious sense a biased sample; but that does not render these subjective attitudes worthless. (Zander 1972, 155)

There are, as has been said previously, many difficulties with such attitude research. For example clients may be evaluating client-handling rather than case-handling. (Ladinsky 1976, 217) That such interrelationships can be problematic is apparent from other research. Thus, Casper has shown that in the United States defendants overwhelmingly prefer retained criminal lawyers to appointed Public Defenders, despite the fact that there is little difference in the outcomes of equivalent cases handled by each. (Casper 1972) Another anecdotal example comes from Silver. (Silver 1969, 217, 224) The Public Defender of Alameda County, California had a very good reputation with clients, including those incarcerated, but the Probation Officer assigned to investigate those incarcerated, for a Rehabilitation programme for welfare fraud crimes found that 90% had pleaded guilty on the Public Defender's advice, but the officer formed the opinion that 25% were either completely innocent or a conviction would have been improbable at trial.

Again, the measureability of outcomes has a number of advantages over measuring attitudes to client satisfaction or to outcomes. For example, clients may not know what has been achieved for them. In Toronto it was found that 51% of charges were withdrawn through negotiation, but 35.4% of the benefitted defendants did not know that this had happened.

The same study found that 75% of convicted defendants were satisfied with their sentences, but that the lawyer had prior thereto been "a key contributor to a client's anxieties". (Ericson and Baranek *op cit* 113) Campbell had found the same tendency in Scotland in the 1960s. (Campbell *op cit*)

Another difficulty is how to interpret such findings. The American Bar Foundation national survey tested people's attitudes to outcomes on a variety of problems:

I   'As sought'
            Crime 58% (90% + : 4 problems)
II   'Adequate, but less than sought'
            Crime 28% (20% - : 3 problems)
III   'Adverse'
            Crime 14% (Median)

One could focus solely on:
I (satisfaction)
II (dissatisfaction)
I-III (net satisfaction/dissatisfaction)
I-II-III (net satisfaction). On the two latter measures the results differ significantly in their context. Thus, I-III for Crime is 44% which lies in the middle range, whereas I-II-III is 16%, which is the least of all net satisfaction. (Curran 1977 T5.11)

Competence rating by clients also has its drawbacks, since competence may well be confused with satisfaction and satisfaction may be a function of released anxiety. Further, professional 'peer' ratings of competence may be in sharp contrast with client opinion. As has been shown, the Toronto defendants were mainly satisfied with their outcomes. However, the Ontario Attorney-General had complained to the Advocates' Society about some of the low quality advocacy, describing a typical defence lawyer as "a warm body with a legal pedigree". In his defence, the Chairman of the Criminal Division of the Advocates' Society, David Humphrey said: "Some are so inexperienced, that they have to take a cab to court because they don't know where it is and they have to hope the cab driver does". (<u>Toronto Star</u> 21/1/1978)

Nevertheless, it remains the case that:

"the most significant factor in satisfaction was the outcome of the case, which accounted for 52% of the variance throughout the sample." (Arafat and McCahery 1978, 198-205)

Perhaps more important in the context of this study:

"the fact that the accused judged their lawyers largely on the basis of outcomes is not surprising. It is much easier to judge by visible outcomes than by the often invisible and normally mysterious means by which lawyers and crime control agents achieve them..." (Feeley *op cit* 333, Curran *op cit* 19)

It does seem that, with all its limitations, focus on outcomes is the least risky way of approaching legal need and responses to it.

It was not until 1984, over a decade after endorsing the legal services movement, that the Lord Chancellor's Legal Aid Advisory Committee, in its review of the criteria for eligibility, recognised the importance of testing consequences. Their criterion was that the greater the gravity of consequences for a criminal defendant, the greater their legal need and vice versa. However, they did not suggest that consequences should be compared between those in receipt of Legal Aid and those without. (34th Legal Aid Annual Report 1983-84 HC 131 VI paras 193, 240)

One significant statement that appears to move towards the position developed in this book came from the Lord Chancellor, Lord MacKay of Clashfern. It was made during his participation in the Institute of Judicial Administration Conference on the Green Papers on Reform of the Legal Profession. In supporting the view of Jenny Levin, Head of the Law Department at the South Bank Polytechnic, that from the consumer perspective advocacy could not be considered an exclusive specialist skill, he urged:

"Those who practice advocacy to realise that the position that it should be an exclusive specialism, which we adopt in the Green Papers, is not self evident at all." (NLJ5/5/1989.603)

In conclusion, it should be repeated that consequential comparison is a negative test. It can only show where a particular adjectival, legal, need does not exist. It does not follow that need exists, inferentially where such a negative test is passed.

Zander's influential views on unmet need in criminal justice are stated in his book 'Legal Services for the Community' published during the Royal Commission on Legal Services. He gave several examples of such need, which will be analysed below along with other relevant material. These examples are: that the unrepresented plead guilty more than the represented; that the represented are twice as likely to be acquitted before Magistrates; that the majority imprisoned by magistrates are unrepresented. To this list should be added the relative grant of Bail for the represented and unrepresented. Zander commented that "obviously the effect of such disadvantages is likely to be serious in criminal cases." (Zander 1978, 274-280) Clearly these situations could constitute a significant amount of unmet legal need and that the comparative need asserted does, in fact, contain a significant differential between the various outcomes of the professionally represented and others.

The method to be used here, is the application of the critique developed earlier in relation to representation and attendance before welfare tribunals. This will be restated and then tested by a few British and American studies: representation (and attendance) correlates with successful outcome (and vice versa).

There are 14 limitations:

1) The curve is not absolutely reliable in all studies.
2) There are risks in generalising from welfare tribunal evidence.
3) Significant variations exist: over time; from locality to locality; and between individual judges.
4) Representatives may not be a single homogeneous type. (For example barristers before the Magistrates, or solicitors in Crown Court).
5) Representative groups may be present too infrequently to allow for significance testing. (This could be true of barristers before some Magistrates, and solicitors before the Crown Court).
6) The topics contested may not be homogeneous.
7) The relationship between those represented and unrepresented is problematic.

8) Outcome may not be the only relevant test. Satisfaction may be equally apposite. There may be a relationship between outcome and satisfaction. ('Care' hypothesis)

9) Outcome should be considered against the preceding stages of the defendant's trial career. For example, it is abundantly clear that defendants have already been selected and form a biased population. This filtering occurs at the stages of suspicion, interrogation, arrest, and charge. Those kept within the system despite this process of attrition, may have special characteristics relevant to representation for the charges typically made. The characteristics can include age, gender, race, class and previous record.

10) The analogy between "Supercessions" in welfare claims and "plea-bargaining" in criminal justice - that is the negotiation of compromised outcomes primarily for administrative reasons - which do not result in a full trial, should not be ignored.

11) 'Over-representation'.
The analogy here is between Repeat-Player prosecutors and One-Shot unrepresented defendants.

12) Intensity of representation: for example number of witnesses called, or length of cross-examination.

13) Psychological factors: activism, combativeness, repetition.

14) Acceptance as a client.

Some introductory examples are now considered briefly within this framework.

These kinds of limitations and even falsifications of the general assumption of legal need can be demonstrated further from Zander's large study (1969, 643) of London defendants. He surveyed one Assize, two Quarter Sessions, and fifteen Magistrates' Courts with a sample of 1565 cases before 1140 magistrates, on which the study concentrates.

Appearance in person occurred in three-quarters of the cases. For some offences the cell size is too small for further consideration (3, Living Off Immoral Earnings, to 16, Firearms).

Sentence variety by Magistrates for the self-representing was also surveyed. The range was from 0 (Prison 12 months +) to 100% (Detention Centre; Prison 1 month -). If the insignificant samples are again removed,[1] the range becomes 53% (Prison 6-12 months, 15) to 97% (Fine £10-, 167). Again the salient factor is 'under'-representation, but the findings are, again, in other respects weakened since sentence was not related to charge or plea nor refinements such as court or comparison between types of representative.

In one sense, an authoritative rather than purely empirical answer to these problems has already been discussed. It is the Privy Council's majority opinion in

Robinson v R. In that case the defendant appeared in person alongside his legally represented co-defendant on a capital murder charge. The trial judge explained to the unrepresented defendant what jury challenge was, but this offer was not taken up. There do not appear to have been material differences in the two defences. The most important aspect of the defence was that counsel for the co-defendant failed to shake the chief prosecution witness in cross-examination. The split between majority and dissentients occurred largely over the consequences of lack of representation for Robinson; the majority took the view than no unfair disadvantage had occurred. These views are themselves speculative, but in the context of law and criminal justice they can be said - on the particular facts considered - existentially and dogmatically to dispose of the assumption of legal need as equalising consequential disadvantage in outcomes.

The section that follows is the first attempt at systematic analysis of outcomes between defendants legally represented and appearing in person. Material from 5 Common Law jurisdictions is used and analysed in relation to the stages of plea, venue choice, bail, verdict, mitigation and sentence. These materials have not been brought together and discussed previously. In addition, there are two further analyses of a comparative nature produced by this researcher, one of which, on the sentencing of convicted thieves with and without lawyers, follows immediately after the international material on sentencing.

Taken together this evidence will test the 'Cure' hypothesis developed in the previous chapters:

> Those legally represented will achieve significantly better outcomes at each stage in the criminal process than those appearing in person.

If this comparative-consequential method falsifies the hypothesis in general or for particular outcomes then further examination will be required of what weight representation has in the process and what is the significant element in judgments.

Footnote

1. 2: Prison 12 months - to 8: Detention Centre, Prison
    1 month - .

12 Applying Comparative-Consequential Method

Comparative empirical evidence on Outcomes

(i) Plea

Although not strictly an outcome, plea is crucial to foreclosing trial and the possibility of acquittal. It is, therefore, considered at this stage. A concluding summary of this evidence appears at the end of this section, and this format will be repeated.

Plea - Australia

1. A study of Victoria's Magistrates' Courts strongly linked appearance in person with Guilty pleas compared to those legally represented: 69% 88.1%. There were, however, considerable differences in the plea rates for different offences, ranging from 14% Not Guilty pleas for theft charges to 50% for assault, but the researchers did not relate these to type of representation. (Douglas 1975 Ch 7, T7.2)
2. The Australian Government Commission of Inquiry into Poverty found a similar pattern, with a much lower rate of Not Guilty pleas for those appearing in person: 23.5%; 64%.
This finding was, however, based on a tiny sample. (Cass and Sackville 1975, 56)

3. In a study of New South Wales Magistrates' Courts it was found that as the legal representation rate increased, so did the general rate of Not Guilty pleas. (Cashman 1982, 194, 205)

Plea - Canada

1. Hann's Toronto study found a significant differential between the pleas of those appearing in person and those legally represented at trial in the Provincial Court. Those legally represented maintained more Not Guilty pleas: 51.8%   61.9%. (Hann 1973, T9.5)
2. Wilkins' Toronto study covers this topic more exhaustively than any others. Two observations of plea behaviour were made, at original appearance and at trial. There was considerable inconsistency between the two. His study is also valuable for demonstrating the lack of homogeneity between the varieties of legal representatives: Duty Counsel, Legal Aid attorney and privately retained attorney. This difference holds true for plea, but will not be discussed here; plea practice for the self-represented will be compared with that of those represented, without reference to the differences within that group.

At the time of first appearance, the self-representing were the least frequent Guilty pleaders, at 42.8% (av 53.1%). (Wilkins 1975 T7.4) By the time of trial this had moved to 72.2% (av 68.8%), a shift upwards of 30% against an average shift upwards of 15% (*Ibid* T7.6) but not at a significantly higher rate than for those represented.
3. In a study of 3 Magistrates Courts and 2 County Courts in Halifax, Nova Scotia, with a sample of 1033, it was found that 66% of those appearing in person pleaded Guilty, double the rate for those legally represented. (Renner and Warner 1981, 62, 69) This differential reduced for those with previous records of multiple charges.

Plea - New Zealand

In the District Courts surveyed by the Department of Justice those represented by attorneys pleaded Not Guilty to 28.3% of charges, double those not represented: 13.2%. (Oxley 1981 Apdx 6, T15) Similarly, in the Children and Young Person's Courts, those represented by attorneys pleaded not guilty to 23.8% of charges compared to 10.4% of those not so represented. (*Ibid* T4.6)

Plea - U.S.A.

1. The one lower court study shows that, although there was a differential for race between Black and White Americans for Guilty pleas when self-representing (B 59.8%   W 71.1%) that was not the case for the plea

decision in general as Guilty pleas again correlated with self-representation and Not Guilty plea with legal representation (B 25.2%, W 23.5%). (Warren 1971, 326, 332)

2.   The American Bar Foundation survey is not easy to interpret, but the following conclusion can be safely drawn, though it is now of historical significance only. Defendants appearing without legal representation were most likely to enter Guilty pleas. (Silverstein 1965 I T29, 91-2)

Plea - U.K.

1,2. Two studies by Zander are relevant.   In the first, the differential between Guilty pleas for the represented and self representing was 31%, at rates of 55% and 86%. (Zander 1969, 633 T10) In the second, the average Guilty plea rate before the magistrates sampled was 87%, but for the represented it was 9%.   It was noted that this pattern varied quite considerably with the variety of charge.   For example, those accused of being drunk, and of obstruction pleaded Guilty at an even higher rate than average (95%, 96%); whereas those accused of loitering with intent did so in half the cases. (Zander 1972, 1041)

3.   In Dell's study of female prisoners, the general pattern was maintained.   Those without legal representation before magistrates pleaded guilty much more than those with such representation (86% 57%) and pleaded Not Guilty four times less (7% 28%).   The same occurred before Quarter Sessions and Assizes (86% 47%, 14% 39%). (Dell 1972 from T6)

4.   The Sheffield study found that 99% of the unrepresented pleaded Guilty to summary charges, whereas with the represented this response was less striking at 81%.   There was little variation with charge in this sample. (Bottoms and McClean *op cit*)

5.   A research report for the Royal Commission on Criminal Procedure showed that 95% of defendants in cases of 'private' prosecution appeared in person; the great majority in the 12 magistrates courts studied were charged with summary offences, pleaded guilty, and were fined. (Lidstone *et al* 1979, 30) This is not strictly a comparative example.

6.   Edwards studied women defendants in Manchester.   In 1981, there were 4471 female defendants.   Of those represented about half pleaded Not Guilty compared to 1.9% of those represented. (Edwards 1984 T8.6) Of the 298 accused of loitering and soliciting, 90% of those legally represented   (70.8%) pleaded Guilty compared to 98.9% of those appearing in person. (*Ibid* T2.1)

7.   Bridges surveyed adult (non alcohol or Road Traffic Acts) defendants in 6 magistrates courts.   The Guilty plea rates were

24% for those represented by private solicitors
45% for those represented by duty solicitors
73% for those appearing in person. (Bridges 1982, 12)

8.   Finally, the Lord Chancellor's Department examined
3000 cases in 59 magistrates courts with special
reference to Legal Aid applications.
The Not Guilty plea rates were:
    Non-applicants   7%
    Refused-applicants-In-Person   27%
    Refused-represented privately   33%
    Legally Aided   34% (LCD 10/1983 T15)

This shows very clearly the link between plea,
combativeness and type of representation.

Conclusion: Plea

Five common law jurisdictions have been examined through
17 studies, half in England and Wales.   They show a
general pattern both of pleading Not Guilty less and
pleading Guilty more, by those appearing in person, than
those being represented.   Representation may be
considered to embody combativness and appearance in
person acquiescence;   these interpretations should,
however, be distinguished from effectiveness.   The
general pattern may be modified for particular charges
and types of defendant.
    One cannot interpret plea behaviour easily as an
outcome, since that assumes a causal relation with lawyer
contact.   Obviously at one level plea, particularly the
Not Guilty plea leads on to trial, venue choice, and the
possibility of acquittal; further there is evidence in
the Crown Court that plea is not the only significant
correlate with sentence for all types of offences.
(McConville and Baldwin 1981 Ch 7, T10)

(ii) Venue - U.K.

As with plea, venue is not strictly an outcome, but
because it is linked with full trial by jury, also by a
greater statistical chance of acquittal, and a virtual
guarantee of Legal Aid, it can be examined at this stage.
It is only in those offences classified today as
Intermediate, that the option arises to select between
the Magistrates and Crown Court.
1,2. There are two British studies of this topic.   One is
the Sheffield study, already frequently cited.   The other
is a Home Office Study for the James' Committee on the
distribution of work between the Crown Court and the
Magistrates.   There are no significant differences
between the findings of these surveys.
    Where defendants have a choice, they overwhelmingly opt
for the Magistrates (95%). (Bottoms and McClean *op cit*
T2) Women opt for summary trial more than men, (*Ibid* 78)

but this may be linked to their offence patterns. The Sheffield study found that there were significant differences around the 5% average Crown Court choice. These ranged from 0 (Meter - Theft; Drugs) to 11% (Sex) and 14% (Assaults). (*Ibid* T4.2)

It seems that the major link with the venue selection is plea, but both surveys had limitations with sample sizes on some points and timing of plea. With these reservations it can be said that Crown Court selection has a strong association with Not Guilty pleas (69%) and magistrates with Guilty pleas (88%). In term of image, and of advice, Crown Courts are linked with acquittal on a Not Guilty plea to a greater extent than magistrates (48%   30%). (*Ibid* 79, T4.12, Gregory 1976 para 2.1.1, 2.1.2)   From the earlier discussion of plea it can be seen that venue is a function of plea - as is representation - and that two populations are involved. The majority population comprises Guilty pleaders before magistrates, without legal representation; the minority population comprises not guilty pleaders with legal representation, and on some charges they will be tried before a jury in the Crown Court. Recidivism was not relevant as a sub-population, except insofar as their reasons for choosing summary trial differed from those without previous convictions. Those with legal representation pleading Guilty before magistrates chose that venue because of the possibilities of a lighter sentence twice as often as others attending the magistrates (44%   23%), but recidivist-strategists did so twice as often again (89%   44%), (Gregory *op cit* T5) and were much less concerned about the alleged lack of delay in the magistrates' courts.

In the minority of cases where the Crown Court was chosen, it was selected as being the 'fairer', more 'professional' court - regardless of plea or previous record. (*Ibid* T3.2, 4.10)

Lawyers were far more involved in advice-giving in the Crown Court than the magistrates (78%   17%). But it was clear that legal advice was not the dominant element in the venue decision. Speed of process was the dominant reason, with sentence important to recidivists as a secondary reason. When lawyers were involved they saw the Crown Court in similar terms to their clients; as the venue for a real Not Guilty defence to a serious charge, principally because of the jury.

Venue - Canada

One study in Toronto found that representation had no statistically significant effect on venue choice. (Hann 1973 350, 358)

Venue - New Zealand

A Government study found that those without legal representation opted for summary trial at a rate of 74%, whereas those with legal representation opted for full trial at a rate of 65.6%. (Oxley *op cit* Apdx 7 T14)

Venue - U.S.A.

A study of state grand larceny defendants found no general difference in the rates of choice for jury trial between pro se defendants and those legally represented (30%, 31%), however urban defendants without counsel made that choice much less, at 20%. (Nagel 1982 T1)

Conclusion: Venue

Four jurisdictions have been surveyed and 5 studies examined. There is some disparity between the British, New Zealand and North American studies. In England and Wales the venue choice is significantly correlated to two variables, plea and representation. The general tendency is for those who wish to plead Guilty to remain unrepresented and to appear in person before magistrates. The opposite tendency occurs for those seeking jury trial. There may be some modification for such matters as gender, offence and recidivism, but they are not significant. As with plea one cannot be dogmatic about venue choice as an outcome in the direct sense, but with that reservation, it is clear that the legally represented maximise risk. It may be desirable to evaluate venue choice along with verdict and sentence, rather than on its own.

(iii) Bail
Bail - Canada

1. Hann's Toronto study found a differential in favour of bail for those appearing in person against those appearing with legal representation at first appearance:

Remanded in custody:
	Represented	In Person
	90.8%	98.3% (Hann *op cit* T8.3)

However at final appearance there was a dramatic alteration:
	Represented	In Person
	58.9%	27.5%

There were considerable differences between rates for various offences; at the extremes:
	Represented	In Person
Drugs	13.3%	7.3%
Liquor	84.5%	70.8% (*Ibid* T8.5, 8.6)

Hann took a special interest in the decision to request bail. Here there was a small but statistically significant advantage to those appearing in person for grant of bail:

71.4%   77.4% (Ibid 299)

Hann's evidence was that defendants were less likely to ask for bail if there was a high probability of conviction (Ibid 302); such requests correlated significantly with not having a previous career in court, and with liquor charges. There was no support from the hypothesis that defendants with legal representation were more likely to request bail. (Ibid 303) Hann's study was undertaken before the Ontario bail reform.

2.   In Wilkins' later study in Toronto, made after the bail reform, the self-representing defendants were on custodial remand in 29.5% of their cases, against an average of 34.9% of all cases. It follows that they were at a marginal disadvantage compared to those with representation. When bail was granted, security ordered was lowest for the self-representing, with 40% in the $0 - $199 bracket (average 26.3%), and 27.1% in the $500 - $10,000 bracket (average 44.3%). (Ibid T4.15) Thus the self-representing were not disadvantaged.

Bail - New Zealand

The Department of Justice study found a marginal advantage to those without legal representation (71% Bail: 69.8% private lawyer: 64.5% Legal Aid). (Oxley *op cit* T19) The situation was similar in the Children and Young Persons' Court, with bail for 98.5% of those without legal representation (95% private lawyer: 87.2% Legal Aid). (*Ibid* T4.9)

Bail - U.S.A.

1.   The only study to examine bail in misdemeanour courts found an insignificant advantage for pro se defendants over those with legal counsel (75%, 73%). This latter gross figure masks a significant difference between the bail rates from those with private attorneys (82%) and court assigned attorneys (58%). (Bing and Rosenfled 1970 TD)

2.   Another study of state grand larceny defendants found that those with legal counsel were more likely to be bailed: 53%   36%; this was intensified for the non-indigent: 74%   37%. However, those with counsel, including those remanded in custody, were more affected by delay (more than two months from arrest to bail): 60% 89%, and again this intensified with the non-indigent: 57%   96%. (Nagel *op cit* T1)

3. A longitudinal study of felony defendants remanded in custody in Baltimore Jail, showed that those without legal representation increased considerably between November 1975, May 1976 and August 1977: 20.8%, 26.3%, 46.4%. (Alpert and Huff 1983 254 T10.1) However, advice and assistance in the Jail rose from two thirds of cases to three quarters, and pre-trial release service cases rose from half to two-thirds, but no significant effects on bail reduction or release occurred. The authors commented:

> "Whilst not statistically significant, this is problematic from the effectiveness of counsel." (*Ibid* 256)

Bail - U.K.

1. Dell's study of women prisoners in Holloway found significant differences for length of pre-trial custody. There was equality for both groups for detention up to 15 days (59%, 61%). Detention between 16-22 days was slightly associated with the unrepresented (27% 20%), but remand for longer periods were associated with represented defendants (20% 12%). (Dell *op cit* 74)

2. The studies by Zander do, however, show an important context in which representation is advantageous. As has been stated above, the gross rates were practically identical for both groups in one study (76%, 75%). (Zander 1969, 633 T10)

3. However, his earlier study with Glasser (on a very small sample) showed that in 38.3% of the sample police objected to bail. In those circumstances the unrepresented (69%) received bail in 20.6% of their cases as against 50% for the represented minority of two defendants. (Zander and Glasser 1967, 816) The point is amplified in a later study of 597 magistrates' cases. Where the police opposed bail at first appearance, the grant rate was 37% for the represented and 20% for the self-representing; at later hearings the differential was 29% to 9%. (Zander 1971, T5) The value of representation correlated with the tenor of information put before the magistrates. The represented had less negative information adduced (39%; 48%) and more positive information adduced (40%; 26%) than the self-representing. (*Ibid* T15) The possible link with offence type was not examined.

4. King's Cobden Trust survey, of 782 cases, in 76 courts found that in gross terms the self-representing had a slight advantage over the represented in bail applications (88%; 81%):

> "These figures, however, may merely reflect the fact that defendants facing more serious charges tend to be represented and it is in such cases that the police are most likely to oppose bail."

Although the questionnaire did ask whether the police contested bail in each case, the responses were found to be unreliable, so it was not possible to take the analysis any further. (King 1976, 11)
5.   The Sheffield survey also considered this issue, examining uncontested bail, and contested and uncontested remand decisions. On all three topics the represented came out ahead where the plea entered was Guilty:

	Unrepresented	Represented
Uncontested	23%	53%
Custody contested	36%	41%
Custody Uncontested	23%	28%

Bottoms and McClean concluded that representation was linked to contest, rather than outcome, in which the key factors were the offence charged, sex of defendant, and previous record. (Bottoms and McClean *op cit* T8.7)
6.   All these studies were made before the Bail Act 1976 came into operation, which introduced objective criteria such as, 'community links' within a Due Process philosophy, with the intention of reducing the pre-trial custodial population. (Robertshaw 1983, 329) One study of the impact of that legislation is relevant. (Cutts 1982, 1089) Cutts used a sample of 63 cases in 1976, and 157 in 1981, both from a North West Midlands city. He found that, as expected, the bail grant rate had risen from 40.5% to 59.8%. He also noted that self-representation had risen from 11% to 17%, but did not relate the two phenomena statistically, though he did conclude that neither representation nor offence type were now relevant to the increased grant rate. This suggests that self-representation is not a disadvantage in gross terms under the Bail Act, but as has been suggested, that was already the case. Like Zander (1979, 108) he noticed that under the Act police objections to bail had dropped from 54% to 34.3%. However, again in line with the Act's objectives and with Zander's impact study, the success rate for defendants of contested application had risen sharply from 7.6% to 26.1% (with an increase in conditions imposed on the bail granted). The samples of contested cases both in 1976 and 1981 were very small (14, 23) and were not related to type of representation.
It can be said that self-representation at bail applications has historically been a liability in the minority of cases where police objected to bail. It is likely that the procedure laid down by the Bail Act, has reduced or even eliminated that disadvantage. This is attributable to the mandatory quasi-inquisitorial procedure that the court must now adopt if a defendant in unrepresented in a contested case, and also because the criteria generally assist defendants regardless of representation.

Conclusion - Bail

Bail is an important outcome, not merely because of the desirability for defendants to remain free before trial, but because of the link between pre-trial custody and conviction. (Simon and Weatheritt 1976; Foote 1966; Rankin *et al* 1963, 67) If there is a link between representation and bail, then one may hypothesise a further link between representation and acquittal. Four jurisdictions have been surveyed and 13 studies examined. It is not easy to draw conclusions from those studies. The most important reason for this is that it is often difficult for the studies themselves, or for an interpreter of them, to ascertain whether defendants arrive at legal representation with bail, or whether this status is achieved by such representation. In addition, one is not always comparing like system with like system. For example, historically both Ontario, and England and Wales, moved to a more liberal bail procedure around 1974-1976, so the studies in each system before and after those dates are not properly comparable for testing the impact of representation. In addition, the American and Canadian bail systems are based on direct money payments, or bonds, which the British (outside Scotland) is not. Bail in those jurisdictions may therefore, as indeed representation, be a function of wealth rather than representation.

With these caveats, what emerges is that there are marginal advantages to defendants without legal representation in some studies and marginal disadvantages in others - in other words, no significant difference overall. More important is the relationship between police objections to bail and those objections being contested. The rate of objection is in part determined by the statutory background; in this minority of cases there is evidence of advantage to those with legal representation. However, where those legally represented are remanded in custody, they are remanded for longer.

To draw a general conclusion here is not easy. One may suggest that there is no apparent and clear advantage to those legally represented under a bail regime which operates a presumption in favour of bail.

(iv) Verdict

Verdict - Australia

1. The earliest study has, at first sight, striking findings from a large sample in New South Wales Courts of Petty Sessions. Vinson and Homel found that representation rates were virtually the same, at about a third, for both recidivists and those with no previous convictions. However, they found one striking difference between the 'one-shot-players' with and without legal

representation. Acquittals for the former where at a rate of 11.3% against 1.7% for the latter, almost a sevenfold differential; however, this differential is probably overstated, because no attempt was made to consider outcome against plea. (Vinson and Homel 1973, 132 T1) Although they did test outcome against a variety of three charge types, and demonstrated strong differentials, those findings where marred by small numbers. (*Ibid* T2; Apdx A) In short, this early comparative study only clearly demonstrates that few are acquitted by magistrates, and many of those had legal representation. It did not demonstrate how that representation occurred and whether it in turn achieved anything that its absence would not have.

Cashman has commented:

"No doubt because of the dramatic impact of these findings the results have been uncritically accepted and reiterated in almost every Australian report and publication which has sought to examine the need for Legal Aid in criminal proceedings since they were reported."

In particular he urged caution in relation to the multiplicity of relevant variables, and that "outcome varies dramatically across offence categories". (Cashman 1982 Ch 8, 203-7) Cashman's own work will be considered below.

2. The second Australian study was an official one. It demonstrates a link between both legal representation and plea (Not Guilty), and self-representation and plea (Guilty), and also between Plea and outcome, with acquittal rates higher for those represented at trial. However, the samples are so minute (14; 24) (Cass and Sackville *op cit* 37-8) as to be of no statistical value.

3. The La Trobe University Legal Studies Department study of Victoria's magistrates and justices shows, again, that one needs to refine beyond gross acquittal rates. As far as Not Guilty pleas were concerned, the acquittal rates for the legally represented were marginally higher than for the self-represented (18.5%, 15.4%) (La Trobe 1980 T7.2) However, as with Wilkins' Toronto study, what was far more significant was charge withdrawal practice. These researchers saw representation as the key to negotiation of withdrawal rather than acquittal through advocacy. Indeed, they were somewhat scathing of the standards of advocacy (*Ibid* Douglas 47) and concluded that in terms of both decision and sentence "in most cases nothing a lawyer can possibly do is likely to make much difference." (*Ibid* 100-1)

However, the study shows that the introduction of other variables does have a link with acquittal, when combined with plea and representation. One example is type of judge. The rate of representation was not significantly different before lay Justices or professional Magistrates

(10.2%, 8.2%) but the offence tried and acquitted on Not
Guilty pleas differed markedly before each type. The
Justices acquitted 19.2% of such traffic charges, of
which the Magistrates received none; whereas the
Magistrates acquitted 27% of such theft or violence
charges, of which the Justices received none. (*Ibid*
T10.1) This theme will be taken up later in the context
of 'Inverted Need'.

Further, there was a link between rate of Not Guilty
pleas for type of offence and Acquittal rate:

Offence	NGP%	Acquittal at Trial%	NG%
Assault	50	13.1	6.6
'Other'	30	7.0	2.1
Traffic	27	5.1	1.4
Theft	14	4.5	0.6 (*Ibid* T7.2)

4.   This aspect of Cashman's work on magistrates justice
in New South Wales is presented by him in such a way that
no conclusions can be drawn from it directly. However,
by combining the statistics from different tables one can
relate representation patterns to conviction patterns and
draw some limited conclusions. (Cashman *op cit* T6C, 6E)
The limitations are that there are no statistics for the
outcomes of particular offences, nor for plea.

If one examines the various districts one finds first,
that in only 4 of the 27 districts is the conviction
proportion for those appearing in person higher than the
representation proportion, and in only one of these is it
'significantly' higher (5%+).

If one then examines those districts where their
conviction proportion is significantly lower (5%+) than
the representation proportion, there were 9 of such
districts.

There were also 14 districts where the advantage to
those appearing in person was not significant (0-5%).

Since these patterns are simply the reverse of those
for the legally represented, the inferences to be drawn
are that in general, the representation pattern is
irrelevant to outcome at trial (14: 27); in a further
third there is no 'need' for legal representation if
(average) outcome is the paramount issue (9 : 27); and
that in only one district was there a significant
advantage to those legally represented.

There is, however, a more basic point to be made, which
concerns the absolute rate of conviction in each of these
categories.   If one links the absolute conviction rate
with the representation rate, it becomes apparent that in
those districts where those appearing in person are
convicted less, the absolute conviction rate is lower
than the majority of districts (where the representation
pattern is not significant to outcome) and that this in
turn is less than that of the 4 districts where the
conviction rate is higher for those appearing in person.

Thus:
9 districts (In person conviction rate significantly lower)   Abs. conv.prop 66.5%
Av Conviction rate (in all 27 districts)   72.2%
14 districts (In person conviction not significantly lower)   Abs. conv.prop 74.9%
4 districts (in person conviction significantly higher)
                                                Abs. conv.prop 84.3%

It follows that conviction rates correlate positively with legal representation and vice versa. Thus:

4 Districts with conviction proportion marginally higher than that for those appearing in person:

4 Districts	In Person%	In Person Conv.%	Total Conv.%
Bankstown	47.2	47.4	75.9
Lidcombe	64.4	65.7	88.2
Waverley	8.7	9.5	91.6
Belmont	52.2	64.2	81.3

4 Districts	In Pers Conv Rate%	Rep Conv Rate%	Totalav
Bankstown	76.1	75.7	72.2
Lidcombe	89.3	86.9	72.2
Waverly	92.4	90.8	72.2
Belmont	93.4	69.2	72.2

9 Districts with conviction proportions at least 5% less than rate of appearance:

9 Districts	In Person%	In Person Conv.%	Total Conv.%
Balmain	48.4	42.2	64.0
Burwood	53.3	48.2	63.0
Campsie	55.6	49.9	63.2
Central	54.2	47.6	72.5
Newcastle	39.4	33.7	70.9
Newton	68.1	56.1	50.8
N. Sydney	41.1	32.3	62.7
Wyong	36.9	31.1	69.7
Pt. Kemble	42.1	31.8	81.7

9 Districts	In Person Conv Rate%	Rep Conv Rate%	Total Av Conv %
Balmain	57.8	70.2	72.2
Burwood	57.9	68.1	72.2
Campsie	57.5	68.9	72.2
Central	65.9	79.1	72.2
Newcastle	65.2	76.6	72.2
Newton	38.8	62.8	72.2
N.Sydney	53.9	71.5	72.2
Wyong	63.9	75.5	72.2
Pt Kemble	71.4	92.0	72.2

To recapitulate, these reconstructed statistics are not controlled for other variables - in particular offence-

charged variations between the districts - but they
demonstrate overall a rather striking disproof of the
assumption of representation-effectiveness underlying
legal need theory. In only one district, Belmont, out of
27, does the negative test fail.

Verdict - Canada

1. Hann's Toronto study found a statistically
significant lack of difference in conviction rates
between those with and without legal representation:

	In Person%	Represented%
At first appearance	56.1	55.5
Last appearance	58.0	53.3
or on Not Guilty plea alone	19.5	24.0

His conclusions are very strong. In general it is the
type of offence that has a significant effect on verdict
even after other variables have been controlled,
including legal representation. (Hann *op cit* 405)
Neither of the two regression analyses performed showed
that having legal representation at first appearance was
a significant factor in determining the probability of
verdict. 'This is certainly not the result one would
have expected.' (*Ibid* 406) Once again, the results do
not indicate that the accused's chances of obtaining a
favourable verdict are increased by having legal
representation at the appearance at which the verdict is
most likely to be handed down. (*Ibid* 409)
Finally, the coefficient of the legal representation
variable was consistently insignificant. In other words,
the result of the statistical analysis did not disprove
the hypothesis that having legal representation has no
effect on the verdict to be expected in a case. This has
the implication that the 'costs' of not having more
extensive systems of legal aid are not as high as one
would otherwise suppose:

> 'Some of the aforementioned results are consistent
> with the prevailing 'wisdom' or 'myth' regarding the
> administration or justice - others obviously are
> not. The latter category of results certainly
> include the findings that having legal
> representation at either first of last appearance
> are both insignificant in their effects on the case
> verdict.' (*Ibid* 418)

2. Wilkins' Toronto study also found that the total
guilt rates, by plea and trial, were not significantly
different between those appearing in person and those
represented (75.2%, 71.9%). (Wilkins *op cit* T7.1). Where
multiple charges were laid, those without legal
representation were convicted more on the most serious
charge (68.8%, 61.4%); in addition those representing

themselves were far less often convicted on one charge and acquitted on others (13%; represented groups 27%, 48%). Wilkins noticed that the strategies differed for each group and that the patterns signified the absence of plea-bargaining by those representing themselves. (*Ibid* T7.7, 115-7)

Where defendants maintained Not Guilty pleas the conviction rate between the represented and unrepresented groups varied a little, depending on the bail status of the defendant, but those legally represented were convicted more than those without attorneys:

Conviction:	In Person	Represented
Remand	55%	60%
Bail	52%	62.5% (*Ibid* T3.2)

3.   Renner and Warner's study of defendants in Halifax, Nova Scotia, found no significant difference between the conviction rates of those pleading Not Guilty to summary charges, whether or not legally represented. (Renner and Warner 1981, 62, 69)

Verdict - New Zealand

1.   In the Department of Justice survey, the total conviction rate by trial or plea was significantly higher for those appearing in person at 83.9%, against 70.9% and 67.6% for the legally aided and privately represented. In the Children and Young Persons' Courts this adverse differential only existed against those with Legal Aid:

Unrepresented	89.4%
Private representation	89.3%
Legally aided	78.2% (Oxley *op cit* T20, T50)

However, if one excludes plea and limits observation to conviction at trial on a Not Guilty plea, there is a considerable advantage to those appearing in person: 9.7%   ;   31% private;   39.1% Legal Aid.   The pattern was different in the Children and Young Persons' Courts with much the lowest conviction rate being for those privately represented, at 25%;   40% appearance in person;   66.7%, legally aided. (NZ Dept of Justice *op cit* T51)

Verdict - U.S.A.

1.   In the Boston survey the unrepresented come out ahead of the represented in gross terms for conviction on Not Guilty pleas (48%   56%).   When the gross figures for representation are broken down, the unrepresented are equal to those with private attorneys (48%, 49%) and ahead of those with assigned attorneys (48%;   65%). (Bing and Rosenfeld *op cit* TD)

This study is valuable for adding further variables to representation and Not Guilty plea. The first was venue, the site of the trial at three urban or three suburban courts, will be considered later in more depth as 'Inverted Need'. There were wide differentials in the acquittal rate from court to court, both for those assigned lawyers (0 Court V 'Suburban' - 34% Court II 'Urban') and for those without a lawyer (14% Court I 'Urban' - 74% Court IV 'Suburban'). There were also wide differentials between the rates for the lawyers and self-representing groups within each court ranging from 2% (for self-representation: Court VI 'Suburban') to 50% (Court V 'Suburban'). But the salient fact to emerge is the advantage to the self-representing in five of the six courts. (*Ibid* TI)

That advantage is in general carried through when the offence variable is added, though this was not correlated against venue. On the Not Guilty pleas the self-representing were acquitted more on four of six 'major' offences: Assault (63%   29%), Thefts (35%   16%), 'Public Regulations' (47%   26%), Non-Support (32%   16%). On two other such offences there were no significant differences: Danger to Persons (7%   9%), narcotics (19%, 18%). On robbery the sample was too small for significance to be attached. (*Ibid* TJ)

2.   Warren's Detroit survey tested for two variables, representation and race. Race was clearly irrelevant to outcome compared to representation. However, neither plea nor offence was considered.

	Black			White	
	Attorney	No Attorney		Attorney	No Attorney
Guilty	59.3%	73.1%	=	59.2%	74.6%
Guilty of lesser offence	1.3%	2.1%	=	1.0%	1.2%

(Warren *op cit* T5)

3.   These findings are only partly supported by another study of a general court in a Mid-Western metropolis when the conviction rates were:

	Black			White	
	Attorney	No Attorney		Attorney	No Attorney
Guilty	61%	=	59%		37%	65%

4.   At trial, state grand larceny defendants in one study were acquitted at a rate around 10%, except for urban defendants appearing in person, whose acquittal rate was 5%. (Nagel *op cit* T1)

5.   Feeley's work, limited to one major city is sceptical in its conclusions on advocacy, 'only slightly more favourable Nolle rates and sentences for defendants with counsel'. (Feeley *op cit* T5.5) He also made a multiple regression analysis of 24 legal, social and

structural factors relating to verdict. As can be seen, lack of representation was relatively high in the ranking, but of light weight.

1.   Number of charges   123.77
2.   Bail   10.44
3.   Prior Arrest record   8.62
4.   Arrest on Warrant   8.45
5.   Defendant not represented   3.39
6.   Age   2.96
7.   Weapons in possession   1.70   (*Ibid* T5.1)

Feeley commented:

> "Those who had some prior acquaintance with the victim, were represented by attorneys and were younger, were all more likely to receive Nolles than their counterparts." (*Ibid* 132)

also, that a use of alternative statistical techniques upheld the relevance of number of charges and type of attorney, but was of no relevance to appearance in person. (*Ibid* 135)

Verdict - U.K.

1.   Three studies by Zander are relevant. The first had a small sample: 60 Not Guilty pleas at Bow Street Magistrates' Court, London, in which 8.5% were acquitted. There was an even split between the represented and those without representation. (Zander 1967, 815)
2.   The second study covered 1018 trials and 720 magistrates. There was a marginal advantage to the represented, at 57% convictions, against 62% for the unrepresented . However, the study did not test for the variables of venue, charge or type of representative, despite producing such information in the survey. (Zander 1969, 633 T9)
3.   The final study was of 840 magistrates' cases, 13% of which involved Not Guilty pleas, of which 37% were represented. Those represented at trial achieved an acquittal rate of 64% against a rate of 30% for those representing themselves. It is clear from the study that there was a wide range around the average of 13% Not Guilty pleas (4.6% Obstruction - 50% Loitering with intent). Unfortunately the study does not carry through to relate plea, representation and outcome to type of charge. (Zander 1972, 1041)
4.   In Borrie and Varcoe's West Midlands regional study they produced a reasonable sample 73 for 'Court C' on pleas. Typically, more of the represented pleaded Not Guilty than the unrepresented (23% 5%). The resulting acquittal rate is a tiny sample, 9, in which both the represented and unrepresented achieved a 33% success rate. They commented: "the legally assisted defendants

include a higher proportion of those likely to plead Not Guilty before the question of legal advice regarding the plea ever arises." (Borrie and Varcoe 1971, para 214)

5.   In Manchester in 1981, Edwards found a very similar rate of acquittal on Not Guilty plea by 4471 women defendants, both legally represented and appearing in person: 48.8%, 51.2%. For the specific offence of loitering and soliciting there were only 5 defendants pleading Not Guilty and appearing in person, so no comparison should be made. (Edwards *op cit* T8.6, T2.1)

6.   The Lord Chancellor's Department Survey of Legal Aid in Magistrates' Courts found that the acquittal rates in the 59 courts on Not Guilty pleas were:

Refused Legal Aid - Appeared in Person	30%
Legally Aided	42%
Av	44%
Refused Legal Aid - Private representative	52%
No Application - Private representation	52%

(LCD *op cit* T17)

This shows a clear disadvantage to those denied Legal Aid and conducting their own defence, though there is no evidence here on the outcomes for particular offences.

Conclusion - Verdict

Five jurisdictions have been surveyed and 20 studies examined.

If one limits focus to the gross acquittal or conviction rates for those without legal representation, those with legal representation have a clear advantage. However, if conviction on Not Guilty plea at trial is considered, the picture blurs. A tentative set of conclusions is:

-    offence charged is very significant
-    where negotiation occurs it is usually where there is legal representation, and it can produce advantages not available to those excluded from negotiation. (Baldwin and McConville 1978 T1, T2)
-    at trial, the classical test for advocacy, there are differences from area to area
-    in general at trial there are no significant disadvantages to those without legal representation

As Nash put it:

" all causal conclusions regarding representation and acquittal should carry a government health warning." (B. Nash, The Guardian 28/1/1980)

Verdict, it must be repeated, is the first stage in the criminal justice process where the 'cure' hypothesis for legal representation can be said to have been unequivocally tested. Sentence is the other.

(v) Mitigation

Mitigation - England

Since the large majority of defendants plead guilty, and the majority of those tried are convicted, the practice of making statements or giving evidence in mitigation of the offence can, without exaggeration, be considered the most important routine act of advocacy. The first study to consider this process with regard to the unrepresented defendant was the Sheffield survey. The survey classified such mitigation on a three-level scale: extended statements, brief statements, and no statement or 'nothing worthwhile'. It was found that:

>   2% made extended statements
>   28% made brief statements, and
>   70% said nothing, or nothing worthwhile. (Bottoms and McClean op cit 163)

Only one study concentrates on this important topic. Since it compares both represented and unrepresented defendants, and the Crown Court and magistrates together, they will be considered here.

Shapland studied statements regarding or attempting to mitigate the gravity of the offence, attitude to the offence, the defendant's personal circumstances and the court and related processes. She also analysed the sentencing suggestions put forward by or for defendants.

The average number of <u>gravity of offence</u> factors can be calculated from the number of factors cited divided by the number of speeches:

```
Crown Court GP represented: 36 factors/29 speeches: 1.2
Crown Court NGP         "   15    "   /14    "       1.1
Magistrates GP          "   25    "   /43    "       0.6
Magistrates GP unrepresented 3    "   /21    "       0.1
(Shapland 1981 T3.2)
```

<u>Attitude to offence</u>
```
Crown Court GP represented: 61 factors/29 speeches: 2.1
Magistrates GP          "   60    "   /43    "       1.4
Crown Court NGP         "   15    "   /14    "       1.1
Mags. GP unrepresented      12    "   /21    "       0.6
(Ibid T3.3)
```

Personal circumstances
Magistrates GP represented:102 factors/43 speeches   2.4
Crown Court GP   "   57   " /29   "   2.0
Crown Court NGP   "   13   " /14   "   0.9
Mags. GP unrepresented   2   " /21   "   0.1
(Ibid T3.4)

Court and other legal processes
Magistrates GP represented: 43 factors
Crown Court GP   "   40   "
Crown Court NGP   "   13   "
Magistrates GP unrepresented   0

Sentencing suggestions
Crown Court GP represented   28/29 : 96.6%
Magistrates GP   "   40/43 : 93.0%
Crown Court NGP   "   9/14 : 64.3%
Magistrates GP unrepresented   1/21 :   4.8% (Ibid 83)

This uniform pattern of low involvement of Guilty
pleaders before Magistrates has an effect on the judicial
reasoning at the sentencing stage:

Mean sentencing reasons given
Crown Court NGP represented   : 7.2
Crown Court GP   "   : 4.6
Magistrates GP   "   : 1.7
Magistrates GP unrepresented   : 0.8 (Ibid T6.2)

and the place of mitigation factors in that reasoning:

Magistrates GP represented   : 27.8% of reasons
Crown Court GP   "   : 18.8%   "
Crown Court NGP   "   : 8.5%   "
Magistrates GP unrepresented   : 6.7%   "

With this latter group reference to the defendants'
antecedents predominated at 40%, compared to the other
groups: 16.5%, 15.9%, 0.
   Shapland makes a number of comments on this situation
and disparity.   Possible explanations put forward
include:

-    the situational rules governing behaviour in court
     and the form of the invitation to the represented
     defendant as inhibiters of response. (Ibid 59)
-    the ignorance of such defendants, for example they
     will probably not know which mitigations could be
     effective and will not know the sentencing opinions
     and policy regarding particular offences. (Ibid 83)
-    they are 'outsiders' to the courtroom culture and
     its practices and will be disadvantaged, as are
     visiting advocates. (Ibid 87)

In reviewing Shapland's work, Hall Williams sums up:

> "The advantages of being legally represented even
> when there is no dispute about responsibility for
> the offence, are clearly indicated. The
> unrepresented defendant may be seriously
> disadvantaged." (Hall 1984, 498-9)

and former Chief Justice Parker is recorded as having
said "an effective mitigation in person is rare". (Home
Office 5/1961)

From the perspective of this work one must be less
enthusiastic, without in any way wishing to disparage
Shapland's pioneering study. There are five problems to
be raised, some of which reduce one's ability to draw
strong conclusions.

First, by no means all defendants in person are
'outsiders'. As 'repeat players' they may well know the
situational rules and operating policies of a court and
be content to abide by the sentence expected. As
Shapland showed, 40% of magistrates' sentence reasons
related to antecedents, more than for any other group.

Second, for most courts and for most offences a
'tariff' operates, so it is only at the margins of
particular tariff outcomes that mitigation can be
effective.

Third, there may be positive advantages in non-
participation and relative silence to a defendant. As
Shapland points out, the unrepresented pleading guilty
never mentioned aggravating factors, whereas
representatives do draw attention to them in mitigating
them. (*Op cit* 82) The defendant has, according to
Shapland, 'all the information', but without
representation nobody will speak for him. (*Ibid* 120)
This, however, may equally work to the defendant's
advantage as detriment. (Baldwin and McConville 1978,
544)

Fourth, there is no information in Shapland's work on
the actual sentences passed on these mitigating
defendants. Comparison of such sentences would be
essential to verify empirically the hypothesised
centrality of the mitigation process. Such comparison is
made below both from the British and comparative Common
Law jurisdictions available, and also from a survey
carried out by this writer.

Finally, there is a technical limitation with
Shapland's study. Although two groups have already been
eliminated here because their cell sizes were so small,
it must be added that, with the exception of those
pleading Guilty, and with legal representation before
magistrates, 43, the other groups are also weak in this
respect: 29, 14, 21. One should not, and Shapland does
not, draw any statistical generalisations from such small
numbers.

Social Enquiry Reports (SERs)

These documents can be important in the mitigation process. The mitigation process can be considered to be the central moment in criminal justice, since the great majority of defendants plead or are found guilty.

In two good samples of imprisoned females, Dell found that there was little difference between the represented and unrepresented before Magistrates, where SERs were made in slightly over half the cases (59%, 55%). However, before higher Courts the unrepresented received such reports much more (85%; 60%). (Dell *op cit*)

In a very small sample in the same year, White also found that the unrepresented cases had them introduced more than the represented (75% - 33%). However the unrepresented defendants never received a copy and never questioned the Probation Officer on them. By contrast the represented did get copies in a quarter of the cases and the Probation Officer was always questioned on it. (White 1971, 690)

In New Zealand those without legal representation appeared with Probation Service reports much more than those with privately retained or legally aided representation, (84.5%; 66%; 42%). (NZ Dept of Justice *op cit*)

It can be speculatively concluded that for some, Social Enquiry or Probation Service reports are a substitute for or variety of representation. What cannot, however, be concluded from the New Zealand survey, any more than from Shapland's work, is whether these reports actually affect sentence. The risk here is the confusion of 'care' and 'cure'.

(vi) Sentence

Sentence - Australia

1.   The earliest Australian survey, on New South Wales petty session cases appears to find a sharply defined advantage for those with legal representation, both for verdict and sentence. The survey concentrated on the defendants with no previous conviction, 'one-shot-players'. For such defendants Discharge is available at the discretion of the court in certain charges. Those with legal representation received such a Discharge over twice as often as those without (16.4% - 7.5%). (Vinson and Homel *op cit* T1) These differentials carried through to particular offences, or groups of offences:

        Larceny   26.7% - 8.8%
        Driving   19.8% - 6.1%
        Summary   33.5% - 8.0% (*Ibid* TII)

When linked to class for those aged 25-39 years, the differential increased consistently:

AB	23.6% - 0
C	19.8% - 3.3%
D	35.2% - 8%

However, above the age of 40 years, Discharge was awarded in half the cases regardless of representation. (*Ibid* TIII)

The drawback with this study is that it does not link these patterns to plea. As we have already seen plea - Not Guilty plea - is the major correlate of legal representation. In some matters the samples were tiny.

2. The plea variable was considered by Cass and Sackville in their study for the Australian Government Commission of Inquiry into Poverty. For those convicted on a Not Guilty plea they found that those with representation were fined between A$40-400, and tended to consider the fines harsh and severe. Those without representation were fined between A$5-150 and considered that they had been treated fairly. However, this study does not relate outcome to type of charge and it too relied on a tiny sample. (Cass and Sackville *op cit* 58)

3. The La Trobe University Legal Studies Department study of Victoria's Magistrates' Courts overcomes these limitations to some extent. Using the polar outcomes of Discharge and Prison, the former correlates with first charges of theft or violence and a Guilty plea, which is treated as a mitigation for such "severer" offences. The latter correlates with at least three previous charges of theft or violence and Not Guilty plea: an unsuccessful recidivist defendant. "Previous convictions of such offences are the key", (La Trobe *op cit* Douglas Ch 8 B1) rather than representation. "In general, the plea of mitigation appears to be a ritual, rather than a crucial stage in the sentencing process." (*Ibid* 66) Key variables are status: the shabby and unemployed being incarcerated and the professionals not; (*Ibid* T9.1) and venue: the Justices ordering Bonds, except for recidivists who are fined or placed under Probation; the Magistrates ordering fines, and imprisoning recidivists. (*Ibid* T10.1) Both status and venue would have to be correlated to charge to assess their full significance. Venue will be considered further below as 'inverted need'.

4. There is one study from South Australia which produced findings showing a clear advantage to those legally represented:

Legally Represented	- Fine	79.8%	Av Fine	65.3%
In Person	- Fine	64.6%	Av Fine	65.3%
Legally Represented	- Prison	20.2%	Av Prison	34.7%
In Person	- Prison	35.4%	Av Prison	34.7%

(Eggleston 1976, T2.42)

It can be seen that there is a marked apparent advantage to those represented. Since over 95% of defendants appeared in person, it is reasonable to consider other variables. This, Eggelston does. His study is in fact of what was at that time a virtually dichotomous legal system for aboriginal and white South Australians, in terms of charges, representation, judges and sentencing. Representation in this case may be seen as an effect rather than cause.

5. Cashman is critical of Vinson and Homel's path-breaking study, mainly because they ignored the considerable differences in custodial rates from offence to offence, from 2%-33% and the variations from year to year. In Cashman's study 'for all 11 offences represented defendants were more likely to be sentenced to imprisonment than those without representation'. (Cashman *op cit* 206-8) In 1977, in the New South Wales districts studied, those legally represented received 3.7% custodial sentences, compared to 1.8% of those without attorneys. Actually this masked an important differential, since privately retained lawyers achieved the same rate as those without lawyers, the rate for Legal Aid lawyers was double.

In conclusion, Douglas comments from his study of thieves and violent offenders: (Douglas 1980, 240, 246 T3)

> "participation (cross-examination) may lead to the exposure of information damaging to the defence case. If this were so, one would expect legally represented defendants' participation to be more strongly and favourably related to sentence than unrepresented defendants' participation. There is no evidence to suggest that this is so."

Sentence - Canada

1. The Halifax, Nova Scotia study found that particular sentences correlated with appearance in person and with legal representation.

	Fine	Suspended/Discharge
In Person	80%	20%
Represented	36%	64%

Fines were also positively correlated with summary rather than indictable offences, (63% - 12%), (Renner and Warner *op cit* T2) and as has been seen above summary charges were positively correlated with appearance in person rather than representation (59% - 10%). Unfortunately, none of the other patterns found in this study can be referred to here, either because they no longer coalesce suspended sentences with discharges or because they do not relate the sentence to representation.

2.   Hann does not display the data of his study, but he
does recount the results of his regression analysis of
sentence.   He concluded that representation is

> "still not shown to have any significant effect with
> regard to type of sentence or sentence in relation
> to particular crimes." (Hann *op cit* 428, 437)

Further, legal representation was not shown to have any
effect on the length of any potential prison term. (*Ibid*
446)
3.   Wilkins' Toronto survey is also relevant.   If one
were to examine the sentence outcomes for the represented
and self-represented in his survey in isolation, it would
appear superficially that the self-representing are able
advocates.   The statistics are highly significant and
show a low incarceration rate compared to the legally
represented (12.9% - 25.6%), a high rate of sentence
without fine or prison (33.7% - 25.6%) and an above
average rate of fine with prison alternative (53.5% -
48.9%). (Wilkins *op cit* T7.10)   In addition, prison
sentences for the unrepresented tend to be short, 30.3%
being under 7 days (average 24.2%), but as has been
suggested previously, this is simplistic.   Wilkins' study
enables   us   to   understand   how   the   defendants   are
channelled through various choices to these particular
outcomes.   We know that the self-representing are less
often charged with jury choice offences, and offences
with a maximum sentence in excess of two years, (*Ibid*
56-7, T4.2) that they tend to be minor public order
charges (*Ibid* T4.7) with Bail, at a low sum (*Ibid* T4.14,
4.15); and they tend to plead Guilty. (*Ibid* T7.4, 7.6)
     It is hardly surprising that the sentence outcomes
listed above occur in a particular pattern.   They simply
reflect the population channelled towards that decision -
outcome.   Each type of legal representative similarly
fits into a particular client population, with regular
verdict and sentence outcomes characteristic to that
population.

Sentence - New Zealand

In the Department of Justice study the fine was highly
correlated with appearance in person: 73.5% - 56.7%,
private 31.5%, legally aided.   (Oxley *op cit* T23)
Further, if these outcomes are controlled by seriousness
of charge by limiting observation to those with maximum
penalties of 3 months, 1 year and 7 years' custody
respectively, the differential increased to 78.8% and 77%
for 3 months and 1 year, but reduced to 61.1% for 7
years' custody. (*Ibid* T24, 25, 26)
     Those appearing in person had the lowest custodial
rates at sentencing, but only narrowly less than those
privately represented.   The largest differential was with

those legally aided: 15.9%, 18.6% - 40.1%. (*Ibid* T23) In the Children and Young Persons' Court appearance in person correlated strongly with suspension orders on conviction, at 66.7%. (NZ Dept of Justice *op cit* T54).

Sentence - the U.S.A.

1. The Boston survey examined the sentence outcomes of all those pleading guilty and found guilty.

Those without legal representations were jailed much less than average (12% - 23%) and far less than those with court-assigned attorneys (35%). They were put on probation more than average (13% - 8%) and more than those with assigned attorneys (6%). They were ordered to pay fines or make restitution marginally above the average rate (26% 23%) and much more than those with assigned attorneys (10%).

In gross terms, it appears that having no legal representative was a positive advantage in terms of avoiding prison and receiving the 'softer' sentences. The only sentence where there was approximate equality between the two groups was suspended prison (38%, 41%, average 35%). However, the study did not interrelate its findings on type of pleas, type of charge, or venue. (Bing and Rosenfeld *op cit* TG, W)

2. The Detroit survey surmounts most of these problems. First, it is possible to construct some notion of the significance of charge type in the sample, although it is only related to the variable of Race and not carried through to procedural variables. Thus, the major charges were Larceny, in which Blacks predominated over Whites (29.9% - 13.2%). On the next most frequent charge, Assault, there was approximate parity (B 9.3%, W 11.7%). The other charges where there were parity were Soliciting (B 7.3%, W 7.8%) and Malicious Destruction of Property (B 2.1%, W 2.4%). Blacks predominated in Non-Support of Family (10.1% - 3.8%), and Illegal Occupation (4.2%, 1.7%), Whites marginally predominated in Vagrancy charges (4.5%, 1.2%). (Warren *op cit* T1)

As stated above, the study did not statistically link the charge patterns with those for sentence, but it is clear that the profiles are different - such as the link between Whites, drink and vagrancy - and that this will have some link with sentence. The study does show in some detail the link between sentence, race, and representation, and discloses patterns of bias which might be accounted for in the patterns of charge, especially as the study disclosed no bias in verdicts. (*Ibid* T5)

The survey examined outcomes on four groups of corrections.

(a) On Probation the outcomes were equal for Blacks, with and without legal representation, and for Whites with representation (50.5%, 50.5%, 49.2%). Whites without representation received Probation less (35.5%).

(b) For prison, those without legal representation were incarcerated most, but within each segment there was no consistency for race: No representative, W 24.7% - B 18.6%; Represented, B 13.3%, W 5.9%. Length of incarceration was not investigated.

(c) Concerning Fines, those with legal representation predominated, regardless of race (B 23.3%, W 21.2%), against those without legal representation (16% B 12.4% W).

On the 'softer' sentences of Fine, or suspended prison term, or psychiatric care, Whites came out ahead, almost regardless of representation (Without: 27.3%, With 22.8%) against Blacks (Without: 14.8%, With: 22.8%). (*Ibid* T1, 6,7)

It is likely that these variations are related in part to plea and charges. Warren introduces another variable, status, measuring by three indicators of dress. (*Ibid* T8-10) It is clear that these indicators were highly significant, but equally it was not clear whether they were independent or dependent variables, for example informal appearance may have been no more than corroboration that the defendant was a drunk, vagrant, white, rather than a signal for the exercise of class bias by a bespoke suited justice as Warren suggests.

3.   Nagel found that those convicted of state grand larceny were more likely to receive the 'soft' sentences of suspended custody or probation if represented by counsel (47%; 37%) and this pattern intensified for non-indigent convicts (58%; 38%).

He also found that those imprisoned were more likely to be in custody for less than a year if represented by counsel: (48%; 22%). However, this pattern reversed for non-indigent convicts: (37%; 46%). (Nagel *op cit* 135) When treated statistically for their independent effect the differentials for 'soft' and 'hard' sentences reduced to 7% and 17%. (*Ibid* Apdx I)

4.   Clarke and Koch's study of 798 burglars found that those without lawyers went to prison least, at 29% regardless of their income. Those with Court assigned counsel were imprisoned at rates of 36% (low income) to 53% (high income) and those with privately retained counsel were imprisoned at rates of 19% (high income) to 34% (low income). (Clark and Koch 1976, 57, 83)

5.   By contrast Feeley's New Haven study, not limited to any type of offence, concluded that the :

"presence or absence of an attorney made no measurable impact on the severity of the sentence".

In his multiple regression analysis of factors relevant to outcome, his variable of representation did not figure at all as significant to severity of sentence:

1.   Type of charge; public order   10.59
2.   No previous convictions   6.94
3.   No court appearance   5.18
4.   Sex of defendant   5.15
5.   Political party of judge   4.77

Again, the application of alternative statistical techniques produced nothing additional or contradictory, and underlined the weakness of this variable.   He concluded that:

> "there is no conventional explanation for this variation"

and

> "it has been argued that an attorney is indispensible to a defendant at sentencing, but in fact neither type of counsel nor presence nor absence of counsel seemed to make much difference at sentencing, and only a slight difference at adjudication". (Feeley *op cit* 132-5, T5.1, 5.5)

6.   A study of the sentencing practice of Oklahoma courts examined the effects of defendant's race and 'defence strategy' in particular plea and type of counsel - including its absence - in relation to 385 burglars and 356 homicides, against 6 other variables. Variance in sentence length was explained by race to between 1-3%. For burglars 'defence strategy' explained 16.5% of variance, but this was accounted for entirely by plea rather than type of representation. For homicides the type of representation was a relevant explanation but only as to 3% of the variance. (Kelly 1976, 241)   Thus, it appears that the type or absence of representation was marginal to sentence length.[1]

7.   Lizotte had reached similar conclusions in a study of prison sentence length for 816 convicted defendants in Chicago in 1971 against 8 variables including type of representation. He concluded:

> "Those with no attorney get slightly shorter sentences than those with private, non regulars, whilst Public Defenders secure the longest sentences for their clients." (Lizotte 1977, 565)

8.   By way of footnote Zeigler and Hermann's study of Pro Se actions by convicted prisoners shows very high rates of summary dismissal of their efforts, 'against the determined opposition of state attorneys in almost all cases':

	1968/69	1970/71
Habeas Corpus	69.5%	83.1%
s.2255 (Civil Rights)	85.2%	93.3%
Complaints	91.8%	86.7%

(Zeigler and Herman 1972, 159 T6)

but success rates of 71.4% and 61.1% and 50% for Habeas Corpus petitions that survived to full consideration in both District and Federal Circuit Courts. (*Ibid* T8)

U.S. Juvenile Courts

1. There are two studies that show the relevance of representation to sentence in juvenile courts. The earlier study did show differences in outcomes between those with and without lawyers. However, the study is more noteworthy for showing, through full experimental method, the different outcomes between two courts. At 'Gotham', with long established judges, the traditional American 'social work' orientation to juvenile cases was maintained, whereas at 'Zenith' recently established judges operated a 'legal' model, with a juvenile public defender and legal aid office. Although there were significant differences within each court for outcomes in relation to type of representation, the differences for each type of representation were greater between courts. (Stapelton and Teitelbaum 1972, 52, TIII, 4-6) Again, this is relevant to 'inverted need' discussed later.
2. The other study of the Charlotte and Winston-Salem, North Carolina juvenile courts, demonstrated the low chances of those appearing in person being commited to a training school or being transferred to a superior court for sanction, compared to those represented by private or court assigned counsel or by juvenile defenders. (Clark and Koch 1980 263 T11) This study also constructed a 'risk' index regarding commitment to a training school, based on five levels comprising previous record, seriousness of offence, the type of complainant, home situation, and parent's attendance at court. Those appearing in person were least likely to receive such an order in the third (15% - Av. 20% - 28% Private) and fourth highest bands (15% - Av. 40% - Assigned Counsel 50%). In the highest band those appearing in person were most likely to be so committed (0 Private - 90% Av. 98%). (*Ibid* 300)

However, the authors comment:

"In our study ... youngsters unrepresented by counsel were a predominantly medium and high income group ... those who did without counsel probably did so by choice or by their parents' choice ... a possible explanation is that the courts may have regarded attorneys as an impediment." (*Ibid* 305)

Sentence - The U.K. Evidence

There is little British evidence on this topic. As was stated in the introduction to this section, Zander's pioneer study in 1969 on the relationship between representation and sentence did not investigate this topic comparatively. The Home office study on 'Sentencing Practice in Magistrates' Courts', which focussed on the wide variations in sentences from court to court, was silent on the representation variable. (Tarling 1979)

1. Borrie and Varcoe's West Midlands study, showed approximate equality between the two groups for all terms of imprisonment, for fines, and for conditional discharge and dismissal. Defendants with legally aided representation were sent to Quarter Sessions for sentence, given suspended prison sentences, and probation far more often than those representing themselves.

However these findings were not related to charge or plea, and were based on a tiny sample. (Borrie and Varcoe *op cit* T14)

In addition, they analysed the sentences for 82 defendants convicted of "relatively serious offences" at "Court C":20.2% of the defendants were legally represented with Legal Aid, 11.9% with private solicitors and 67.9% represented themselves:

(i) A quarter received custodial sentences, amongst whom the legally aided were over-represented (35.5%);

(ii) 30% were fined, of whom the legally aided were markedly under-represented (5.8%) and the self-representing over-represented (38.6%);

(iii) 10.7% were conditionally discharged or dismissed. Both groups of legally represented were over-represented (17.6%, 20%).

(iv) The only group to be linked to a specific charge were the five defendants sent to Detention Centres, all of whom were unrepresented and were charged with drug offences. (*Ibid* T15)

But, against this evidence that legally aided representation is positively correlated with imprisonment of its clientele, Borrie and Varcoe conclude,

"the picture painted by this Table is most disturbing and shows that Legal Aid is still not reaching a significant number of those who require it at this court." (*Ibid* pa 121)

2. Dell's study of women prisoners elicits a different point. Dell's is the original study of the plight of the unrepresented, amd does show striking contrasts between the represented and unrepresented in the Magistrates' Courts. Those imprisoned or sent for Borstal training comprised 17% represented and 81% unrepresented defendants, a picture which only modifies slightly if remands are taken into account: 17%; 69%. However, it is contradicted for those imprisoned in lieu of paying a

fine (81%; 19%) and for those sentenced by Quarter Sessions and Assizes (81%; 19%), even when remands are taken into account (74%: 14%). (Dell *op cit* T1) Further, when length of sentence is considered, the missing values in the study are suggested. For sentences under three months the unrepresented are greatly over-represented (85%; 15%). There is marginal inequality between the two groups for intermediate sentences of 3-6 months (53%: 47%) but for sentences of 6-12 months and in excess of one year, the represented defendants significantly predominate (29% 71%; 14% 86%), as do they in Borstal training (32%; 68%). (*Ibid* T2)

3.   Two other studies also relate sentence to the gender of the offender. The first was limited to Theft Act offences, with a sample of 408 cases decided by the Cambridge magistrates' court in 1979. The researchers conducted a dichotomous regression analysis covering 17 variables, including representation and concluded that representation and plea were not independently important:

> "The effect of legal representation is probably a function of the fact that it is required in certain cases when severe sentences are likely." (Farrington and Morris 1983, 229)

The most important predictor of sentence severity was the type of offence; previous convictions, age and guilty plea also combined to produce more severe sentences. They did, however, suggest that there was a link between legal representation and reconviction for men, but not for women, and this, it followed, affected sentence. (*Ibid* 244)

4.   Edwards' study of female defendants in Manchester magistrates' courts showed some significant differentials in sentencing dispositions in relation to representation and plea:

Conditional Discharge Av 31.3% NGP - In Person 41.7%
Fine   Guilty - Represented 27%
                        Av. 44.7%
                        NGP - Represented 54.2%
                        GP - In Person 60%
Probation Not Guilty In Person 4.2% GP - Represented 18.3% (Edwards *op cit* T8.6)
For those guilty of loitering and soliciting they were:
Fine   Guilty-represented 32%, GP - In Person 55%
Suspended Sentence   Av 11.4% NGP - Represented 21%
Custody   Av 6.2% Change Plea - GP - Represented 17%
(*Ibid* T2.1) For these female defendants pleading Guilty and appearing without professional representation seems to have been advantageous.

Conclusion - Sentence

Five jurisdictions have been surveyed and 23 studies examined.

Since in all jurisdictions the great majority of defendants are sentenced, either as a result of a guilty plea or conviction at trial, this may be considered the most important outcome to compare, for policy purposes; comparison of verdicts is relatively peripheral to the day-to-day reality of criminal justice.

If one examines the studies as a whole, a generalisation can be made: in nearly all the studies those convicted without legal representation are at an advantage, in that they receive proportionately more 'soft' sentences and less 'hard' sentences than those without legal representation.

It would, however, be misleading to stop at such a conclusion. For example, two of the studies suggest strongly, that with their samples ethnicity was more important than other variables in the sentencing decision. The point already made, that there is a difference for 'soft' and 'hard' sentences needs amplification. It should be obvious now that in general such varieties of sentence will be related to the varieties of charge. One method, which some of the studies attend to, is to focus on specific charges and to maximise the degree of specification for other variables that may be relevant beyond that of representation. The other, rarely done, is to employ a statistical method, such as multiple regression analysis, which can isolate the independent effect of a variable, such as representation against all other relevant variables.

If one considers the studies from these perspectives the following conclusions may be drawn. First, there are considerable differences from district to district and bench to bench. It follows that there may be an advantage for those with legal representation for some offences or sentences, and sometimes the advantage is with those appearing in person. Second, occasionally variables other than offence may predominate.

In general one must conclude with a negative statement: the assumption that legal representation is the appropriate response to legal need at the stage of sentencing is not proven; this is supported by those studies using multiple regression analysis.

(vii) Comparative-Consequential Need in Criminal Justice

Summary of empirical studies in five jurisdictions

Plea

Representation is associated with Not Guilty pleas, though offence and personal characteristics may modify this generalisation.

Although the Not Guilty plea cannot be considered an outcome as such, it is a pre-condition for trial and potential acquittal.

Venue

In general the same points are relevant as for plea.

Bail

Bail is an outcome in its own right and also because it has been shown to relate to acquittal positively.

Much depends on the institutional structure and procedure of the bail decision.

Representation is an advantage where the presumption in favour of bail is weak, and irrelevant when it is strong. Again, offence and defendant characteristics are of some relevance.

Verdict

If one examines trial alone, there is no general disadvantage to those appearing in person, although particular charges do give rise to different patterns.

The advantages for those represented lies in the possibility of negotation pre-trial.

Mitigation

There is only one study and this does not make any consequential comparison.

Those without representation tend to receive Social Enquiry Reports more than those represented, but again nothing is known of their comparative consequences. This is considered in the following section.

Sentence

This may be considered the key outcome to test because although less dramatic than the verdict on trial, it is far the most common outcome in the court; sentence may range from discharge to many years in custody.

What the evidence supports is a conclusion that those appearing in person do receive 'soft' sentences compared to those legally represented, however only a minority of the studies clearly relate sentence to offence charged. In these instances legal representation does not appear advantageous, however there are also district variations and occasionally ethnicity surfaces as a key variable.

Conclusion to the international survey of comparative-consequential outcomes.

The 'Cure' metaphor for legal representation cannot be said to be vindicated. It is a matter of interpretation whether that in itself falsifies the 'Cure' hypothesis. The safest conclusion to draw is one that the hypothesis is 'not proven', that is, that whilst it is definitely not positively supported, neither is it clearly mistaken. What is needed is detailed focus on specific offences, employing as wide a range of variables as can be managed. This follows immediately. The issue of district variation is considered further below.[2]

Footnotes

1. In Texas G. W. Baab and W. R. Furgeson 45 <u>Texas Law Review</u> (1967) 471, 487 reported: "The results indicating that offenders with no counsel are treated even less severely than those with retained counsel could reflect sympathy on the part of the sentencing authority or a bargain which includes waiver of counsel; however these results are based on a comparatively insufficient sample and support no definite conclusion."

2. The only material discovered relating to outcomes in Crown Courts was in H. Levenson 'The Price of Justice' 1981: 85 appeals from magistrates heard by Knightsbridge Crown Court. The cell size for privately retained counsel and for those appearing in person are too small for statistical inferences to be drawn:

	<u>Total Dismissed</u>
Privately retained	(22.2%)
Legally aided	43.7%
In Person	(63.3%)

13 The Impact of Representation on Sentence

A Comparative-Consequential Study of Thieves

Here follows an empirical study with particular emphasis on theft, taking into account other attributes of those convicted and sentenced. It is a continuation of the previously cited survey material.

(i) Representation and Sentence

Sentences imposed were, in order of volume:
Fine   (186),   'Other'[1]   (125),   'Non-specific'(87),[2]
Probation(53), Discharge (49), Custody (44), Committal to the Crown Court for sentence (32), Community Service Order (CSO) (32), Suspended custody (31): 639. Again we can divide them in terms of representation:

	Represented	%	In Person	%	Total	%
Fine	98	8.9	72	54.1	170	28.1
'Other'	95	20.1	23	17.3	118	19.5
Discharge	23	4.9	18	13.5	41	6.8
Probation	42	8.9	10	7.5	52	7.6
Custody	40	8.5	4	3.0	44	7.3
CSO	27	5.7	4	3.0	31	5.1
Non-specific	83	17.6	2	1.5	85	14.0
Committal to Cr.Ct.	31	6.6	0	0	31	5.1
	472	99.9	133	99.9	605	99.8

Chi^2 = 95.76 Sig. p < 0.001 with 8 dsf.

This table is useful for demonstrating the significant correlation between particular sentences and representation, notably suspended and custodial sentences with legal representation and the discharge and fine with appearance in person. It is also clear that to link those patterns with other variables, notably offence, cannot always be attempted. Either one cell is too small as in suspended and custodial sentences, probation, or committal to the Crown Court, or both cells are too small as in discharge and community service orders.

This leaves the fine, the typical sentence, as the only one viable for further investigation, but there is no point in doing so since the number of types of offence will produce sample sizes below viability for such measures.

To reiterate the major assumption of method: over-generalised description in comparative study can be misleading. Equally, refined description requires a large enough pool of material to provide statistically viable cells for every relevant permutation. This presents practical problems that are rarely overcome, however, to skate over these difficulties is not an adequate response. An attempt will be made, therefore, to place only meaningful linking catagories between type of representation and type of sentence. Because there were 14 offence categories and 9 sentence types in the survey it should now be clear that even with a sample of over 600 originally, not many generalisations can be safely made, but where they are made a clear distinction can be made between one statistically reliable and between a judged impression.

(ii) Representation and Bail

The focus of this survey was on sentence, so we do not know what the active relationship between representation and bail status was, but information was available on bail status itself.

Of the 447 defendants, where full information was available, 56 (12.5%) were legally represented and remanded in custody, (8 (1.8%) appeared in person, remanded in custody, 76 (17%) appeared in person on bail, and 307 (68.7%) were legally represented on bail.

The bail rate was 85.7% which is absolutely in line with the national position since the Bail Act 1976. The numbers remanded in custody without legal represention are tiny, as expected, but this prevents any comparisons for that group. The bail rate for those without legal representation was higher than for those with representation (90.5% 84.6%) (Whites 91.5: 86.9%).

Using two comparative measures: proportion within each group, and proportion of the entire category, an estimate was made of the relevance of other possible salient factors in the bail-representation catagories. Later

this can be tested against sentence outcome.   These
factors were:

```
    offence : theft, burglary
    race    : white
    age     : less than 21
    status  : single
```

56:	Remand			(8:	Remand	
	x Representation	10.8%			x In Person	5.7%
(11	Burglary	12.8)		(0		/)
28	Theft	14.9		6		8.0
40	Single	13.6		7		8.0
39	White	8.8		6		5.5
27	-21 years	19.3		2		3.4)

307:	Bail			76:	Bail	
	x Representation	84.6%			x In Person	90.5%
59	Burglary	84.3		(2		100.0)
99	Theft	77.9		42		87.5
178	Single	81.7		48		87.3
260	White	87.0		66		91.7
130	-21 years	82.8		39		95.1

All Not sig. p < 0.05.

It can be seen that those appearing in person are
slightly more likely to be bailed than those legally
represented, and more so if aged under 21 years. Theft
is an offence where those legally represented are less
likely to be bailed than if appearing in person. However,
none of these statements have statistical significance,
though if presented as a progression table, limited to
those with bail, it appears that those appearing in
person, charged with theft, are at a marginal advantage
to those legally represented, and more so if aged under
21 years:

```
Bail:   21 years - x In Person    95.1%
        White     x In Person     91.7%
        Av        x In Person     90.5%
        Theft     x In Person     87.5%
        Single    x In Person     87.3%
        White     x Represented   87.0%
        Av        x Represented   82.8%
        Single    x Represented   81.7%
        Theft     x Represented   77.9%
```

(iii) Representation, Employment and Sentence

The employment status of a convicted person has some
significance in a regime where the fine is the principal
sanction for the majority of offences. That status also
must have significance in a culture where work is a prime
measure of status and of personal acheivement, if not of
survival - that is the more so where most defendants are

male with no alternative recognition and status from
unwaged household work.

In this survey, information was gathered on employment
status in relation to representation and disposition.
Information on offence linking those relationships was
not available; however, if it had been the cell sizes
would have been too small for analysis, except perhaps
for theft and the fine.

There were:

      75 in full-time employment, legally represented
      23 in full-time employment, appearing
                            in person (23.5%)
17.2% 98
    305 unemployed and legally represented
     81 unemployed and appearing in person (21%)
68% 386
     47 in part-time employment, legally represented
      3 in part-time employment, appearing
                            in person (6%)
8.8% 50
     21 in full-time education, legally represented
     13 in full-time education, appearing
                            in person (38.2%)
6.0% 34
     568

It can be seen that the unemployed are massively present
as convicted defendants. Both they and the fully
employed are legally represented in line with defendants
in general. However, those in part-time employment are
almost always legally represented (94%) unlike thos in
full-time education (61.8%). No reason for this can be
put forward on this information.

*Disposition Patterns of the Legally Represented in
Relation to Employment Status.*

Sentence	F.time	%	Unempd	%	Pt.time	%	(F.t.Educ.%)	
Probation	5	6.7	31	10.2	1	2.1	1	4.8
Discharge	2	2.7	16	5.2	2	4.3	5	23.8
Fine	31	41.3	58	19.0	4	8.5	3	14.3
Suspended	11	14.7	20	6.6	3	6.4	0	/
CSO	4	5.4	22	7.2	2	4.3	0	/
Custody	5	6.7	33	10.8	2	4.3	1	4.8
Committal	5	6.7	24	7.9	3	6.4	0	/
Non-specific	7	9.3	39	12.8	22	46.8	0	/
Other	5	6.7	62	20.3	8	17	11	52.4
	75		305		47		(21)	

It can be seen that employment status is extremely important in relation to disposition where the defendants share the characteristic of legal representation.

Full-Time
Employment :   Fine 41.3%, Suspended custody 14.7%
                     Least: 'Other' 6.7%
Unemployed :   Custody 10.8%, Probation 10.2%
                  Committal 7.9%, CSO 7.2%
                  (Fine 19%, 'Non-sp' 12.8%, Other 20.3%)
Part-Time
Employed   :   Non-specific 46.8%
                     Least: Probation 2.1%, Fines 8.5%

Disposition Patterns of those Appearing in Person in relation to Employment Status

Sentence	(F.Time %)		Unempd %		(Pt.Time %)		(F.t.Educ. %)	
Probation	2	8.27	5	6.2	0	/	2	15.4
Discharge	1	4.3	12	14.8	0	/	2	15.4
Fine	16	69.6	44	54.3	2	66.6	5	38.5
Suspended	0	/	0	/	0	/	0	/
CSO	1	4.3	3	3.7	0	/	0	/
Custody	0	/	2	2.5	0	/	0	/
Committal	0	/	0	/	0	/	0	/
Non-specific	0	/	0	/	1	33.3	0	/
Other	3	13	15	18.5	0	/	4	30.8
Totals	(23)		81		(3)		(11)	

Suspended, Committal to the Crown Court and 'non-specific' sentences 0

Unemployment, representation and sentence

Comparison can only be made fully for the unemployed, as their statistics were highly significant (Chi^2 = 67.64, sig. at p. 0.01 with 8 degrees of freedom). For those in full time employment the findings are **not** statistically significant (Chi^2 - 12.086 with 8 degrees of freedom) since 7 of the 9 cells total less than 8 defendants. A Chi^2 test is therefore invalid.

Apart from Probation (10.2%, 6.2%), CSOs (7.2%, 3.7%), and Other (20.3%, 18.5%) there are significant differences in the rates of every disposition. For two sentences these are very large. Those appearing in person are fined at the rate of 54.3%, compared to 19% for the legally represented, and were never awarded 'non-specific' sentences, compared to 12.8% for the legally represented. Discharges occur more often for those appearing in person than for the legally represented (14.8%, 5.2%). Suspended prison sentences - often custody - all occur with legal representation (6.6%, 10.8%, 7.9%: 25.3%) and never for those appearing in person.

Theft, Representation and Sentence

This, typical crime provided enough cases for a more detailed comparative examination that would be statistically viable.

But the limitations must, nevertheless, be acknowledged. First, to repeat the point made earlier: there is no information on plea, and it is not normally known which type of court the defendants were convicted in. In addition, the term theft covers both attempts at one end of the scale and robbery at the other end. On the other hand deception, burglary and handling are excluded, so on balance it is a relatively homogeneous category. As has already been said, the prior conviction rate was nearly always 2 or 3, so no further attention will be given to defendants' records. Finally, there is no information on the value of items stolen by these thieves, value almost certainly being relevant to disposition in some circumstances.

The general pattern of theft dispositions is presented first.

	Theft Represented		Theft In Person		Other Crime Represented		Other Crime In Person	
	N	%	N	%	N	%	N	%
Probation	20	9.9	5	6.8	22	7.6	5	8.3
Discharge	17	8.4	9	12.3	6	2.1	9	15.0
Fine	34	16.7	41	56.2	64	22.1	31	51.7
CSO	11	5.4	2	2.7	16	5.5	2	3.3
Suspended	6	3.0	0	/	26	9.0	0	/
Custody	18	8.9	0	/	22	7.6	0	6.7
Committal	16	7.9	0	/	15	5.2	0	/
'Non-specific'	19	9.4	2	2.7	64	22.1	0	/
'Other'	40	19.7	14	19.2	55	19.0	9	15.0
Totals	203		73		290		60	

Theft:Fisher's exact Chi^2 = 47.24 <u>sig</u> p.<0.001 with 8 d.f
Other: " " = 58.14 <u>sig</u> p.<0.001 with 8 d.f

If we restrict ourselves to thieves, those appearing in person are fined at a massive rate compared to those legally represented, who receive custodial sentences, are committed to the Crown Court for sentence and receive 'non-specific' sentences at a greater rate. One hypthesis that might account for these divergences would be the value of the property stolen.

With certain dispositions there are no significant differences: probation, discharge, Community Service Orders and suspended sentences.

Theft, Representation, Bail and Sentence

For the past 20 years it has been recognised that there is a strong positive association between remand and custodial outcome. Those defendants bailed prior to trial are more likely both to be acquitted and to receive a non-custodial sentence if convicted.

In the present survey the sample size does not allow for double-correlation tests - for example bail and gender or age or ethnicity - against variables other than Representation and one further variable at a time. In this instance the cell sizes for remanded defendants are too small to allow for comparison: 27, 5. It follows that the comparison can only be made validly for those with bail.

Theft, Representation, Bail and Sentence

		Represented - Bail %		In Person - Bail %
12	Probation	12.5	4	10.3
6	Discharge	6.3	6	15.4
13	Fine	13.5	17	43.6
(4	CSO	4.2	1	2.6)
(4	Suspended	4.2	0	/)
(5	Custody	5.2	0	/)
(5	Committal	5.2	0	/)
13	Non-specific	13.5	1	2.6
34	Other	35.4	10	25.6
96			39	

Chi^2 = 23.9 sig p.< 0.01 with 8 d.f. so not valid for CSO, Suspended, Custody, Committal.

It can be seen that three custody-related dispositions taken together occur for those with bail and legal representation (4.2%, 5.2%, 5.2%) 14.6%, but never occur for bailed thieves appearing in person. In addition non-specific and 'other' sentences are awarded more against the legally represented (13.5%, 35.4%: 48.9%) than those appearing in person (2.6%, 25.6%: 28.2%.)

Those appearing in person are discharged more than the legally represented (15.4%, 6.3%) and fined on a massive scale by comparison (43.6%, 13.5%).

For Probation (12.3%, 10.3%) and CSOs (4.2%, 2.6%) there are no significant differentials related to representation.

Theft, Representation, Social Enquiry Report (SER) and Sentence

	SER				No SER			
	Rep'd	%	In Person	%	Rep'd	%	In Person	%
Probation	13	20	2	9.5	0	/	0	/
Discharge	5	7.7	4	19	7	10.6	4	10.3
Fine	9	13.8	8	38.1	20	30.3	26	66.7
CSO	7	10.8	2	9.5	1	1.5	0	/
Suspended	1	1.5	0	/	3	4.5	0	/
Custody	13	20	0	/	3	4.5	0	/
Committal	12	18.5	0	/	4	6.1	0	/
Non-specific	0	/	0	/	14	21.2	2	5.1
Other	5	7.7	5	23.8	24	36.4	7	18.4
	65		21		66		39	

Chi^2 = 15.72 with 8 d.f. <u>Not</u> sig.

Here there is such a preponderance of valueless cells that significance statements cannot be made. The only remark worth risking is that those legally represented and with a Social Enquiry Reports, tend to be steered away from the fine; those appearing in person without a Social Enquiry Report have a very high chance of being fined; we do not know by how much.

Theft, Representation, Gender and Sentence

	Males	Representation %	Males	In Person %
Probation	13	9.2	3	4.9
Discharge	12	8.5	8	13.1
Fine	28	19.9	34	55.7
CSO	8	5.7	2	3.3
(Suspended	4	2.8	0	0)
(Custody	16	11.4	0	0)
(Committal	16	11.4	0	0)
Non-specific	13	9.2	2	3.3
Other	31	22	12	19.7
	141		61	

Chi^2 = 37.96 <u>sig</u> p.< 0.001 with 8 d.f.

Although one can make comparisons between men and women with legal representation, which could yield statistically significant correlations, the cell size, 11, of women appearing in person is too small to make comparisons between the two female groups possible, so these comments are limited to male offenders.

Those legally represented are very much less likely to be fined (19.9%; 55.7%) than those appearing in person, and more likely to be sentenced to the 'non-specific' (medical) sentences (9.2%; 3.3%) than those appearing in person. Although the individual cell totals for suspended sentences, custody and committal to the Crown Court are too small for statistical comment, one can say that their aggregate shows a marked disadvantage to those legally represented (25.6%, 0).

The differences in either direction for probation, discharge, community service and 'other' offences are not marked.

Theft, Representation, Race and Sentence

	Representation		In Person	
	White	%	White	%
Probation	19	13	4	7
Discharge	12	8.2	7	12.3
Fine	29	19.9	30	52.6
CSO	7	5.0	0	0
Suspended	6	4.1	2	3.5
Custody	16	11	0	0
Committal	10	6.8	0	0
Non-specific	13	8.9	1	1.8
Other	32	21.9	13	22.8
	146		57	

Chi^2 = 32.93 sig p.< 0.001 with 8 d.f.

Comparison between Whites and Non-Whites with legal representation is not possible because the cell size for Non-Whites appearing in person is too small for statistical use. Comparison here is therefore only between Whites with and without legal representation.

Those Whites with legal representation incurred probation more than those without (13%, 7%) and also Community Service Orders (5%, 0) and 'non-specific' outcomes (8.9%, 1.8%). Against this they received all the custodial sentences and committals to the Crown Court for sentence (11%, 6.8%: 17.8%; 0, 0: 0).

Those appearing in person were fined on a large scale (52.6%, 19.9%).

In certain instances the type of representation was not associated with outcome. These were discharges (8.2%, 12.3%), suspended sentences (4.1%, 3.5%) and 'other' sentences (21.9%, 22.8%).

Theft, Representation, Age and Sentence

So as to preserve viable cell size for comparison, the sample was divided into those subject to the Children and Young Persons Act procedures of the Juvenile Court, and those subject to adult procedure.

	CYPA				20 years +			
	Rep'n	%	In Person	%	Rep'n	%	In Person	%
Probation	6	8.8	3	8.3	14	13.5	2	6.5
Discharge	7	10.3	5	13.9	9	8.7	4	13
Fine	13	19.1	21	58.3	17	16.3	17	54.8
(CSO	2	2.9	0	/)	8	7.7	2	6.5
(Suspended	1	1.5	0	/)	(4	3.8	0	/)
(Custody	3	4.4	0	/)	(14	13.5	0	/)
(Committal	6	8.8	0	/)	(10	9.6	0	/)
(Non-specific	12	17.6	0	/)	(6	6.7	1	3.3)
Other	18	26.5	7	19.4	22	21.2	5	16.1
	68		36		104		31	

CYPA Chi² Fisher's Exact = 24.53 sig p.<0.01 with 8 ds.f.
20+ " " " = 24.48 sig p.<0.01 with 8 ds.f.

Probation is statistically more probable for those aged above 20 years and with legal representation.

For discharge, neither age, nor type of representation is significant.

For fines, age is irrelevant, but appearance in person has a marked effect on its probability.

For 'Other' medical sentences, age is irrelevant, however legal representation has a small but statistically significant effect on the chances of being awarded these options.

Theft, Representation, Marital Status and Sentence

The cell sizes for those appearing in person who were married or of 'other' status were too small to allow for comparison, so comparison here is only of single persons legally represented or appearing in person:

	Single Represented	%	Single In Person	%
Probation	7	6.4	2	3.9
Discharge	11	10	6	11.8
Fine	21	19.1	29	56.9
(Suspended	3	2.7	0	/)
CSO	7	6.4	2	3.9
(Custody	14	12.8	0	/)
(Committal	8	7.3	0	/)
Non-specific	11	10	1	2
Other	28	25.6	10	19.6
	110		51	

Chi² Fisher's Exact = 32.19 sig p.< 0.001 with 8 d.f.

It can be seen that single persons appearing in person are fined at a massive rate compared to those legally represented (56.9%, 19.1%).

Those legally represented received custodial type sentences at a high rate whereas those appearing in person never did (2.7%, 12.8%, 7.3%: 22.8%; 0, 0, 0: 0).

Those legally represented received 'non-specific' and 'other' sentences at a higher rate than single persons appearing in person (10%, 23.6%; 2%, 19.6%).

For probation, discharge and community service there is no significant difference between the groups.

Theft, Representation and Sentence:
The Effect of Other Variables - Constructing Progression
Tables

So far the effect of representation against a single linked variable at any one time has been demonstrated. It is clear that there is no simple correlation for all purposes between representation and outcome even in relation to a relatively homogeneous crime category such as theft. The procedure to be followed now will bring together these discrete items of information to show synthetically their combined effect. These tables include all variables where the cell size was sufficient to allow for effective comparison.

The tables are presented in order of rank from assumed 'softest' to 'hardest' impact on defendants.

Discharge (range 3% - 19%; 16%)

(2.1	Non-theft x Legal Representation)
3.0	'Other' Marital x Legal Representation
6.3	Bail x Legal Representation
7.7	SER x Legal Representation
8.2	White x Legal Representation
8.4	All Thefts x Legal Representation
8.5	Male x Legal Representation
8.7	20 years + x Legal Representation
10.0	Single x Legal Representation
10.3	CYPA x Legal Representation
10.3	No SER x In Person
10.6	No SER x Legal Representation
11.8	Single x In Person
12.3	White x In Person
12.3	All Thefts x In Person
13.0	20 years + x In Person
13.1	Male x In Person
13.2	Married x Legal Representation
13.5	Female x Legal Representation
13.9	CYPA x In Person
14.3	Non-White x Legal Representation
(15.0	Non-Theft x In Person)
15.4	Bail x In Person
19.0	SER x In Person

The pattern for theft differs from other offences, having slightly more spread. The need for convicted thieves seeking this 'softest' of all outcomes is in general to avoid the marginal disadvantage of legal representation, particularly if on bail and with SER. This generalisation does not hold for the married, females and non-whites, since these characteristics overcome the disadvantage of legal representation.

'Non-specific' sentences (e.g. Binding Over, Restitution and Compensation)
(Range 0 - 21.2%: 21.2%)

    (0   Non-Thefts x In Person)
      0   SER x Legal Representation
      0   SER x In Person
      0   CYPA x In Person
    1.8   White x In Person
    2.0   Single x In Person
    2.6   Bail x In Person
    2.7   All Thefts v In Person
    3.3   Male x In Person
    3.3   20 years + x In Person
    5.1   No SER x In Person

    5.7   20 years + x Legal Representation
    7.9   Married x Legal Representation
    8.9   White x Legal Representation
    9.2   Male x Legal Representation
    9.4   All Thefts x Legal Representation
   10.0   Single x Legal Representation
   13.5   Bail x Legal Representation
   14.3   Non-White x Legal Representation
   15.2   'Other' Marital x Legal Representation
   17.6   CYPA x Legal Representation
   21.2   No SER x Legal Representation
  (22.1   Non-Thefts v Legal Representation)

The pattern differs from other offences in that it does not occur at all for those appearing in person on non-theft charges. The need for convicted thieves seeking these 'soft' options is in general to seek legal representation - or negatively, to avoid appearing in person - particularly the bailed, single and juveniles. This generalisation does not hold for those aged above 20 years for whom representation only minutely enhances the possibility of these outcomes.

Fine (range 6.0% - 58.3%: 52.3%)

```
  6.0   'Other' Marital x Legal Representation
 13.5   Bail x Legal Representation
 13.5   Female x Legal Representation
 13.8   SER x Legal Representation
 14.3   Non-White x Legal Representation
 16.3   20 years + x Legal Representation
 16.7   All Thefts x Legal Representation
 19.1   Single x Legal Representation
(22.1   Non-Theft x Legal Representation)
 30.3   No SER x Legal Representation
 35.5   Married x Legal Representation

 38.1   No SER x In Person
 43.6   Bail x In Person
(51.7   Non-Theft x In Person)
 52.6   White x In Person
 54.8   20 years + x In Person
 55.7   Male x In Person
 56.2   All Thefts x In Person
 56.9   Single x In Person
 58.3   CYPA x In Person
```

This is the typical outcome for convicted thieves.

Probation % (range 0 - 24.2%: 24.2%)

```
  0     No SER x Legal Representation
  0     No SER x In Person
  2.9   Non-White x Legal Representation
  3.9   Single x In Person
  4.9   Male x In Person
  6.4   Single x Legal Representation
  6.5   20 years + x In Person
  6.8   All Thefts x In Person
  7.0   White x In Person
( 7.6   Non-Theft x Legal Representation)
( 8.3   Non-Theft x In Person)
  8.3   CYPA x In Person
  8.8   CYPA x Legal Representation
  9.2   Male x Legal Representation
  9.5   SER x In Person
  9.9   All Thefts x Legal Representation
 10.3   Bail x In Person

 12.5   Bail x Legal Representation
 13.0   White x Legal Representation
 13.2   Married x Legal Representation
 13.5   20 years + x Legal Representation
 16.2   Female x Legal Representation
 20.0   SER x Legal Representation
 24.2   'Other' Marital x Legal Representation
```

The pattern of award for this community control sanction is not as tightly bunched as for non-thefts.

For those convicted thieves who seek this outcome - perhaps as a preferred option to custody or fining - there is in certain instances a need for legal representation, but only if it is combined with other characteristics, especially 'other marital' status, SER, being female, aged over 20 years, and to a less extent married or white.

Representation is irrelevant to those bailed and juveniles. Those who are single and without SERs have little or no chance of this outcome, whether legally represented or not.

Community Service Orders (range 0 - 10.8%: 10.8%)

```
   0     No SER x In Person
   0     White x In Person
   0     CYPA x In Person

 1.5     No SER x Legal Representation
 2.6     Bail x In Person
 2.7     All Thefts x In Person
 2.9     CYPA x Legal Representation
 3.0     'Other' Marital x Legal Representation
( 3.3     Non-Theft x In Person)
 3.3     Male x In Person
 3.9     Single x In Person

 4.2     Bail x Legal Representation
 5.0     White x Legal Representation
 5.4     All Thefts x Legal Representation
( 5.5     Non-Theft x Legal Representation)
 5.7     Male x Legal Representation
 6.4     Single x Legal Representation
 6.5     20 years + x Legal Representation
 7.7     20 years + x Legal Representation
 7.9     Married x Legal Representation
 8.1     Female x Legal Representation
 8.6     Non-White x Legal Representation

 9.5     SER x In Person
10.8     SER x Legal Representation
```

This is still a relatively uncommon variety of community control sanction and the rates are virtually identical for those legally represented or appearing in person, regardless of offence.

For those convicted thieves who seek or prefer this outcome, perhaps after a previous career in probation and in preference to imprisonment, the need is to combine particular characteristics with legal representation, but even these, being married, female and non-white are marginal enhancers; and being over 20 years assists, regardless of representation.

However the key to this outcome is better stated as the active support of an SER. Representation is irrelevant once that has occurred; equally the lack of an SER is fatal, regardless of representation.

<u>Suspended Sentences</u> (range 0 - 6.4%: 6.4%)

(0   <u>Non-Theft</u> x <u>In Person</u>)
  0   <u>All Thefts</u> x <u>In Person</u>

  1.5 SER x Legal Representation
  1.5 CYPA x Legal Representation
  2.7 Single x Legal Representation
  2.8 Male x Legal Representation
  3.0 <u>All Thefts</u> x <u>Legal Representation</u>
  3.0 'Other' Marital x Legal Representation
  3.8 20 years + x Legal Representation
  4.1 White x Legal Representation
  4.2 Bail x Legal Representation
  4.5 No SER x Legal Representation
  5.4 Female x Legal Representation
  6.4 Married x Legal Representation
(9.0 <u>Non-Theft</u> x <u>Legal Representation</u>)

The categorisation of the suspended sentence is difficult. It can appear as a 'soft' option relative to custody, however the consequences of breach are draconian. It is clear that this sentence is not available to those without legal representation, but non-thieves receive it more than thieves.

For thieves, certain characteristics enhance the minor chances of being awarded this sentence: being married rather than single, female rather than male, <u>not</u> having an SER and being over 20 rather than a juvenile.

<u>'Other' sentences</u> (eg. Hospital/Guardianship orders)

The importance of this group of dispositions is that they bridge the custodial and 'soft' continua of sentencing: in general terms it is better to locate these sentences within the medical or therapeutic model rather than as 'soft' penal policy. It is interesting to note that this option coincides with personal characteristics of the offender.

<u>'Other' Sentence</u> (range 7.7% - 36.4%: 28.7%)

```
   7.7   SER x Legal Representation
  13.2   Married x Legal Representation

 (15.0   Non-Thefts x In Person)
  16.1   20 years + x In Person
  18.4   No SER x In Person
 (19.0   Non-Thefts x Legal Representation)
  19.2   All Thefts x In Person
  19.4   CYPA x In Person
  19.6   Single x In Person
  19.7   All Thefts x Legal Representation
  19.7   Male x In Person
  21.2   20 years + x Legal Representation
  21.2   'Other' Marital x Legal Representation
  21.9   White x Legal Representation
  22.0   Male x Legal Representation
  22.8   White x In Person
  22.9   Non-White x Legal Representation
  23.8   SER x In Person
  24.3   Female x Legal Representation
  25.6   Bail x In Person

  25.6   Single x Legal Representation
  26.5   CYPA x Legal Representation
  35.4   Bail x Legal Representation
  36.4   No SER x Legal Representation
```

These status altering outcomes may be both carceral and perceived as non-criminal labelling, but equally stigmatic. It is perhaps best therefore to analyse the patterns in terms other than need, simply as behaviour. It occurs over a wider range for theft than other offences.

One factor stands out; those with an SER are very unlikely to reach this disposition with legal representation but highly likely to do so without it. Similarly those without SERs appearing in person are far less likely to reach this disposition than those with legal representation. In this instance bail enhances further the possibility of this disposition with legal representation, whilst marriage depresses it.

Unmarried juveniles without lawyers are less likely to incur this disposition than those with lawyers.

Race and representation are not influential.

<u>Committal to the Crown Court for Sentence</u>
This disposition obviously can only occur in Magistrates' courts. It, therefore, forms a more homogeneous sample. (We cannot, however, assume that all those legally represented were represented by solicitors, nor that all were legally aided.) There is no information on the eventual decision on sentence by the Crown Court, however it is not unreasonable to place this option at the

'severe' end of the sentence continuum as it presupposes the probability of a sentence beyond the powers of magistrates (£2,000 and/or 6 months custody).

Committal to the Crown Court for Sentence (range 0 - 21.2%: 21.2%)

0	All Thefts x In Person
(0	Non-Theft x In Person)
0	Female x Legal Representation
3.2	Married x Legal Representation
(5.2	Non-Theft x Legal Representation)
5.2	Bail x Legal Representation
6.1	No SER x Legal Representation
6.8	White x Legal Representation
7.3	Single x Legal Representation
7.9	All Thefts x Legal Representation
8.8	CYPA x Legal Representation
9.6	20 years + x Legal Representation
11.4	Male x Legal Representation
17.2	Non-White x Legal Representation
18.5	SER x Legal Representation
21.2	'Other' Marital x Legal Representation

Since no unrepresented persons, whether thieves or not, and no female thieves were committed to the Crown Court, the sole question is whether any other factors, besides gender and representation, reduce the risk of this outcome. Married status seems to be the only marginally reductive factor. Three factors have an augmenting effect; not being white, having an SER and having 'other' marital status.

Custody (range 0 - 20%: 20%)

0	All Thefts x In Person
3.0	'Other' Marital x Legal Representation
4.4	CYPA x Legal Representation
4.5	No SER x Legal Representation
5.2	Bail x Legal Representation
5.4	Female x Legal Representation
5.7	Non-White x Legal Representation
(6.7	Non-Theft x In Person)
(7.6	Non-Theft x Legal Representation)
7.9	Married x Legal Representation
8.9	All Thefts x Legal Representation
11.0	White x Legal Representation
11.4	Male x Legal Representation
12.8	Single x Legal Representation
13.5	20 years + x Legal Representation
20.0	SER x Legal Representation

It can be seen that the pattern for prison outcomes is more spread than for other crimes. For those appearing

in person prison sentences did not occur where the
conviction was for theft.

For legally represented thieves, this outcome increases
in probability with the typicality of the defendant:
white, male, single, aged more than 20 years. The
presence of a Social Enquiry Report significantly
increases the risk; one speculates that the SER either
attempts to mitigate and channel away from this outcome,
unsuccessfully, or attempts to channel towards this
option - but mitigages for a particular length of
sentence. On length of sentence, as with quantum of
fine, there is no information here.

Conclusion on Progression Tables

The impression may have been given that the progression
tables presented here comprise an amoral guide to the
immoral consumers of criminal justice. Certainly that
would be one possible use to which such tables could be
put, not only by defendants but also by their legal
advisers, acting quite legally. However, the 'value-
free' nature of such information allows it to be put to
other uses, notably penal advisers such as the Probation
Service, or youth social workers could use such
information if wishing to maximise certain dispositions
that they might consider socially desirable. Equally,
courts might consider whether their sentencing policy is
consistent. The stated function of this research,
however, is to test a particular notion of legal need.
The argument developed earlier is that there are
considerable difficulties with developing objective and
positive definitions of adjectival need, such as legal
need. Instead a more modest negative test for non-need,
comparative consequential need, was proposed. From this
perspective one is limited to stating where adjectival
need is not present, that is where the response envisaged
produces no net benefit in relation to the person with
the problem.

So far we have seen a whole range of such tests, each
highly specific, and intended to be limited to those
circumstances. In the final analysis of this section an
attempt at generalisation will be made, using different
statistical methods.

Theft, Representation and Sentence Severity - Multiple Regression Analysis

Multiple Regression Analysis is a statistical technique
which can isolate the impact of each of a number of co-
existing variables against each other in relation to a
ranking system.

In the context of this study the necessary ranking system was established by constructing a 'severity index' from the 9 types of sentence disposition against the defendants in this survey. It was decided not to follow the Walker-Marsh respondents' model, and instead to use two severity indices from the same types of sentence, thus:

I			II		
	1.	Discharge		1.	Discharge
	2.	'Non-specific'		2.	'Non-specific'
	3.	Fine		2.	Fine
	4.	Probation		3.	Probation
	5.	Community Service		3.	Community Service
	6.	Suspended		4.	Suspended
	7.	'Other' (hospital)		4.	'Other'
	8.	Committal		5.	Committal
	9.	Custody		5.	Custody

The seven independent variables were Social Enquiry Report, Marital Status, Representation, Race, Bail Status, Age, Gender. The 'backward' method of eliminating them was used in the computer programme.

The results were:

I

Step	Indpt Var.	Rank	Zero Order Coefficient	Multiple E Coefficient	Partial Correlation Coefficient
1	SER	5	- .08		- .08
2	Mar Status	4	.02		.08
3	REP	2	* - .22		* - .18
4	Race	7	- .03		.00
5	Bail	1	* .31		* .27
6	Age	6	.10		.02
7	Sex	3	- .06		- .09

$$.38^2 = 14.44$$

* Bail sig p < .005; * REP sig p < .05 with 100 d.f.

II

Step	Indpt Var.	Rank	Zero Order Coefficient	Multiple R Coefficient	Partial Correlation Coefficient
1	SER	5	- .1		- .12
2	Mar Status	3	.05		.12
3	REP	2	* - .25		* - .20
4	Race	6	- .01		.02
5	Bail	1	* .31		* .28
6	Age	7	.09		.00
7	Sex	4	- .04		- .12

$$.42^2 = 17.64$$

* Bail sig p < .005; * REP sig p < .025 with 100 d.f.

Interpretation

For both severity indices, only two variables had a statistically significant effect independent of all the other variables. For both indices they were the same variables in the same order, but in different directions. They were first, bail status, and then representation; for representation the correlation was negative.

The positive correlation with bail status means that those remanded on bail received less severe sentences. Further, this effect was significant in that it occurred independently of all other combinations of variables.

The other statistically significant variable was the concern of this study, representation. Here the correlation for representation is negative, that is to say, counter-intuitive. For representation on both indices, the correlation is between representation and more severe sentences, and between appearance in person and less severe sentences; again this occurs independently of all other combinations of variables.

None of the other variables are statistically significant independently of the others. There is, however, an effect of ranking between them, weakened by the differences in each table. In broad terms, marriage status and gender correlate, the former positively, the latter negatively; that is, the single and female receive somewhat less severe sentences than the married and male. Social Enquiry Reports, age and race have least impact, regardless of direction.

In addition, the multiple regression coefficient squared enables us to state the combined effect of all seven variables against all other possible causes of severity. The two significant variables account for between 10-12% of all possible causes of severity or leniency. The other 5 variables do not account for more than 5% between them, that is about 1% each.

The fact that about 90% of the causes of variance in severity of sentence is not accounted for is not unexpected. The untested variables must include quantum or value of property stolen, plea and court, clerk and judge. It is suggested on the basis of the international research reported in detail elsewhere in this study that those variables, particularly the latter, are much more significant than representation. To conclude, what this analysis shows is that the independent importance of representation is not great, but within that context its value is, at a statistically significant level, negative to defendants seeking lenient sentences through the means of representation. The assumption that representation reduces severity is falsified for these thieves, and their legal needs should be perceived in that context.

Conclusion

The value of multiple regression analysis in the context of this book's theoretical orientation is that it provides an example, however limited, of the falsification test that must occur with a comparative consequential theory of need. Whilst one cannot make dogmatic assertions about the existence of need without resort to consensual devices - which themselves may not be agreed upon - what one can do instead, more modestly, is to make negative assertions about when need may not exist, as here.

The consequences of such falsification of positively hypothesised need as 'Cure' are considered in the ensuing and concluding chapters.

Footnotes

1. Such as ss 60/65 Mental Health Act 1959.

2. Such diverse matters as binding over, adjournment *sine die*, and various medical orders. Deferred sentences have already been excluded as only 17 were recorded overall.

14 Representation, Judges and Decisions – 'Inverted Legal Need'

Introduction

In the preceding chapters a conception of legal need has been developed and tested in relation to defendants in the criminal process.

From that testing two conclusions can be drawn. First, the general assumption behind legal need as representation is 'not proven'. Second, that assumption does survive such testing in particularised settings. From the theoretical perspective developed earlier one can conclude from such survival that a positive proof of legal need has occurred as recognition, but response remains a matter for politics in the broadest sense.

This failure of the general assumption raises a basic question: if legal need as representation is not central to decisions, then what is?

In examining and responding to this question three further assumptions are made here.

First: although the outcomes of earlier stages can weight later stages in a decision process, it is the last stage which is of most importance. In the context of court process it follows that the decision-maker is central to the decision and that other contingencies, such as representation, are relatively marginal.

The second assumption is that of routine. In general the decision-maker establishes, then follows a routine or series of routines prompted by various characteristics in the materials presented; in judicial decision-making this

is further supported by the central notion of Precedent
in the judicial role. It is only at the margin of a
particular outcome that the decision-maker is likely to
be persuadable. This assumption recognises that routines
may vary considerably between decision-makers. An
example of a routine in criminal justice in the sense
used here is the 'tariff' in sentencing, that is of
standardised responses to the average miscreant convicted
of a particular charge, on a particular plea, and
presenting other recognised features, such as previous
convictions.

Third, there is an assumption that the variation in
outcomes between courts and judges is a product of
discretion and rationality mediated by courts and judges,
and not the product of consistent irrationality at each
and every procedural stage in each jurisdiction.

This final assumption is particularly amenable to
empirical observation. Indeed there is a well known
literature in penology on the 'problem' of such
variation. Its concern is with equality in awarding
'like' sentences to 'like' offenders. That literature is
concerned to establish the causes for such variations,
psychological, administrative and cultural. This is not
the place to discuss those issues, except to acknowledge
its existence and that it is well known. (Hood 1962
Hogarth 1971)

The legal need movement cannot have been unaware of
this phenomenon and the discussion it engendered. In
addition, during the major period of legal need
evangelism the wide variations in Bail rates and Legal
Aid grants between different courts were researched and
publicised as relevant to legal need. The weakness of
most legal need research was that it too often neglected
relevant variables. The judicial variable was almost
always omitted when the representation variable was
stressed.

The point here is not so much to make criticisms, as to
point out how these two, continuing, tendencies have
sailed past each other, and have never engaged in debate
despite their obviously related subject matter and
different interpretations of it.[1] Clearly the impact of
both representation and decision-maker on outcome need to
be investigated alongside other relevant variables.

From these assumptions is derived the notion of
'inverted' legal need: that the focus should be 'up' to
the judge, rather than 'down' to the advocate. There are
practical and ethical implications of this conception of
legal need, which will be considered later.

The issue considered here is not solely a matter of
concern for criminal justice. There are many examples
from civil justice as well, including tribunals, county
courts, family disputes, and the Court of Appeal. Dutch
researchers concluded that there are considerable
differences between individual judges' decisions, but
personal characteristics are only moderately influential.

It was, they said, the interaction between personality and case characteristics which produce outcome variation. (Van Koppen and Kate 1984, Bruinsma 1990, 337 T2, T3)

Judicial individuality in Criminal Justice

Before referring to British evidence on district variation it is proposed to reinforce the point made about the importance of judicial individuality by bringing together evidence from disparate sources and which bear on a wide range of criminal justice topics. They are presented so as to mirror chronologically the various stages in process.

Character and workload (U.S.A.)

An American study examined the proportion of cases handled by the eight judges of 'Central Sessions Court' against their general characters, somewhat sardonically constructed by the researchers through observation and interviews. The study does no more than suggest the type of dispositions that might emanate from such judges, and makes no attempt to weigh the impact of representation against these characteristics. Their proportions of cases were:

A	'Workhorse' and 'Intellectual'	34.8%
C	'Workhorse' and 'Routine-hack'	30.4%
G	'Political Adventurer'	9.5%
J	'Careerist'	6.6%
D	'Tyrant-Benevolent Despot'	5.2%
P	'Judicial Pensioner'	4.5%
K	'The Hatchet Man'	3.4%
M	'Judicial Pensioner'	3.2%
L	'Judicial Pensioner'	2.6%

(A. Smith and Blumberg 1967, 96, 105, T1)

Probably up to two thirds of the case outcomes in such a court would be predictable, especially those from Judges C, J, P, M and L, also two thirds of all decisions are made by A and C. Once these traits become established and well known, at least to established 'insider'advocates, the scope for 'tailoring' defendants, defences and mitigations to the particular judge becomes important. There will, however, even here only be a certain amount of room for manoeuvre at the margin of each judge's routines and tariffs. The scope for tactical avoidance by adjournment may be more limited today, with lists controlled by computer to a considerable extent.

'Diversion' and inverted need (U.S.A., Australia)

Reduction of status of charge; Dismissal and Non Recording. Shane-Dubow and her colleagues examined the patterns of decision by individual judges in a number of counties in the state of Wisconsion. One measure that they used was the reduction of a felony charge to misdemenour status, a good measure of leniency. I report here only those findings that were statistically significant. In Dane County Judge G made 14.2% less than average and Judge D 16.4% more than average of such decisions. (Shane-Dubow *et al* 1979 T11)

In three 'upstate' counties one judge DDD made such reductions at a rate of 22.4% above average. (*Ibid* T26)

Two particularly lenient outcomes on convictions are available to Australian magistrates. One is the s.556 order under the Criminal Justice Act which allows for non recording of the convictions on first conviction. The other is Dismissal, the equivalent of an absolute discharge.

In South Australia the rate for the 6 magistrates hearing more than 100 trials included:

Judge	II	III	V	
s.556	69.4	2.9	44.8	%
Dismissal		2.9	20.4	

(Grabosky and Rizzo 1983 Apdx)

Verdict (Australia, India)

The same South Australian magistrates (hearing 48.7% of all cases in their jurisdiction) had acquittal rates ranging from 7.3% to 83.9%. (*Ibid* 152)

In Delhi, India, vagrancy laws are administered by a special Beggars' Court. As a reaction to a reform campaign by law students at Delhi University, Magistrate A was replaced. He could be described as a legalist or proceduralist, and as a consequence a certain amount of acquittals had occurred. His replacement, Magistrate B, could be described as a social controller, and as a consequence even less acquittals occurred than before. (Pande 1983 291, 296-7)

Appeal (U.S.A.)

There is one study of the fate of Habeas Corpus petitions - a form of appeal in the U.S.A. - by long term prisoners to the Second Federal District of New York. Of the 56 judges who had received more than 10 such petitions, 13 had summarily dismissed less than 60% and 17 more than 90%. (Zeigler and Hermann 1972, 159, 197)

Sentencing

Juvenile Courts (U.S.A.)

In a well-known study of juvenile justice in two cities the researchers tested for both individual and institutional differences. The institutional differences were that one court (G) had long established judges with a social work orientation, whereas the other (Z) had newly appointed 'legalist' judges to conform with recent Supreme Court rulings.

The differences between judges at Z were insignificant, but at G they were noticeable:

Discharge	12.3% (B)	22.3% (A)	:	10.0%
Court supervision	25.4% (A)	38.6% (C)	:	13.2%
Probation	34.3% (C)	45.6% (B)	:	11.3%

There were no controls in this study for the type of charge. (Stapleton and Teitelbaum *op cit* TIII.7)

Another American study of juvenile justice in 13 jurisdictions found the following ranges of distribution, all in excess of 50%. (Ferster and Courtless 1972, 195 T3)

Judge A	:	*'No Significant Action'*	:	66.9%
Judge D	:	<u>Community Supervision</u>	:	5.3%
Judge H	:	Removal from Community	:	3.6%
Judge I	:	<u>Community Supervision</u>	:	5.2%
		Removal from Community	:	56.4%
Judge L	:	*'No Significant Action'*	:	11.1%
		<u>Community Supervision</u>	:	57.4%

Misdemeanor Sentences (U.S.A.)

Ryan studied the individual tendencies of judges in Columbus, Ohio in handling 2,764 misdemeanour cases in 1978:

A	Negative correlation for incarceration
C	Suspended part of fine often
D	Informed of sentence to encourage Guilty plea
E	'Middle of the road' - occasional suspension of part of fine
G	'Gives you a good trial'
	Drunk drivers - severe fines
	Theft - severe
	Incarceration - severe
H	As D
J	Traffic - severe fines as charges increase
	Theft - not severe
M	As C, and
	Theft - severe, incarceration

(Ryan 1980-1, 79, 87, 94 T5, T6)

Thus two judges have the same characteristics and five, B, F, I, K and L have no special features.

Sentencing for Specific Offences

Probation for Burglars

In Dane County, Wisconsin, the researchers tested for length of probation on conviction of burglary. Judge E sentenced for 4.8 months less and Judge J, 6.3 months less than average. (Shane-Dubow *et al op cit* T11) In Milwaukee County the range was greater, with Judge CDD giving 17.72 months less than average and Judge HH 18.08 months more than average. (*Ibid* T16)

Incarceration for Burglars

In Milwaukee County, Wisconsin, Judge II incarcerated 10.3% less than average, and Judge HH 10.6% more than average. (*Ibid* T14) The length of incarceration ranged from 13.65 months less than average by Judge CC to 12.21 months more than average by Judge HH. (*Ibid* T15) In the upstage counties the incarceration rate of Judge CCC was 20.2% above average. (*Ibid* T25)

Incarceration for Robbers

In Milwaukee County Judge JJ ordered incarceration 15.8% above the average and Judge HH sentenced to 26.89 months longer than average. (*Ibid* T17, 18)

Shane-Dubow and colleagues concluded that the individual judge was not significant to the type of sentence. For type of sentence the significant determinants were the type of offence and previous record of defendant. For length of sentence the individual judge was significant after type of offence and previous record. However, at the margin the identity of individual judges could be a reliable predictor or outcome, such as Judge HH generally and in the specific contexts instanced Judges G, DDD, E, CDD, II and CC as 'lenient' and D, J and JJ as 'severe'. (*Ibid* 194-7)

It is also important to note that representation was a variable in this study, but it never produced any significant effects.

Rape Sentencing - Judicial Religious Affiliation - New Zealand

Barber studied the relationship between the judges' religious affiliations and their rape sentences against certain variables concerning the victim. The sample was 126 cases for 4 judges. There was also a control of 6 individual judges tested against sentence alone:

Roman Catholic J 100% 5 years. None of the victims suffered 'extensive' injuries.

Rapists of single non-virgins received less custodial sentences (55.6% 5 years) than rapists of single virgins (70.6% 5 years).

Anglican J 40% received intermediate sentences 5-10 years; and 49% received 'severe' sentences, 10 years +, regardless of the degree of injury, and regardless of the victims's status or virginity. There was a slight tendency to lengthen sentence if the victim's moral conduct was 'good'.

Other Christian J 62% received intermediate terms 5-10 years, regardless of the victim's state of injury, status, virginity or conduct.

'Other' J Very similar to 'Other Christian' except that all the rapists of single non-virgins received 5-10 year terms. (Barber 1974, T15, 16)

The general sentencing tendencies of six judges of convicted rapists were also listed:

Soft	B	70%	5 years -		
Intermediate	A	42%	5-10 years		
Intermediate	C	57%	5-10 years		
Firm	D	36%	5-10 years	45%	10+ years
Firm	E	33%	5-10 years	58%	10+ years
Hard	F			75%	10+ years

(*Ibid* T13, 14, 15)

Sentencing - Three types of Crime (Israel)

The earliest example of a study of individual judicial variation is from Israel which used a severity index for sentencing against three categories of offence by 7 judges: (Shoham 1959-60, 327 TII):

Offence range	Judge - Points		Judge - Points	
General	D	30	N	71
Property	J	33	D	72
Person	N	10	A	90

On particular types of sentence the range of variations were:

	Judge		Judge	
Suspended sentence	R	10	D	40
Suspended sentence and fine	D	4	R	57
Binding Over			N	10
Probation			D	10
1 year - Custody	G	18	N	42
1-3 years Custody			L,D	20
3+ years Custody			G	7
(*Ibid* TIV)				

From these tables one can construct profiles of individual judges:

A   'Severe' on offences against the person.

D   'Soft' except on property offences. High on intermediate custodial sentences 1-3 years; presumably this links with property offences. High use of probation in general.

G   Generally against short and in favour of long custodial terms.

J   'Soft' on property offences.

L   'Severe' on offences against the person; presumably this links with high use of custodial terms 1-3 years.

N   Generally 'severe', except on property offences; many short custodial sentences and Binding Over; the latter may correlate with property offences.

R   Favours suspended sentence coupled with fines.

Although there are some obvious methodological limitations with this research, it did pioneer what I now call Inverted Need. A legal adviser could, once the trial listing was posted, give a reasonable estimate of the probable consequences of conviction on say a property offence before judges N, D and J, and of offences against the person before judges N, D, L and A. Such information is particularly relevant to plea-negotiation, and to what is discussed below as 'tailoring'.

Federal Felons, Judicial Workload and Severity Deviation (U.S.A.)

A large study by Diamond and Zeisel considered the sentencing practices of federal judges in Chicago and New York City.

In Chicago there were 8 judges with caseloads ranging from 48 to 385 over the period studied; and in New York there were 12 judges with caseloads ranging from 5 to 201.

In New York the deviations from the group's average was from -21% (Judge I, 61 cases) to +58% (Judge J, 27 cases). In Chicago the deviations were narrower, from -11% (Judge A, 329 cases) to +10% (Judge B, 311 cases). (Diamond and Zeisel (1975) 109 T7, 115)

Sanctioning Draft Resisters (U.S.A.)

One American study examined the impact of a large number of variables on the sanctioning of resisters to conscription to the armed services during the Vietnam war, using two sets of measures. Only three variables were significant at .05 or less, and only two were significant on both measures. They were plea and the particular judge. The judicial variable was significant on both measures at .01 and at a much higher regression than any other variable: -.865 and +.749. (Hagan and Bernstein 1979, 109 T3) An earlier study limited to probation sentences for draft resistance did not consider individual judges, but showed wide differences over 9 successive years in both federal circuits and California districts. (Cook 1977, 567, T1)

Sentencing, Race and the Individual Judge (U.S.A.)

In 1970 the decisions of 7 judges in the 'General Court' of a mid-western metropolis were analysed in relation to the race of defendants. The judges' caseloads ranged from 1%, (G) (who is excluded here):

A (8%) Highest Not Guilty verdicts for Blacks   21%
        Lowest Dismissal verdicts for Whites   11%
        Highest Non-Fine sentences for Whites   85%
        Highest Jail rate for employed and
          unemployed Whites   87%
        Highest Jail rate for unemployed Blacks   100%

B (2%) Lowest Jail rate for employed and
          unemployed Whites   60%
        Lowest Jail rate for employed Blacks   0%
        Highest Jail rate for unemployed Blacks   100%

C (27%) Lowest Not Guilty verdicts for Blacks   7%
        Lowest Not Guilty verdicts for Whites   5%

D (17%) Highest Dismissal verdicts for Blacks   35%
        Lowest Non-fine sentences for Whites   44%
        Lowest Non-fine sentences for Blacks   13%
        Highest Jail rate for employed Blacks   40%

E (30%) Highest Dismissal verdicts for Whites   34%
        Highest Dismissal verdicts for Blacks   35%

F (15%) Lowest Dismissal verdicts for Blacks   20%
        Highest Not Guilty verdicts for Whites   18%
        Highest Non-fine sentences for Blacks   62%
        Highest Jail sentences for employed Blacks   40%

It can be seen that in terms of verdict the disposition of cases by C or E is great significance to defendants. For convicted defendants A is the severest sentencer but the race of those convicted was not relevant. (Atkinson and Newman 1970, 68 T1, 2, 4)

Another study constructed a Discrimination Index for 11 judges in the Superior Court of one County. This was derived by the subtraction from the higher percentage of 'severe' (as defined and controlled) sentences for black or white defendants of the lower percentage of such sentences for the other group, for each Judge. This yielded:

Anti Black   E - 32.1, G - 24.8, H - 18.8
Anti White   I + 55.6
Neutral
(under+/-10)   A, B, C, D, F, J, K.

Incidentally the efforts of defendants' attorneys were seen as having a negative effect on influencing sentence (at -.40) compared to the District Attorney's recommendation (+.09), defendants' attitudes (+.39) and the prior records of defendants (+.63). (Gibson 1978, 455 T5, 7)

Verdict - Differential Conviction Rates

There is also one study of a metropolitan court in the U.S.A. which tested for both judicial and defendant ethnicity; there were 75 white judges and 16 black judges and 30,350 defendants.

The mean conviction rate was 60%. The article discloses percentage differences above the mean. I am here arbitrarily taking differences above 20%, i.e. 72% as significant. The differentials were:

	Black defendants		White defendants	
Excess %	White -	Black judges %	White -	Black judges %
20-29	6.7	12.6	1.4	6.3
30=39	6.7	6.3	1.4	0
40-49	1.7	0	0	0
70-79	2.7	0	0	0
	18.8	18.9	2.8	6.3

It can be seen that black defendants are convicted at a higher rate than whites, however this feature is an effect equally of black and white judges. There is a small group of white judges (5.4%) who convict black defendants at an abnormally high rate.

Sentence Severity (controlled for type of crime):

(Mean 25.5 units)	Black defendants		White defendants	
	White	Black Judges	White	Black Judges
20-29	33.3	37.5	0	0
30-39	22.7	12.6	0	0
40-49	8.0	0	1.4	0
50-59	2.8	6.3	0	0
60-69	2.8	6.3	0	0
70-79	0	0	0	0
80-89	1.4	0	0	0
90-99	0	0	0	0
100-110	1.4	0	0	0
	72.4	62.7	1.4	0

Here the discrimination against black convicts is
blatant, however it is again a feature of both black and
white judges. There is a small group (2.8%) of white
judges with extreme sentences against blacks and an even
smaller group (1.4%) of white judges with extreme
sentences against whites. (Uhlman 1976, T4-3, 4-6)

*Individual Prosecutors and Individual Judges' Severity
(U.S.A.)*

In the U.S.A. the prosecutor may, and usually does, call
for a particular sentence. One may therefore consider
whether this type of advocacy is effective. Comparison
with private and lay prosecutors is not possible in the
U.S.A.
    Green examined the variations in sentencing amongst
those 18 felony court judges in Philadelphia who had
convicted in more than 30 trials in 1960. From the
material provided by him one can construct profiles of
relative judicial leniency or severity. Green, uniquely,
introduced the variable of the individual prosecutor,
which is examined here. All samples of less than 30
cases have been excluded here, and for sampling reasons
only non-custodial dispositions are considered:

Prosecutor			Judge			Non-Custodial %
a			O			63.3
h			G			60.0
k			O			57.4
e			P			53.4
c			G			49.0
k			M			43.4
l			G			43.2
l			O			40.4
i			J			39.2
e			L			39.1
a			P			35.0
h			J			25.6
i			L			25.0
h			I			25.0
j			B			25.0
c			M			16.7
l			I			13.8

One can see that certain combinations involving one prosecutor or judge can be markedly different to that with another, such as hlG or hGJ or aeP or cKM; some are relatively consistent at each polarity such as aklO and hlI.

Using a different sample but with the same judges Green also demonstrates differential in the length of custodial sentence: Of those giving above 3 months custody at a rate in excess of 70% (70.1%-78.8%) the following proportions exceeded one year of custody.

R   52.6%

M   44.8%
I   41.3%
B   40.0%
H   38.0%
J   34.6%

K   19.1%
and those giving above 3 months custody at a rate under 50% (45.8%-49.9%) the following proportions exceeded one year of custody:
G   25.5%
O   25.0%

P   10.4%
D   3.8%
(Green 1961 T7.51, 4.3)

One can conclude that G, O, P were by both criteria 'soft' sentencers and that B and I are 'hard' sentencers.

Sentencing - Lay and Professional Summary Justice (Scotland)

In 'Lay Justice?' (Bankowski, Hutton and McManus 1987, T6.2, 6.4) six lay District courts and their adjunct professional Sheriffs' summary jurisdictions were surveyed. The fining rates ranged thus:

67.9%	Sheriff F
83.4%	Sheriff B

The mean fines variations were:

£57.3	Sheriff C
£95.1	Sheriff F (*Ibid* T6.15)

Custody rates varied:

3.6%	Sheriff B
13.8%	Sheriff F (*Ibid* T6.14)

The length of imprisonment ranged from 78.7 days C, to 101.6 days, F. (*Ibid* T6.16)

From these abstracted statistics one can construct Sentencing Profiles of Sheriffs:

Sheriff B	High rate of fining and low use of custody
Sheriff C	High amount of fines and low length of custody
Sheriff F	High rate and length of custody

The Crown Court - The Individual Judge and Sentencing

An attempt to mount a major study of sentencing individuality in the English Crown Court by the Oxford Centre for Criminological Research was blocked by the Lord Chief Justice with the support of the then Lord Chancellor. (Ashworth 1984, 14-5) The pilot study has however been published.

As might reasonably be expected, the study did discover individual differences, for example in one court two judges differed markedly on their sentencing of drug importers. It transpired that the sentences of one judge correlated with the quantity imported. Perhaps more important is that when their sentencing profiles were presented to them they 'failed to confirm their recollections of their past sentencing practice'. It was also apparent that there were significant variations in compliance with both statutory and Court of Appeal rulings. (*Ibid* 29, 46)

The psychologists Fitzmaurice and Pease were able to analyse the custodial sentence length of 3 Crown Court judges against 'severity' and perceived seriousness of crime indices. They found considerable variation on each measure, but that the polar judges altered with each measure. Thus, on 'severity' the range was from 1 unit for Judge I to 1.70 units for Judge II. For 'seriousness' the range was from 0.45 for Judge II to 0.81 for Judge III. (Fitzmaurice and Pease 1986 T7)

They also tested 6 Crown Court judges on sentencing hypothetical sexual offences and found that the patterns altered with the hypothetical offence. Thus for indecent exposure there was no variation at all on both the indices used (2; 100). However for attempted rape the range was from 2.8 (B, F) to 4 (A, E) on sentence length, and from 140 (F) to 225 (D) on seriousness. For rape the variations were from 3.65 (B) to 6 (A) on sentence length, and from 225 (C) to 510 (D) on seriousness. This suggests that variation reduces with perceived reduction of seriousness, and that at the extremes individual judges can be isolated on several measures (B, A). (*Ibid* T8)

Individual Magistrates, Offence and Sentence: Experimental Psychology

An experiment with 9 magistrates to find the degree of similarity between them in relation to three hypothetical offenders. There was a considerable degree of similarity, but in each case one or two of them did differ significantly.

Case I (Shoplifting)

Magistrate   3 : 0.69 Spearman Correlation Coefficient
               6 : 0.73
(1,2,4,5,7)   0.91 Median
               8 : 0.97

Case II (Threat with Knife under influence of Alcohol)

Magistrate   2 : 0.62
               9 : 0.80
(1,3,4,5,6,8)   0.91 Median
               7 : 0.99

Case III (Larceny of valuable silver)

Magistrate   5 : 0.82
(1,3,4,7,8,9)   0.94 Median
             2,6 : 0.99
(McKnight 1981, 141 T1)

A Preliminary Conclusion

The evidence for the expression of judicial individuality in decision-making is overwhelming. However its effects need to be stated carefully. On each decision item in each bench, court or district there is a norm; this will differ between such ourts. Between courts approximately a third to a half represent the norm on the item; the remainder will differ widely in both directions. Within each court the same occurs. Within the relevant court or district the individual judge in general conforms to, indeed constitutes the norm on the majority of items, but for the remaining items each individual differs both as to what the conformed-to majority is, and the direction in which difference occurs. Representation has a marginal impact on this expression of confirmity and individuality.

As supportive evidence for this conclusion I shall now briefly catalogue the topics where similar conclusions have been reached for bench or district variation, limited to Britain, presented seriatim to mirror the chronoglogical flow of the process.

District Variation

Criminal Legal Aid

Magistrates

As a result of the earliest studies of legal aid rates a debate was held in Parliament in 1970, in which it revealed that the national refusal rate for magistrates was 18% but this masked a range from 0 at Great Yarmouth to 94% at Bootle.

Although these variations have reduced, they continue to be considered politically as a serious flaw in the system, and consideration by the Royal Commission on Legal Services has not made a significant impact.

There is however a particular continuity in this problem which should be mentioned because of its relevance to representation and legal need. Those pressure groups which assert that there may be injustice in low grant rates make a particular complaint where adjacent or neighbouring magistrates courts have widely differing rates. What has not been considered however is the extent that the same advocates also make applications in such neighbouring courts for Legal Aid for representation on behalf of defendants, and whether their applications are responded to differently by these neighbours. If they are it may follow that the court or judges in question are more important than representation.

A recent Lord Chancellor considered that these variations are the most important problem in the Criminal Legal Aid scheme. The Criminal Legal Aid Appeal Committees set up regionally under the Legal Aid Act 1982 were an attempt to reduce this.

Criminal Legal Aid - Juvenile Courts

In the Juvenile Courts these differences are today less marked, nevertheless in districts receiving more than 33 applications in 1988 61 districts from 259, about a quarter had variations in excess of 10%. (Lord Chancellor's Dept Judicial Statistics 1988)

Legal Aid - Crown Court

It is well known that the national average refusal rate for trial in the Crown Court is around 1%. Nevertheless there were and remain deviant centres with considerably higher refusal rates. In 1988 the refusal rate for Appeals to the Crown Court were, at Bristol 11%, Lincoln 15%, Croydon 32% and Durham 33%. (Lord Chancellor's Dept Judicial Statistics 1988)

Legal Aid - Contribution Orders

Magistrates

Crown Court

Criminal Legal Aid Appeals

The grant rates varied between the 15 Area Committees in 1988 thus:

For Counsel in Magistrates' Courts   15%
For prior Authority to expenditure   26%
            Total   <u>31%</u>
Against Refusal of Legal Aid   44%
To Amend a Legal Aid Order   47%
(Lord Chancellor's Dept Judicial Statistics 1988)

Verdicts and Legal Aid

Magistrates

Crown Court and Assizes

Bail

Before the Bail Act 1976 a number of studies demonstrated (and were concerned with) the variation in bail/remand rates between magistrates' courts.

Although studies made after the Act came into force noticed the continuing differences in police bail rates, they did not at first attend to continuing variations between courts. It is however clear now that such variations continue.

A recent Statistical Bulletin (7/1987) from the Home Office shows that this continues with 12.5% of all Petty Sessional Divisions making custodial remands in excess of 25% of cases and 17.2% in less than 5% of cases. In addition I was given access to all the area reports compiled by the Home Office, but which were only issued to the courts of each area. These statistics are acknowledged to contain some inconsistencies due to differing methods of local compilation, but they are nevertheless useful and relevant to this discussion, and so are analysed here. Courts taking less than 70 cases per year have been excluded, which reduces 'freak' averages.

In analysing this data I have used an arbitrary measure: 'Significant Difference' is a range within an Area of Petty Sessional Divisions in excess of 20%:

Circuit	20%+ range	(Indictable)	:	Areas	(PSDs)
SE	5	(2)		12	(130)
London	1	(1)		6	(52)
NW	2	(0)		5	(60)
Mids	2	(0)		4	(46)
NE	2	(1)		8	(67)
E	3	(0)		8	(77)
SW	3	(0)		6	(64)
Wales	2	(0)		9	(52)
	20	(4)	:	58	(548)

It can be seen that for summary offences about a third of the areas have ranges in excess of 20%; for indictable offences this does reduce to under 10%. It is worth pointing out that there are considerable differences between the levels for those areas without significant difference; they are not by any means all uniformly low or high. The overall range was 0-100% for summary and 0-70% for indictable offences.

Venue Decisions by Magistrates on Mode of Trial

Where an offence charged is classified as intermediate, 'either-way', magistrates have a discretion whether to accept or decline jurisdiction under section 19 of the Magistrates' Court Act 1980. A recent Home Office Research Study shows for the first time considerable variations in 4 Crown Court Districts within 2 Crown Prosecution Service Districts. In the 4 districts the rates for declining jurisdiction were:

Durham 21%; Newcastle 31%; Northampton 56%; Leicester 64%

The overall averages in the two CPS districts were 28% (Northumbria and Durham) and 60% (Leicester and Northampton) ranging from differentials of 60% to 69% for fraud/forgery (9%) to 20% to 60% for violence (40%). All differentials were towards Leicester and Northampton, except for sex offences which reversed, 83% to 100%. (Riley and Vennard 1988 T3)

Verdict - Magistrates

Considerable effort has been expended on investigating differences in outcomes in the Magistrates' Courts. Much of this work has been polemical - and ineffectual. It is also the case that some of this work has been undertaken by researchers associated with the legal services movement. This suggests some ambivalence about the scope for representation to achieve the required results.

In 1972 McCabe and Purves made a comparison of plea and acquittal rates in magistrates courts so as to make a further comparison with jury acquittals. The 12 extreme areas were:

Worcestershire	13%	Great Yarmouth	70%
Somerset	19%	Oldham	75%
Norwich	20%	Dorset	78%
Leicester	25%	Walsall	80%
E Sussex	25%	Coventry	84%
Leeds	29%	Monmouth	91%

(McCabe and Purves 1972, T2)

In Edwards' study of prostitutes and criminal justice, she found a range of acquittal rates from 1.6% at Birmingham, through Manchester, London and Sheffield to 13.6% at Liverpool. (Edwards op cit T8.13)

In a study by myself of trials defended by lawyers retained by a motorists' organisation, I examined the acquittal rates in 5 regions for 5 high volume Road Traffic offences. For three offences: Careless Driving, Breaking the Speed Limit and Driving after Consuming Alcohol, there were no statistically significant differences between regions; the variations were 2.6%,

19.9% and 21.4% respectively. For two other crimes the
regional variations were statistically significant:

	SE%	Mids%	W&W%	N%	Range%	Chi^2
Neglect Traffic Ds	54	81	52	63	29	p<0.01
Accident Offences	65	77	82	72	17	p<0.05

Verdicts - Crown Court

The Role of Judges

By no means all acquittals in the Crown Court are by
juries. Judges may acquit in two ways. The first,
Discharge occurs before the jury is empanelled; this may
be on the initiative of the Crown Prosecution Service,
but it is for the judge whether or not to accept it. The
other judicial acquittal is by Direction to the jury,
usually because the case 'fails' in some way through lack
of evidence, or evidence relevant to the particular
breach of law, often witness failure.
    With data provided by the Lord Chancellor's Department
I was able to survey both types of acquittal over two
years in 64 Crown Court Centres in 5 Circuits.

Judicial Discharge

In 1987 nine courts' judges discharged less than 10% of
defendants and twelve more than 20%. The range was from
5.3% at Knutsford, to 35.3% at Doncaster.
    The following year six courts discharged less than 10%
and six more than 30%. The range was from 0 at Durham to
52.9% at Salisbury.
    For defendants remanded in custody - a smaller group of
generally most serious cases - a smaller sample was
available. In 1987 the range was from 2% at Portsmouth
to 14.9% at Sheffield.
    The following year the range was from 0 at Teesside, to
30% at Sheffield and Stoke. Six courts discharged
defendants at a rate under 10% and 4 about 20%.

Directed Acquittals

In 1988 12 courts had directed acquittal rates of less
than 5% and 7 above 15%. They ranged from 0 at
Carmarthen and Newport, Isle of Wight, to 21.1% at
Durham.
    In 1988 6 courts had rates less than 5% and 13 above
15%. The range was from 1.3% at Coventry, to 27.6% at
Carmarthen.
    For the minority of defendants remanded in custody the
range of directed acquittals in 1987 was from 0 at
Stafford and Winchester to 16.4% at Exeter. The following
year it was from 0 at Bolton, Swansea and Winchester, to
19% at Derby.

Sentencing

This measure is of great importance, because it is the final outcome (apart from appeal), and because if one takes Guilty pleas and conviction rates together, about 95% of charges lead to sentence.
Many of the studies have found considerable differences between even neighbouring courts. We are considering a deeply rooted phenomenon since the studies go back as far as the 1930s.
The studies include:

Juvenile Courts including sentence variations for particular crimes.

Young Adults including effect of previous convictions and employment status.

Indictable offences sentenced by Magistrates - Custodial Rates

Magistrates and Sentencing of Specific Offences and Sentencing Policy (including studies of variation)

Binding Over Orders

Local Patterns - Property Crime and Employment

The Crown Court - Sentencing

Recently David Moxon has published a Home Office Planning and Research Unit Study (1988, 57-8) examining 2,077 offences in 18 Crown Courts during 1986 and 1987. His focus was particularly on the differing outcomes of Circuit Judges and Recorders. However the study gives no information on district or Circuit variation.
This does figure prominently in a 1990 National Association of Probation Officers' Survey of 'Crown Courts and Sentencing'. The range for custodial sentences was:

Tier I Court
38%   Ward Green to   Mold   69%
                                Old Bailey   70%
Tier II Court
44%   Durham   Chelmsford   61%
                                Oxford   63%
Tier III Court
33%   Portsmouth   Coventry   63%
35%   Southampton
(*Ibid* Apdx I, II, III)

The range of custodial sentence for three offences is also given by Police Area for 17-20 year olds (Y) and adults (A). (*Ibid* TIII, IV)

Theft and Handling; range:

Y	5.8%	N Wales	Cheshire	15.6%
A	6.2%	Powys	City of London	25.0%

Burglary

Y	22.2%	Dorset	Cheshire	46%
A	29.3%	Gloucester	N Wales*	53.6%

Criminal Damage

Y	5.1%	Powys	Herts	31.6%
A	4.2%	Powys	Cleveland	26.6%

In addition I made a survey of custodial and partially suspended sentences in 64 courts in 5 circuits from data provided by the Lord Chancellor's Dept for 1987 and 1988.

Bailed Defendants | Guilty Plea | 1987/88

	23.5%	Newport IOW	25.5%	Newport
M	43.5%	Burnley	43.9%	Leicester
	<u>60.2%</u>	Coventry⁺	<u>59.5%</u>	Mold
	36.7%		34.0%	

Bailed Defendants | Convicted at Trial

	29.8%	Carmarthen	23.9%	Bodmin-Truro
M	52.1%	Taunton	53.8%	Warrington
	<u>70.7%</u>	Mold	<u>82.5%</u>	Coventry⁺
	40.9%		58.6%	

Remanded Defendants | Guilty Plea | 1987/88

	60.6%	Merthyr Tydfil	67.4%	Newcastle
M	82.1%	Winchester	80.3%	Derby
	<u>94.2%</u>	Caernarvon	<u>88.6%</u>	Aylesbury
	24.6%		21.2%	

Remanded Defendants | Convicted at Trial

	67.5%	Portsmouth	66.7%	Swindon
M	88.8%	Reading	87.5%	Stafford
	<u>97.0%</u>	Cardiff	<u>96.8%</u>	Cardiff
	29.5%		30.1%	

Conclusion: This brief overview of variation in British criminal justice decision making at district or regional level, merely buttresses the international evidence on judicial individuality in such decision making. There do not appear to be any topics immune from it, though some produce more extremes than others.

Footnote

1. This point was made by the late Tudor-Price J,
   shortly before his tragically premature death, in
   addressing Cardiff law students. He suggested that
   3% of cases are lost by bad advocacy and 7% won by
   good advocacy. The corrollary is that in 90% of
   cases advocacy is irrelevant to outcomes.

15 The Implications of Inverted Legal Need

The Weight of Representation in Judicial Decisions

In previous chapters I established that representation and appearance in person do not, when comparable, produce marked differences in outcomes. For example a major American study with very large samples and many variables apart from self representation found a maximum independent effect of type of attorney in either direction of 2%, that is a maximum independent effect of 4%. Apart from denting the cherished American myth that 'money buys the best' it demonstrates the over valorisation of representation with regard to trial and sentence. (Herman *et al* 1977)

The preceding section suggests that the judge is an important, and often the important determinant of his or her own decision; indeed it is remarkable that it is necessary to state that. It raises the question: what weight does representation have amongst all the other variables including that of jurisdiction, court, bench or judge?

There is some evidence that bears directly on this issue from Anderson's study of 'Representation in the Juvenile Court'. (1978) Two courts were studied and the findings presented here are reconstructed from those on sentencing:

Discharge %	Type	Representation	Court
0	Abs	In Person	B
0	Abs	Legal Rep	B
(3	Cond	Legal Rep	A)
(4	Cond	In Person	A)
(9	Abs	Legal Rep	A)
(13	Abs	In Person	A)
23	Cond	In Person	B
29	Cond	Legal Rep	B

Clearly the court is much more important than type of representation.

Fines % £5 -

11	In Person	(B
9	Legal Rep	(B
5	In Person	A)
3	Legal Rep	A)

Fines % £5 +

3	Legal Rep	(B
9	In Person	(B
20	Legal Rep	A)
26	In Person	A)

Again Court B is clearly more lenient than Court A regardless of the type of representation and vice versa.

Supervision %	Type	Representation	Court
0	Social Service	Legal Rep	A)
4	Social Service	In Person	A)
9	Probation	Legal Rep	A)
12	Probation	In Person	A)
12	Social Service	Legal Rep	(B
12	Probation	Legal Rep	(B
15	Probation	In Person	(B
23	Social Service	In Person	(B

Court B is consistently more Supervision orientated than Court A. At Court A type of representation is irrelevant but at Court B there is a slight tendency to award these orders to those appearing in person.

For the custodial orders - Detention Centre, Borstal and Borstal Recall - there were no significant differences attributable to either court or representation.

For Care orders there was a slight tendency towards those appearing in person and those appearing in Court A:

Care Orders %	Representation	Court
3	Legal Rep	B
6	Legal Rep	A
9	In Person	B
17	In Person	A

Overall it is the court which is important for Discharge,
Fine level, Supervision and Care orders. Representation
(in person) is occasionally relevant as a secondary
influence, for Supervision orders at Court B and Care
orders at Court A.

In a study limited to robbery in two years in Greater
Boston, U.S.A., Conklin found that in a regression
analysis of seven variables the type of representation
was seventh, positive at .11, (11% of all) but at a
significance of .10, which is normally considered
statistically insignificant; all the other significances
were under .05. In his regression on verdict the type of
representation did not weigh at all but the trial court
was strongest both in terms of coefficient, at .48 (48%
of all) with statistical significance, at .001. (Conklin
1972 T26, 168-70)

One Australian study used two statistical models for
weighing the impact of several variables. In both models
the dominant variable was the individual judge. Model II
did not include gender or representation, but did examine
particular magistrates. On verdict the conviction range
was from 15.6% (JII) to 60.4% (JVI). Model I controlled
for a number of variables including representation
against the dependent judicial variable. Here the
predominant variable at all times remainded the:

	Chi^2	(Conversion %)
Presiding Magistrate	262	73.4
Age	37	
Arrest	20	
Representation	20	5.6
Employment	18	
	357	

(Grabosky and Rizzo *op cit Fig I., T5*)

The weight of the Presiding Magistrate is 13 times that
of representation in the decision. The study also
examined New South Wales through the looser variable of
court location rather than judge or Presiding Magistrate.
This test raised the value but not the relative place of
representation. (*Ibid* T8, 9)

Another Australian study examined judicial variation in the sentencing of drunk drivers in 9 courts in New South Wales. The variations were:

	s556A %	Restrd lic %	Prison %	$ M. Fine	M. Days Disq
Min:	0	0	0	107	94
Max:	20.9	49.3	9.4	223	450
Range	20.9	49.3	9.4	$116	356 days

In this study Homel's analysis showed that one third of the total explanatory power of the model was contributed by previous drink-drive convictions and a quarter by magistrate variations. A general toughness-leniency dimension was evident. Most magistrates clustered at the lenient end of the spectrum, but one magistrate appeared to be particularly severe. He had the highest rate of imprisonment and length of disqualifications orders. 'Tough' magistrates could be further divided into two groups. First, those individualising the penalty through using restricted licences, heavy fines and longer than average disqualification. The others simply levied a tariff of above average severity, but normally without imprisonment. Sentence style also affected the perception of relevant criteria, thus there was a bigger difference between 'lenient' and 'tough' magistrates for first than for second offenders. 'Tough' magistrates were also harder on 18 year olds than 'lenient' magistrates. Legal Representation correlated with disqualification period and imprisonment when the presiding magistrate was 'tough' rather than 'lenient'. (Homel 1982, 225, 238-9) This suggests that representation is resorted to or offered in an attempt to limit penalites expected, but that this is not usually successful. This view is supported by a British study of gender and sentence. It was limited to Theft Act offences, with a sample of 408 cases before Cambridge magistrates' court in 1979. The researchers conducted a dichotomous regression analysis covering 17 variables including representation and concluded that representation and plea were not independently important:

"The effect of legal representation is probably a function of the fact that it is required in certain cases when severe sentences are likely." (Farrington and Morris 1983, 229)

In the U.S.A. Feeley's New Haven study, not limited to any type of offence, concluded that the:

"presence or absence of an attorney made no measurable impact on the severity of sentence."

In this multiple regression analysis of factors relevant to outcome, his variable of representation did not figure at all as significant to severity of sentence:

1. Type of charge; public order   10.59
2. No previous convictions   6.94
3. No court appearance   5.18
4. Gender of defendant   5.15
5. Political party of judge   4.77

Again, the application of alternative statistical techniques produced nothing additional or contradictory, and underlined the weakness of this variable. He concluded that:

> "there is no conventional explanation for this variation" and
> "it has been argued that an attorney is indispensible to a defendant at sentencing, but in fact neither type of counsel nor presence or absence of counsel seemed to make much difference at sentencing, and only a slight difference at adjudication". (*Op cit* 132-5, T5.1, 5.5)

Using two models Grabosky and Rizzo examined judicial variation in South Australia and court location in New South Wales.

South Australia (*Op cit* T10)
Independent influences on penalty:

Variable	Model A	B Chi²	(Conversions %)	
Magistrate	390	345	59.3	77.5
Previous Adult Conviction	78	51		
Arrest/Summons	55	Not Sig.		
Legal Representation	38	31	5.8	7.0
Employment status	36	18		
Gender	25	/		
Age	18	/		
Origin	18	/		
Plea	Not Sig.	/		
	658	445		

From both models Models A and B those defendants with prior convictions received harsher sentences, particularly imprisonment. Those defendants who were legally represented were more likely to receive an order or a bond without supervision, while unrepresented defendants were more likely to be fined. However individual magistrates dominate the other sentences; two of the six studied being severe.

In general, as the conversions show, the individual magistrate is 10 times more significant to penalty than representation.

New South Wales (*Ibid* T11)

Variable	Model A	B Chi²	(Conversions %)
Employment status	145	77	32.0	23.1
Gender	122	76	27.0	22.8
Bail	77	57	17.0	17.1
Legal Representation	57	73	12.6	21.9
Court location	52	51	11.5	15.3
Plea, age	Not Sig.	/		
	453	334		

On both models 'court location', a vaguer variable which includes the judicial variables is signficant but at a low level. In the first model legal representation is outweighed greatly by employment status and gender, whereas in the second it appears to have equal weight with those variables.

Legally represented defendants received both more severe and more lenient penalties than the unrepresented, especially Recognizances and Prison.

The general conclusion of this study was that after the magistrate, age was the most important factor regarding outcomes in both South Australia and New South Wales. Controlling for other factors, defendants who were legally represented fared better than their unrepresented counterparts at both decision and sentence stages. However, legally represented convicted defendants, in both states, who were not ordered to make Bonds with supervision, stood a greater chance of going to prison. (*Ibid* 159) So on balance representation was not of great independent value.

One conclusion not drawn from the evidence is that the individual judge has more explanatory weight than the locality in which s/he sits along with and alongside other judges. Another Australian study found that the type of judge was of significance to sentencing rather than representation: Justices ordering Bonds, except for recidivists who were fined or placed on Probation; the Magistrates ordering fines, and imprisoning recidivists who were fined or placed on Probation; the Magistrates ordering fines and imprisoning recidivists. (Douglas *op cit* Ch 8 T9.1, 9.4, 10.1)

One recent British study of four English magistrates' courts divisions contains information on the influences on their sentences handed down for juveniles and for young adults. The influences noted include those of prosecution and defence. The measures are rather imprecise, in particular defence is stated as the percentage of defendants with legal representation when defence is mentioned as an influence. The data was responses to questions on influences on sentencing. The tables covered 'most frequently mentioned', 'most frequently mentioned major' and 'major influences' towards a more severe or more lenient sentence. It is also unclear what method, if any, prosecutors might use to influence sentence.

Here I give an example and how I have reconstructed it:

'Influences on More Lenient Sentence'

Yellowtown	Juveniles %
School Report	43
Social Enquiry Report	37
Moral Assessment	23
Defence	23

So, the range is 23-43 on 4 items, total: 126. Defence influence: 23/126 = 18.2%. This may or may not be confirmed by the other tables on 'frequency' and 'major' influence. In the above example it was as a 'major' influence, 10.5%, but not as 'frequent'.

For simplicity I have discounted those influences on 'lenient' or 'severe' sentences where no such confirmation occurs.

Influences on more severe sentences

Juveniles			Confirmed
Yellowtown			0
Redtown: PROSEC. 40/119	PROS. 33.3	'Major'	17.2
(Greytown: PROSEC. 13/60	PROS. 21.6)		NOT
Bluetown			0

Young Adults			
Yellowtown			0
Redtown: PROSEC. 79/161	PROS. 50	'Major'	26.3
Greytown			0
Bluetown: PROSEC. 37/107	PROS. 34.5	'Major'	18.5

Influences on more lenient sentences

Juveniles			
Yellowtown: DEF. 23/126	DEF. 18.2	'Major'	10.5
Redtown			0
Greytown: DEF. 27/92	DEF. 29.4	'Major'	15.4
Bluetown: DEF. 43/192	DEF. 22.2	'Major'	14.9
		Freq	19.3

Young Adults			
Yellowtown			0
Redtown			0
Greytown: DEF. 20/80	DEF. 25.0	'Major'	21.0
Bluetown			0

Thus, albeit crude and impressionistic, one can estimate the influences on sentences thus:

```
PROSECUTION      Redtown - Young Adults
                 Redtown - Juveniles
                 Bluetown - Young Adults
DEFENCE          Bluetown - Juveniles
                 Greytown - Young Adults
                 Greytown - Juveniles
                 Yellowtown - Juveniles
```

The Prosecution appears to have no admitted influence in Bluetown Juvenile Courts, and at Greytown and Yellowtown generally.

The Defence lawyers appear to have no admitted influence in Bluetown and Yellowtown Young Adults Courts; nor in Redtown generally. (Parker, Sumner and Jarvis 1989 T5.1, 5.2)

Important work on this topic has been done by the Australian psychologist Lovegrove. He examined all the sentences on Robbery, Burglary and Theft defendants in the state of Victoria convicted after a Not Guilty pleas over a two year period.

There were quite wide variations in the length of sentences:

		Range
Theft	11 - 18 months	(7 months)
Burglary	16 - 25 months	(9 months)
Robbery	28 - 44 months	(16 months)

On rate of custodial sentence "it appeared that there were a few deviant judges" (out of 16 in 1978 and 19 in 1979).

As for preferred maximum and minimum sentences:

"on these points, marked and consistent individual differences were found".

On the maximum, 28% of variation in 1978 and 23% in 1979 was attributable to the individual judge.

"It is important to stress that these figures undoubtedly underestimate the importance of the judicial factor because they represent the percentage of total variance rather than reliable variance." (Lovegrove 1984, 161, 164-73)

Conclusions on the Weight of Representation

The general conclusion to be drawn from these studies is that the individual judge is the predominant influence in the decision. Representation is at most a second order influence and even then only in combination with other second order variable in particular contextual patterns.

For example:

> "How little of the variance (between judges) in sentencing is explained by these variables, such as race, age and gender, including type of representation." (Lizotte *op cit*, 565, 578)

Again on sentencing:

> "Previous convictions of such sentences are the key rather than representation. In general the plea of mitigation appears to be a ritual rather than a crucial stage in the sentencing process." (Douglas *op cit*)

More generally:

> "The most unexpected result from the regression analysis related to legal representation. Over all the decisions considered, whether or not the defendant had a legal representative was a significant factor only in the decision to request additional remands.... This has serious implications for defendants, deciding whether or not to retain a lawyer; for model builders deciding whether or not to include information on legal representation...." (Hann *op cit* II, 453)

A recent Dutch study confirms these conclusions from Australia, Britain, Canada and the U.S.A. The study examined discussion in chambers of two benches in different District Courts on verdict and sentence in 25 cases. They found virtually no influence at all from the trial lawyers with one exception, points of law - but they were rare. (Van Duyne and Verwoerd 1985)

'Tailoring'

By reintroducing the judge as the dominant figure in his or her own decision one has not displaced the representative nor legal need, but it certainly needs redefining, more subtly and modestly. The role of the lawyer may be far more circumscribed than some legal evangelists have suggested, but that role does exist as a meaningful function though perhaps at the margin rather than the centre of the stage. There are a few hints in the literature that lawyers and clients understand this. When they do it can present ethical problems:

> "A clique may have close relations with members of the prosecutor's office and get most of their cases tried before a certain judge from whom preferential treatment is anticipated." (Wood *op cit* 163)

A speculative example is provided by the North Eastern Circuit. This Circuit has had the highest 'productivity' rate for Crown Court practice for a decade, in terms of use of judges, staff and Legal Aid. This is achieved by its consistently high Guilty plea rate compared to the national average: 79% in 1983 and 1984 compared to national averages of 68% and 70%, and 36% and 40% in London. This has been attributed by a Circuit Administrator to "robustness of the bench and the legal profession and a good dollop of northern common sense". (Huebner 6/1986) A commentator has given a conflicting interpretation of this account, only part of which is now reported:

> "A Leeds solicitor told us that the local bar was not prepared to fight enough cases. They come from the same chambers as the judges and were afraid to pursue anything which might prove fruitless ... One of the reasons I use London counsel such a lot is because they are willing to fight cases - and win 9 out of 10 of them ..."

A similar account was given for Sheffield. (136 NLJ 27/6/1986, 601) Another disturbing example arose from the prosecutions in Nottingham during the national miners' strike. The Disciplinary Tribunal of the Bar had to decide on cases which, inter alia, revealed considerable differences between the approaches to defence of London counsel defending 22 Nottingham miners and Nottingham counsel defending 20 Yorkshire miners on riot charges. The disciplinary matter arose from the reactions of London counsel to the information that the Nottingham counsel had gone to lunch with the local prosecutor who shared chambers with the leading defence counsel. As a result the Nottingham counsel were absent from a discussion which resulted in a point of law on 'riot' being argued which had not been taken earlier. As a result the jury eventually retired for 10 minutes and acquitted all the miners, both those from Nottingham and Yorkshire. (D. Leigh, The Observer 11/1/1987)

Sometimes 'tailoring' is impossible, but all repeat players share instead very high routine expectations of tariff behaviour. An example of this is the study of 'Womens' Court' by Lipetz. In this Chicago court presided over by the same judge at all times, the judge, state attorneys, police, public defenders and prostitutes all conformed to their mutual expectations of each other. (Lipetz 1984)

In Scotland Sheriffs' individual summary jurisdiction is considered by defence agents to be more predictable than the lay justices. (Bankowski et al op cit 157) This produces responses both prior to court and in court.

> "Once the foibles of judges are established this affects the 'marking' practices of fiscals

(prosecutors) and this produces lay justice." (*Ibid* 148)

But where there is a choice, for example through the venue decision or sometimes an adjournment, a minority either decide to stay wth a particular judge or make the venue decision to avoid a judge. In Ericson and Baranek's Toronto study 20% of defendants took decisions on this basis. (*Op cit* 101-4)

In an unpublished survey of law centre's criminal practice, one law centre worker who had considerable experience of local criminal courts informed me that the 'track record' of the full time Stipendiary magistrates was well known. In particular in drug possession cases Stipendiary A would routinely fine £15 whereas Stipendiary X would fine £140 and £40 forensic costs, despite admitted possession of a named substance. Some defendants would maintain a plea of Not Guilty so as to increase the chance of a different judge taking the case after the adjournment. (Interview, N. Kensington 8/7/1986) In addition Ashworth writes:

> "Our pilot study suggests that flexibility and responsiveness to the judge during mitigation may be the crucial element in the Crown Court ... What appears to be crucial is the interaction between judge and counsel ... the good mitigator must be able to engage in a dialogue with the judge ... commonly presenting certain clues ..." (Ashworth 1984, 38)

One can take Inverted need back one stage. If the individual Court, bench or judge may be crucial, it becomes important to understand the process of allocation of cases to individuals; 'tailoring' may occur at this stage. Lovegrove has also studied these practices in England in 9 Crown Court centres. He found considerable scope for discretion by the Clerks and Listing Officers with 30 variables operating, under 7 headings:
Management, such as Practice Directions and directions of the presiding judge;
Court efficiency, including judicial in expertise and attempts by counsel to adjourn so as to avoid a particular judge or because a particular judge is unwilling to hear a particular type of case;
Relevant judicial characteristics: judges who are considered competent sentencers may receive a greater caseload of guilty pleas;
Judicial personality: incompetent counsel may be matched to competent judges;
Judicial Job Satisfaction:
Prevention of Injustice:
Personal justice - of the person making the list.

Lovegrove concluded that most cases are routine, but there are real differences between listers, particularly over the role of the 'personal'; 7 of the 9 listers took non management factors into account and some of their decisions were non or pre rational. (Lovegrove *op cit*, 738-44)

Developments in the Lord Chancellor's Department's administration of the listing process may reduce the possibilities for variation linked to the personal characteristics and attitudes of listing officers. As a result of a management scrutiny of the listing process in 1983-84, the Department has now issued its concusions for implementation. The emphasis throughout is on 'efficiency' and the maximum use of judge's time in court. There are, however, two clauses which can be interpreted to allow for some judicial choice of cases on the grounds of interest, specialism or attitude. They are:

> "The overall objective of listing is redefined to state that:
> "The listing of cases is subject to judicial authority and direction...and
> "In consultation with Presiding Judges, Circuit Administrators will give increased attention to enabling designated judges to spend as much time as possible at their designated courts..." (LCD 1/1987, 2.1, 5.2)

It is particularly interesting to note in this context the emphasis on 'inverted' need and 'tailoring' in the Law Society's Criminal Advocacy Training Course.

Such references occur in the Outline of the Lecture on Preparation and Presentation; Notes for Group Leaders; Notes for Course Leaders on Mock Trial for Theft and Notes for Group Leaders in Bail Exercises. In total there are 11 such references, such as 'foibles'. (1987 Version paras 9.3, 9.4, Cases F, G; paras 3.6, Cases A, C)

Conclusion

My major finding has been the marginality of legal representation in affecting court outcomes. The evidence on 'tailoring' only enables a speculative conclusion. It is that tailoring is that margin. Failure to tailor may account for the worse outcomes for those legally represented compared to those appearing in person.

16 Re-Thinking Legal Need

The Clinical Analogy

This book has concentrated on the most easily measured, objective, aspects of the crminal process: outcomes. In so doing it has frequently resorted to the medical analogy of 'cure'. That was deliberate because legal services evangelists originated the analogy of 'clinical legal education' - admittedly emphasising the link between legal practice and legal education, rather than developing any specifically medical metaphor. But if one is to take clinical or medical analogies seriously one must admit that there is more to it than cure or successful outcome. In particular there are further roles allied to that of cure which have not been investigated. These include: immunisation and prevention; diagnosis and counselling; and care.

(1) Immunisation and Prevention

Immunity' has a very special meaning in criminal justice, linked to the slang 'supergrass'. Because of the ethical and practical risks in immunity deals between criminal informers and the police and prosecution there are now decisions from the Court of Appeal (Criminal Division) strongly discouraging broad use of this ploy. DPP v Turner (1975) 61 Cr App R 67, R v Mathias NLJ 20/10/1989, 1147. Mathias in particular brings the practice within the scope of legal need by ruling that admissions so made will not be admissible unless the informant has had the opportunity of discussing the deal with a solicitor. The difficulties are highlighted by the example of Clifford Barnes who sued Scotland Yard for failing to provide him with an allegedly promised new identity after he assisted in the breakup of a nationwide petrol and credit card fraud. (Mail on Sunday 1/10/1989) Further Agar (Daily Telegraph LR 11/9/1989) rules that such deals are objectionable if a consequence is to prejudice the defence of those informed on.

Immunity as a legal prescription has therefore today a very narrow ambit; the great majority of intelligence contracts with criminals fall now under the rubric of 'negotiation' and the sentence discount. (R v Afzal The Times 14/10/1989)

Immunisation is in fact an incorrect analogy because it does not precede the 'illness' of the crime. Tax-proofing by avoidance schemes is a more apposite example. Similarly when one talks of preventative medicine in the context of criminal law practice, we are in practice considering ex post methods of harm reduction by preventing worse consequences for the client, given the existence of criminal charges. Nevertheless such practice is important and is preventative in the sense that it may obviate the possibility of the outcome occurring at all, such as through charge reduction, plea negotiation, and so on.

In Britain both the Birmingham and Sheffield studies found that negotiation before and at court was common. Ericson and Baranek's Toronto study found that 51% of charges were withdrawn through negotiation - though 35.4% of the benefitted defendants did not know that this had happened. (Op cit 113) The test however in the context of legal need is whether such negotiation leads to more favourable outcomes than for those without lawyers. Wilkins' Canadian study suggests that this is so (Op cit T7.1, 7.7, 115-7) as does the La Trobe study in Victoria, Australia. There the legally represented achieved charge withdrawal in 12.8% of cases compared with 2.4% for the self representing; also charge withdrawal on a Guilty plea occurred in 17% of represented cases, compared with 5.8% for the self-representing. These researchers saw representation as the key to negotiation of withdrawal rather than acquittal through advocacy. (Douglas 1980 Ch 7)

(ii) Negotiation

At first glance the medical analogy may appear irrelevant to lawyers' negotiations. However as has just been shown, the analogy holds good for 'prevention'. One can also cite the value of medical negotiation, where such 'insiders' can act for patients' benefits, for example in making referral to an appropriate specialist; in negotiating place or transfer on the waiting list system;

or by selecting one of a number of ethical diagnoses for an effective industrial injuries claim.

Apart from these examples, the research has from time to time produced evidence of the negotiator role of defence lawyers. It is not always easy to measure the existence or impact of such activity, especially under the more or less secret conditions required by the British law. (R v Turner (1970) 54 Cr App r 352; PD [1976] 1 WLR 799) On balance, the evidence is that negotiation, whether of the rational mutual presentation of views pre-trial by experienced advocates, or the much criticised 'horse trading' of absent clients, does yield some benefits for most defendants - though it cannot be certain whether the same outcomes would have occurred eventually without negotiation. Baldwin's study of the pre-trial conference experiments in Nottingham and Leeds found that about one third of defendants altered their plea to guilty and about one fifth of charges were dropped by the prosecution; actual negotiation only occurred in about one tenth of all cases. (Baldwin 1985) Earlier work by Baldwin and McConville on the relation between negotiation and sentencing is rather disturbing. The framework in which negotiation occurred was important; the process was extremely erratic; deals were sometimes empty or broken; examples of 'imputed' need enforced on defendants occurred; victims were ignored. (Baldwin and McConville (1978) 544; Giller and Morris (1982) 29)

(iii) Counselling: Diagnosis and Advice

The research presented here has not systematically investigated the relationship between counselling, representation and outcome. For example, defendants who appear in person may have received legal advice from various sources. Sometimes such advice may be perfunctory, but on other occasions it may be all-embracing; and there are occasions when such advice is not followed. From civil justice we know that the proportion of clients before tribunals who appear in person differs between tribunals and topics, but in addition the proportion of them receiving advice also varies. The willingness of Court administrations to actively support the provision of advice can also vary. It is also suggested that advice can promote the withdrawal of cases, against rent defaulters and the withdrawal of hopeless appeals by benefit claimants. Hard and fast conclusions cannot be drawn from such limited evidence, except that they do make the term 'appearance in person' problematic.

In Victoria, Australia it was found that 70% of lawyers had advised criminal defendants to appear in person on occasion, 7.5% between 11-21 cases per year and 4% in more than 21 cases per year; where Road Traffic offences were charged 90% did so. Their reasons were similar to their clients for appearing in person. One American study of the 'Criminal Lawyer' found that specialist, successful, trial lawyers would usually advise clients who intended to plead Guilty to appear in person. (S. Fitzgerald 1977, 31)

Another study does consider the relationship between advice and outcome: bail at Baltimore. Between November 1975 and August 1977 in-court representation for Bail decreased from 80% to 54% but the provision of legal advice for those remanded in custody under two schemes increased from two thirds and a half, to three quarters and two thirds. However no significant effects on Recognizances or the release rate occurred. The researchers concluded that: 'whilst not statistically significant this is problematic for the effectiveness of counsel'. (Alpert and Huff *op cit* 254-6, T10.1) Also relevant is the Home Office study for the Committee on the distribution of work between the Crown Court and the magistrates. It provides evidence that there is a positive link between legal advice or its absence and plea in the magistrates' courts:

	GP Unrepresented	GP Represented	NGP % Represented
Lawyer advice	0	34	44
No advice	81	57	38
	81	13	6

(Gregory *op cit* T6, 7)

This evidence is rather equivocal. On the one hand plea but not representation is significant in Crown Court sentencing. On the other hand, legal advice is the key to Not Guilty pleas in the Magistrates' courts, but the Not Guilty plea rate for the represented occurs in under half the cases and is only 6% more than those with no advice. It is difficult to draw strong conclusions in any direction from this evidence.

One should not conclude cynically from these examples that advice has little value, not least because the mere provision of relevant and timely information is a measurable gain in itself to the client, but also because such advice can be subsumed under the amorphous but over-arching notion of 'care'. It may also be difficult to extract actual examples of such positive interraction, which often is not visible to researchers. An example - incidentally of 'tailoring' - is from Case 6046 in the Sheffield study (*Op cit* 129):

'The barrister (one of the most senior counsel practising in the Sheffield area) saw the defendant and advised him to plead guilty, because the judge he was to face was a very lenient one, and he (counsel) would be able to bring out the facts of the first jury being unable to agree. Counsel apparently said he would not advise this course if the defendant had been scheduled to appear in Court Two, where a much harsher judge was sitting, but in Court One it was the best policy. L was sentenced to borstal training; counsel apparently told him that had he pleaded guilty at the outset of the first trial he would have probably received 3 years' imprisonment.'

This brief account cannot pass by the one institutional procedure which patently espouses the counselling role but eschews the direct advocacy of outcomes.   This was the McKenzie ([1971] P.33) in-court assistant now threatened by the recent decision R v. Leicester City Justice ex parte Barrow (NLJ 25/1/1991, 93 QBD). Further assistance had been provided by the 1988 Guidelines for Legal Aid (Green Form) advisers. ([1970] 3 All ER 1034 Law Society Gazette 14/2/1988) There is now one practice in Britain, in Bristol, which formally and consistently gives priority to these sorts of methods. (F. Gibb, The Times 27/2/1991)

(iv) Care

In practice care cannot be separated from 'cure', neither in medical nor legal contexts, but it is a useful analytical distinction. It becomes more important if the 'cure' function as consequential need is demonstrated to fail or is not positively proven. The evidence on this aspect is a part of 'felt' need research but is thin and unsystematic. Some of it is damning, notably Blumberg's evidence on co-opted 'insiders' in the American courtroom subculture. Against such an account can be put notions of the defence lawyer as 'hand holder', 'flak catcher' or even as 'choreographer' in Carlen's mordant account of Inner London magistrates' courts. (Carlen 1976)
  The Duty Solicitor schemes have from the beginning been promoted as 'care' institutions. They can be seen as a lifeline to the angry, bewildered, confused and dazed, typical first time or occasional defendant. (King 1976, 13-4, 30-2) On the other hand they can be seen as part of the management of the production line problem in magistrates' justice. Recent research by the Insitutute of Judicial Administration (Sanders *et al* 1989, Sanders 1990) found that in a survey of 800 cases in 10 police stations, 20% of responses to calls for assistance in serious cases were solely by telephone (30% for non serious);   the use of representatives rather than solicitors was widespread; there were wide variations in practice between localities; and that standards were higher where 'own solicitor' responded.   It was not a flattering   picture   of   this   'care'   institution. Nevertheless it exists and does provide 'care' today. In Canada Ericson and Baranek at Toronto asked defendants about their dis/satisfaction with their attorneys. Their

findings were counter-intuitive on two of the three
measures, two of which are clearly 'care' measures; the
other is directly related to 'cure'. On two measures
Legal Aid attorneys were perceived more favourably than
privately retained attorneys:
On being kept informed about the situation and the
possibilities available ('Care'):

NET (Positive-Negative) %	Legal Aid	Private
	+ 17.2	+ 37.5

On the effort put in on behalf of the client ('care'):

	Legal Aid	Private
	+ 3.4	- 9.4

On the outcome achieved ('cure'):

	Legal Aid	Private
	+ 44.8	+ 34.3

(Ericson and Baranek *op cit* T3.2, 113)

Walters' study of leading defence advocates in the USA
emphasises the distance between professional and lay
client, with only 17% involving the client in the
preparation of the final speech to the jury. (1988, 70)
Taken together these net opinions of satisfaction cannot
be said to evidence a high degree of perceived 'care' by
clients, and lawyers were perceived as 'a key contributor
to a client's anxieties'.

In the UK the earliest similar study was by Borrie and
Varcoe and tested the attitudes of defence solicitors,
court clerks, and defendants on the effectiveness of the
formers' mitigations. (*Op cit* paras 217-9) They found
that half the defendants thought that the mitigations
were successful in half their cases compared to 10% who
believed that the mitigation had increased the sentence.
In this small sample 84% of those legally represented and
dissatisfied still wanted legal representation in future.

In the Sheffield study defendants were asked whether
their lawyers had helped a little, or a great deal, or
had not helped at all or made matters worse.

Lawyer-Court	Positive	Negative	NET + %
Solicitors Summary	93	6	87
Solicitors Higher Courts	64	35	29
Barristers Higher Courts	70	30	40

It can be seen that the perceived service by solicitors
in the magistrates' courts was good, whereas in the
higher courts (principally the Crown Court) for both
solicitors and counsel a third of defendants had
unsatisfactory experiences. (*Op cit* T6.11)

There is also interesting material in another American
study of the role of perceived injustice in the
defendant's evaluation of courtroom experience. (Tyler
1984, 52) This study did not attend to the

representative variable, the focus being on the outcome
and judicial handling of the trial. Satisfaction was
found to be less related to outcome than in previous
studies, the defendants' perception of fairness being
significantly related to the quality of the judge's
handling of the case, 'care' it appears is relevant to
the judicial as well as the advocate's role in the
outcome.

In the last two years a change of climate has occurred
in Britain with regard to these sorts of issues. The Law
Society for example makes references to client care in
its Criminal Advocacy Training course.[1] However standards
of care are not yet consistently high, and solicitors'
views on what 'care' is may contradict those of their
clients.[2] A survey by the National Consumer Council of
the legal services used by clients of 46 CAB over a 5
month period found that the most common complaint was of
poor communication by solicitors (NCC 1989); an image
echoed by the Annual Report of the Solicitors Complaints
Bureau. (NLJ 13/4/1990, 307) The Law Society commissioned
its own report on 'Public Use and Perception of
Solicitors' Services' which found a 14% dissatisfaction
rate and which ranked solicitors well above accountants,
bank managers and estate agents for non 'care',
efficiency aspects such as honesty and reliability. (Law
Society Gazette 21/9/1989, survey of 2,609 adults) The
latest survey was by Easi-Bind International which found
that the public perception of solicitors is as poor
presenters - only 8% of whom were above average. (NLJ
9/6/1989, 797)

That there is a problem of professional competence in
this area has been acknowledged by the General Secretary
of the Law Society (Daily Telegraph 27/6/1989, 6/7/1989)
by the creation of a Law Society annual letter drafting
competition and by developments in major 'path breaking'
firms. (The Times 30/5/1990) Pannone-Napier, the disaster
law Manchester based firm, has achieved British Standards
Institute accreditation for its services - a consistent
and continuous quality control method. (Law Society
Gazette 25/8/1989, 39) Nabarro Nathanson, the London
commercial law firm, has invested £125,000 in a training
centre designed by Mediapro consultants which will
emphasise personal presentation and communication skills.
(The Independent 25/6/1990)

Some Structural Considerations

The Positive Residue of Legal Need

The general tenor of the empirical work presented and
analysed through the course of this book has been that
the orthodox pre-entry unmet legal need criterion is not
soundly based in the theory of need; that the appropriate
criterion for defining an adjectival need, such as legal

need, is consequential comparison, and that legal need, from that perspective, is in general terms not proven or must be narrowly specified. In previous chapters it has been argued that 'inverted' need, the judicial variable, is a much more powerful determinant in the decision process than the advocate.

There are however a number of qualifications that must be made explicit, before some of the structural issues arising from these findings can be discussed.

First, the method used in this book relies on Popper's falsification principle in the philosophy of science: it is a negative proof. It can only indicate where adjectival, legal need, defined in a terms of a comparative consequentialism criterion, is not met. It follows that where a particular need assertion survives this test, all the problems of positive definition discussed at the beginning of this book remain. Three approaches to that problem can be canvassed. One would be demand side consumer sovereignty in terms of felt and/or expressed need. Another would be supply side professional domination, as normative need, with the attendant risks of imputed need or failed take up also discussed earlier. A third approach would be the attempt to find or construct consensus definitions. It is these that are examined now.

Attempts to Transcend the Problem of Definition: Consensual Need

It has been argued that adjectival needs, such as legal need, are particularly difficult to define positively. A shorthand description of the problem is that need is an 'essentially contestable' concept.

Difficulty however does not obviate the necessity of continuing the search for an appropriate method or methods, because need, however defined, remains so central as both a social problem and a problem for social policy. The discussion of the pragmatics of need underline these points.

It has been hinted that there does in practice exist today a dominant paradigm of need definition, and in a sense this dominant paradigm is a consensus definition. I refer here to normative, expert or professional definition, or perhaps to the consensus that may be constructed within a profession and by it upon government. Such normatively constructed consensus may be more effective to the extent that it achieves an official status, such as the Widgery criteria in Criminal Legal Aid. However such a consensus masks a silence in that a consensus, properly described, involves the voice of all concerned, not merely an interested segment of the public.

Normative consensus is however unstable. For example, as has been illustrated, the public may not conform to the behaviour encoded in the official definition, or may express contradictory attitudes and behaviour in different topics. Further there may be competing normative definitions from other professions or political interests.

Nevertheless consensual definitions will remain attractive as long as the basic philosophical problem remains unresolved. It is proposed now to examine such proposals. For example the philosopher Condren suggests that a practical way round these difficulties would be to search not for needs as such but for non-contentious need claims and then move, by appropriate methods and measures, towards a hierarchy of claims. From this he suggests one could frame priorities and responses, which might even include rights. However, he emphasises that this is a pragmatic solution, which simply obviates the Humean gap between 'is' and 'ought', by replacing it with 'oughts'. (1977 Ch 14, 254) Such consensus solutions do not validate need as such but they may legitimate responses to need claims. This ought not to be complained of, provided it is acknowledged for what it is, since the concept of need covers both 'is' and 'ought', but does not provide a logical bridge between them.

Minimalist Approaches

One set of approaches has the political attraction of being cheap, relatively easy to administer and do not openly yield to subjectivity. These are minimalist consensus definitions.

An example comes from the former Director of Legal Services Program of the USA Office of Economic Opportunity. He estimated that there were at least six million problems per year amenable to legal solutions affecting persons below the official poverty line. These would require 12-15,000 fulltime lawyers at a cost of $350M per annum. To provide this service would mean a sixfold increase in the legal services programme, a quite unrealistic proposition. (Johnson 1978, 235) As a result a variety of methods are used to reduce eligibility or limit the benefitting populations. My purpose here is only to point out that this is a misuse of the term 'need'. If, by whatever criteria, there are 6 million unmet legal problems a year, then there are 6 million such problems a year. If one does not or is not able to respond to that need and one devises rationing or priority systems that is another matter. This is perhaps the one difficulty with Williams' attack on the 'needologists'. As an economist he properly insists that price is always relevant to services and that methods of assessment which ignore it or exclude it are vitiated to that extent. He continues his argument:

"Thus we could think of other people having a 'Demand' for some individual having or not having care." (Williams 1974 Ch 4, 69-73)

Such an attitude can be put into a need matrix under a 'social' axis. However, there is a preliminary difficulty. How do we determine who or what counts as 'social'? There are already difficulties in allowing a 'normative' axis, in that we can never be sure if the expert is an expert and we may not know if the expert is also a supplier of the service needed, so to add a social axis may increase the problems. There has been one carefully constructed approach to creating a method of discovering 'social need', (Mack and Lansley 1985) which is discussed below, but in general the weakness in introducing a social axis is that the generalised donor replaces or adds to the expert supplier in deciding on the donee's need, and the donor is, as such, not in a value free position for judgment. The other weakness which is intimately linked with the first is that it confuses and conflates recognition of need with response to need.

A similar difficulty abounds in Wilkins' 'Consumerist Criminology'. (1974, Chs 8, 9) Wilkins' empirical study in achieving a consensus is predicated on the general public being the consumer of criminal justice. At the very least that assumption needs careful delineation. In general the public as non-deviants are not consumers of criminal justice but its indirect suppliers.

There are two continental writers who have fairly similar minimalist approaches to need, which are analytically rigorous, though whether they would yield a consensus is moot. Blankenburg would limit need to the voluntary supply of services which the legal profession can and will provide to active unsolicited demands for assistance.

Reifner's contention, derived from his survey evidence, is that legal need occurs only when individuals do not have enough social power to solve their problems themselves and the legal system is their sole opportunity to pursue their rights or interests and the method selected does not violate their moral beliefs. (Blankenburg 1980 *op cit* Ch 17, 237, Reifner *ibid* Ch 4, 41) This is the typical 'last resort' perspective, which is much criticised for producing too few legal responses with too few resources, too late.

A *Cumulative* Approach

Bradshaw, whose taxonomy of need has so much influenced my discussion, is a relativist because his analysis clearly distinguishes the client's views and actions from those of suppliers and responders to need. Nevertheless in an undogmatic way he does take the view that consensual definition is desirable and even achievable; however he would concede that such consensus would not thereby become an objective definition, even if officially recognised or sanctioned. (Bradshaw, New Society 1972, 640-1)

His view, shared by Cass and Western in Australia, (op cit 18) is that the greater the degree of identity of opinion of both demand and supply sides, coupled with supporting action from the demand side, the stronger the argument for need is. Thus: Normative + Felt + Expressed + Comparative + can be called positive consensual need, whereas: Normative - Felt - Expressed - Comparative - can equally be called consensual non-need. The problem remains that there is a large range of intermediate possibilities in which all the difficulties of this topic remain unaltered, and questions of manipulation and internal supply side politics remain.

It is interesting to note that in (English) Criminal Legal Aid the 'Widgery criteria' for eligibility operate cumulatively in this way and that the approach of the Royal Commission on Legal Services was simply to reverse the presumption but not to undermine the method.

A Referendal Approach

Klein argues from his considerable experience in the study of health economics and administration, that the achievement of consensus regarding need is very difficult in practice. Since there are analogies with Legal Aid it is necessary to repeat his argument.

Professionals, Klein proposes, are ethical individualists responding to the individual client rather than the community; they give priority to acute needs and are relatively unconcerned about opportunity costs. Consumers are even less homogeneous than the professional but share their ethical individualism. However, their hierarchy of values within that framework is frequently different and they may give priority ranking to different matters. Since they have difficulty evaluating the professionals and their services, these priorities may not be rational, but that does not reduce their significance. As far as potential clients are concerned, costs are more likely to be recognised by them than the professionals, and to that extent they are ethical collectivists. Generally professionals tend to seek the concentration of resources, whereas the consumers want their diffusion. Administrators by contrast, are concerned with abstract norms and are therefore utilitarian cost-effective maximisers; this can conflict with both professionals and consumers. The politicians' concern may reflect differing ideology and local political considerations, but what they share is a need for visibility, often in the form of architecture or technology; these priorities will frequently satisfy one constituency, whilst frustrating others.

Klein concludes that if the decision to define an item or service as need is analysed from these standpoints, consensus, whilst not an impossible aim, must be recognised as very difficult to achieve. (Klein 1977, 88, 91)

A major attempt to overcome these problems and the problems of objectivity and relativity in defining need was published in 1985 by Mack and Lansley, based on a national representative survey of 1,174 people by MORI and commissioned and shown by London Weekend Television as 'Breadline Britain'. The survey 'normatively' put forward a list of 35 items for respondents to consider; however these items were already established from previous surveys as being closely connected with respondents' perceptions (Felt need) of necessity and poverty. None incidentally could be called directly legal needs. The aim of the survey was precisely to obtain a picture of consensus and non consensus on these items as necessities from all social classes, thus transcending the problem of definition by uniting those with and without them and by uniting those who might be (tax) donors and donees of them. This approach to consensus I call referendal. Its virtue is that it openly admits to the existential necessity of acting as if need can objectively be defined, and at the same time recognises the ultimately political nature of such decision, but provides information that decision makers have every right to know and use with regard to the public's attitude to necessity. What the survey could not do is provide any objective cut off point for the definition, such as 51% or 66% or 75% consensus on a particular item as need.

The average consensus on the 35 items was 64.1% and this ranged from:

97%   Heating to warm the living areas of a house.
96%   Indoor toilet, not shared with other households.
96%   Damp free home.
94%   Bath.
94%   Separate beds for all in a household.

Clearly housing, broadly interpreted, is perceived consensually as a crucial focus of need. Analysis of the 13 items with above 66% consensus shows a strong tendency, 8 items, towards identifying necessity with housing conditions.

The least consensual items were:

33.32%   Friends/family round for meal once a month.
34.22%   Car.
35.14%   Packet of cigarettes per day.
(*Op cit* T3.1)

In fact there was considerable variance between social classes outside the first 5 items listed above; such variance occurred both for relatively high and low consensus items. On 4 items it exceeded 20%:

```
New, not secondhand clothes    53%  AB   79%  D
2 hot meals per day            46%  AB   69%  C1, D
Garden                         41%  AB   61%  D
TV                             37%  C1   64%  D
```

With only 2 items was need perception significantly greater than possession:
Heating 92%   perception 97%:
Damp free house 85%   perception 96%. (*Ibid* T3.3)
    In addition the study tested variations in consensus against age, household type, and political identification. Each item produced some degree of variation, for example:

```
Telephone         32% (15-24 years)   60% (65+ years)
Dressing gown     15% (15-24 years)   48% (55-64 years)
                                      (Ibid T3.5)
Dressing gown     29% ('Others')      57% (Pensioners)
2 pairs all-      63% (Single)        84% (Households
weather shoes                         without children)
Adults: 2 hot     56% (Pensioners)    76% (Single
meals a day                           Parents)
                                      (Ibid T3.6)
Meat/fish every   58% (Labour)        78% (Lib SDP)
other day                             (Ibid T3.7)
Washing machine   50% (Single)        71% (Single
                                      Parents)
Washing machine   61% (Conservatives) 73% (Lib SDP)
```

Since political constituencies are relevant to possible decisions regarding the public provision or subsidy of such items or their cash equivalent it is interesting to note the degree of consensus across political parties:

```
66%- 75%  All 3 Parties: Celebrations for special
                         occasions
85%- 90%       "         2 pairs all-weather shoes
90%- 95%       "         Beds for all
                         Bath
95% +          "         Damp free house
                         Indoor toilet
                         Heating
                         Holiday
```

There were 6 items with 10-20% variation between parties (Conservative-Labour-Liberal SDP). However an innovatory aspect of the study was to ask respondents, with their political allegiance in mind, whether the government should raise the tax level by 1 p in the £ to provide necessities. The responses were positive:

```
        Conservative      79%
        Liberal SDP       77%
        Av.               74%
        Labour            73%   (Ibid T3.8)
```

The value of that finding is that, in general, it shows that those voters already more likely to be in possession or receipt of the items and more likely to be taxpayer donors than donees are prepared not only to describe items as necessaries ('Felt Need') but to respond behaviourally ('Expressed Need').

However there are problems of interpretation which must be borne in mind even with a referendal approach.

First, a comparative study with Denmark suggests that one should not expect such elicited definitions to remain static; and there may well be significant regional differences not tested here.

	Danish	British
2 pairs all-weather shoes	64%	78%
Separate bedroom for children	66%	77%
Refrigerator	94%	77%
Roast once per week	50%	67%

(*Ibid* T3.9)

Second, one could take a 'bottom line' approach that not only should the average on an item exceed a particular percentage, such as 50%, but that no identified group response - itself a matter of political choice - should be less than that percentage. If we take the earlier list demonstrating group variation in response to items from Telephone to Washing Machine, then Telephone and Dressing Gown would fail to qualify, despite their strong constituency amongst the old.

Finally, the survey exemplifies, yet again, the extremely difficult epistemological problems of attitude research to 'felt needs'. Respondents were asked with regard to items which they themselves had defined as necessities whether:

(i) They 'had the item and could not do without it?'
(ii) They 'had the item and could do without it?' and
(iii) They 'did not have and did not want the item?'

I define these possibilities as (i) Need, (ii) Want and (iii) Not-Need, but it must be remembered that all respondents had already defined the items as necessaries. If we limit ourselves to the higher response of the last two questions and deduct that from the response to the first question, one can calculate a net consensus, which is considerably smaller than the original response as 'necessaries'. Some examples are:

Item	(i) Need	(ii) Want	(iii) Not Need	: Net
Public Transport	96	78		+18
Bedrooms for children	87		60	+27
Toys for children	87		76	+11
Roast, once per week	89	59		+30
Hobby/Leisure activity	82	52		+30
Telephone	65	21		+44
Dressing gown	72	23		+49

The problem raised by these interesting combinations of questions is that the respondents appear to hoist themselves on their own petard. If politically a decision was taken that even an item with 51% consensus qualified for government support through revenue distribution, not one of these items would qualify. On the other hand there is nothing politically to prevent a decision to act on gross rather than net felt need; it is just that the basis for consensus would be radically altered.

There is a further theoretical point to add in conclusion. It is transparent that many of the items above are decidedly ethnocentric needs or wants. If we take as an example toys for children or the weekly roast or a hobby, it is possible but very difficult to demonstrate that harm arises in the material sense if they are lacked. However at the symbolic level harm may be perceived, which may in itself be sufficient measure, to constitute need in the sense that those deprived are seen as ethnic amputees or cripples. The concept of comparative need as developed in this work does not attend to these issues as such. This is because such a criterion is pre or irrational, which does not reduce its political importance, but philosophically the case remains that if no adverse consequences can be demonstrated need does not exist, and should instead be described as 'want'.

This symbolic need relates to some standard of relative social deprivation. That standard presumably is citizenship, which may be the unarticulated major premise of a referendal approach. If assumptions about citizenship do not in fact rest upon a political consensus it is hard to see how referendal testing for need can transcend such divisions.

Conclusion: Referendal Approaches to Legal Need

It is necessary, however obvious, to point out that needs for legal services never appear amongst the 35 items analysed above. It follows that at the broad level of need in general neither donors nor donees rank legal services above 33%.

On the other hand there is no reason why referendal method should not be applied to an hypothetical Legal Services budget. In this case the interviewed groups must include representative samples of the potential donees and of potential non-donees within the criminal justice system; for example a careless driving defendant intending to plead Guilty before magistrates, and a first time defendant on a theft charge to the value of £1.75 intending to plead Not Guilty before magistrates, and so on. The balance of the sample would cover the general population in the normal way for social class, age, gender and regional balance. It must be repeated however that the questionnaire examples could only include those crimes where comparative consequential need had been shown to exist. Even here the problem remains as to what territorial limit to test since there is so much local and individual judicial variation. Presumably a Circuit or Legal Aid Area would be administratively simplest.

Further Structual Considerations

(i) The Place of Advocacy

The importance of the judge, as 'inverted' need, appears to render representation marginal in terms of outcomes. (Bellow and Kettleson 1978, 337, 339) This does not, as the discussion of 'tailoring' suggested, render representation meaningless, and it is important not to take the notion of inverted need too far. As has been suggested inverted need can give the legal representative means for meeting client's needs in ways which are not amenable to comparative consequential research. An anecdotal example from the writer's knowledge can illustrate this. Several years ago a 'Beauty Queen' was charged, after being apprehended in flagrantè dèlicto, attempting to smuggle, as a courier, several kilos of heroin. She was remanded in custody. When the case was listed her counsel took the view that the trial judge was 'fair minded but very severe in sentencing'. The advice to the defendant was followed: bail was not sought and a Guilty plea maintained. The defendant's former boyfriend, who had used her to carry drugs on several occasions, was considered to be an important organisational link in a large international drug combine. Her family was advised to move away completely from their home area and to start a new life in a different country. The defendant then informed the police with the fullest details of the boyfriend's activities and associates, whereupon he was arrested, charged and later imprisoned for a long term. All this was put to the trial judge who then sentenced her to a lengthy term in custody, but 10 years less than counsel had originally anticipated.

There is another value of representation which should not be ignored. Although the evidence surveyed and presented in this research in general falsifies the hypothesis that representation produces more favourable outcomes for defendants, it is the represented cases which set the general standard, the ethos, of any courtroom. Bell, whose work has been one of the acknowledged foundations of my method, noticed the cursory consideration of applications made by invisible claimants who did no more than write into tribunals, and that as attendance and participation increased so did quality and advantageous outcomes. As Feeley puts it:

> "To suggest that there is little difference between outcomes in cases with and without attorneys does not imply that the outcomes would be the same if no one at all had an attorney." (*Op cit* 184)

Much that has been written here suggests that the Rule of Law notion of equal access to representation is rather empty formalism. One can judge for oneself from the evidence whether that is a whole or partial case, but without lawyer access or the possibility of adversarial procedure the trial process is likely to be marked by unremarked and unchecked variability, local and personal, and arbitrary particularism. From that risk legal access is a necessary preventative measure.

(ii) Legal Aid: Welfare or Subsidy?

Another issue that flows from the generally not proven status of legal need as a comparative consequence, is the political definition of legal need. The institutional responses to legal need, such as Legal Aid, the law centres and duty solicitor schemes, have previously been defined consensually as welfare, whether charitable or as a public service publicly funded. The issue is whether that definition is correct - ignoring here the ancillary aspects of 'care' just discussed. This is not a trivial issue since half a billion pounds per annum are involved. It does seem to flow from the hypothesis tested and falsified here and the complimentary material on inverted need and the weight of representation that this received definition of legal need as welfare is problematic. To the extent that the various responding services do not meet the legal need on which they are predicated should the public funds involved be to that extent redefined as a public subsidy to a private group? Further, should those public funds be reallocated?

Apart from raising these questions, it is suggested that it does not follow that reallocation is a necessary conclusion. First, it might be that on those topics which have survived the negative test greater allocation than is currently the case might be required, for example to level upwards the rates of pay between criminal and matrimonial practice, or to some notional 'fair and reasonable' rate. In addition the scope of response might be augmented, for example by a rule that joint defendants never share advocates. Again, it does not follow that any reallocation should necessarily be away from legal services, including criminal justice, for example for the establishment of a prison duty solicitor service or the provision of salaried public defenders where no duty solicitor scheme exists as in West London. Again, as far as take-up of benefits and rights are concerned, there are clear indications of comparative need where typically the person in need will remain in a state of lack without the assistance of a responding agent, including targetted advertising, such as a law centre which postively channels that person to the appropriate benefits. These examples do raise an allied issue however, whether the same output of benefit could be achieved with greater cost-effectiveness by other agencies which are not adjectively characterised as 'legal'.

(iii) Other Types of Legal Need in Criminal Justice

The focus of this thesis has been on the legal needs of defendants before and during trial. In that focus it does no more than mirror the received tradition of what is normally understood by legal need in the context of criminal justice. However even accepting this focus on crminal defendants may be too limited. Until the passage of the Costs in Criminal Cases Act 1984 Part II and section 16 of the Prosecution of Offences Act 1985 it was generally considered[3] that section 3 of the Costs in Criminal Cases Act 1973 did not meet the economic needs of acquitted defendants, and that vindication was not complete without financial support.

Another recent discovery is the special needs of witnesses in criminal trials both inside and outside the courtroom. (Justice 1986)

From a much broader perspective the discovery of rural legal need as a separate social problem may be briefly mentioned. The legal services movement has been an almost exclusively urban phenomenon, and implicit in its programme and its action was a concentration on the problems of the urban deprived. Whereas that social movement achieved recognition between 1968 and 1972 as valid political currency, rural legal need did not impinge on public consciousness until some point between 1976 and 1984. Further that development was associated with different groups. It remains at the periphery of public consciousness. (Rural Advice and Information Committee 1984)

However the discovery of the decade in criminal justice has undoubtedly and deservedly been defendants' victims, specifically as persons with problems before and during trial in the criminal process. (National Association of Victim Support Schemes 1988)

The established system for meeting the needs of victims, apart from vindication by the conviction of the wrongdoer and possible civil action for damages, is by compensation, either from the courts or the Criminal Injuries Compensation Board. Compensation is an economic response to a wrong which may have other than economic impacts.

The original provision for compensation was in section 1 of the Criminal Justice Act 1972 which has been successively amended in terms of its scope and relation between court ordered compensation and that payable under the prerogatival Criminal Injuries Compensation Board. Both Crown Court and Magistrates have tended to use these powers more over the course of time, and to order higher payments and for more offences. Encouragement and guidelines for consistency have been issued by the Magistrates' Association. The Home Office has also reminded and encouraged the police and Justices' Clerks to inform victims of their rights and the relevant procedures. (HO 27/1983, pa.4) Various proposals for the increase and improvement in take-up have been put forward by a wide variety of sources and experts. The Criminal Justice Act 1988 gave for the first time a right to compensation for victims.

(iv) The Mode of Criminal Justice

There is however another approach to the needs of the victim which is broader in its outlook than the narrowly economic issue of compensation. It can be said that this approach is developing into a reform lobby in much the way the legal services movement took on an evangelistic tone in the late 1960s. It raises radical questions about both the trial itself and the assumptions of the penal system as modes of criminal justice. This tendency or movement originated in the early 1970s in the USA. It is sometimes known as the 'Informal Justice movement' or 'Alternative Dispute Resolution' movement and sometimes as the 'Mediation movement' or movement for 'Restorative' justice. The premises upon which it is based contrast sharply with those underlying the classic adversarial trial. The latter can be characterised as public catharsis, the expulsion of the convict from the social body; whereas the former is therapeutic, the reintegration of the victim **and** offender, and therefore the healing of the social wound. (Griffiths 1970, 359)

There were negative reasons for the promotion of such approach, such as the widespread cynicism with the vast scale of American plea bargaining and the ineffectiveness and expense of the prison sentence, so there has been some official support for alternative approaches, at least as experiments, from the beginning. (LEAA 1973) As a result hundreds of experiments have occurred with a bewildering variety of scope and approaches. (Alpert and Nichols 1981) Debate continues over the philosophy of the mediation movement; one issue being whether informal justice is covertly as oppressive as that which it attempts to replace, and whether a 'family model' of criminal justice is in fact possible in society divided by social class and historic divisions of ethnicity, gender and region. (Abel 1981, Matthews ed 1988) If one can typify the mediation approach to criminal justice at all, one might generalise that victim and offender are brought together before an independent person who encourages them to express their feelings about their experience of the delinquent event, and if possible to reach some agreement acceptable to the victim in terms of apology, restitution, reparation or some other type of personal service; there may also be agreements in relation to future conduct.

In Britain the first reference I have found to mediation occurred in the First Half Yearly Report of the Paddington Law Centre. (Para 33) Their large criminal law caseload was described as being 'predominantly petty' and mediation to produce reconciliation was considered as being an appropriate response. This proposal does not appear to have been taken any further, either by the minority of law centres specialising in criminal law, nor by the law centre movement generally.

The Home Office interest has shifted markedly with the political climate, but interest has continued from as early as 1975. The initiative and drive have come from the National Association for the Care and Rehabilitation of Offenders and the National Association of Victims Support Schemes with the National Association of Probation Officers. The first experiment was made in coventry in 1980, and a variety of further experiments continue, with much emphasis on juvenile delinquency and all following conviction or admission of guilt.

Five varieties of approach can be isolated: dispute settlement within the community; police based mediation usually aimed at diversion from court process; police based juvenile lay panel reparation; probation service run reparation, combined with intermediate treatment; and probation service, court based, reparation schemes. (Marshall and Walpole 1985) In the autumn of 1984 a national lobby and education group emerged, F.I.R.M., the Forum for Initiatives in Reparation and Mediation, which has organised a number of conferences and provides training for mediators. It produces a quarterly journal, Mediation, now in its eighth year.

In an important respect this lobby, which is no more of a social movement than the so called legal services movement, appears to differ from other evangelistic groups in criminal justice: it is markedly more self critical, perhaps because it attempts to view delinquency from the perspective of both victim and offender.

This book has developed a critique of the received notion of legal need which has put into question both legal representation as a response to defendants' needs, and the courtroom process itself through the empirical evidence of 'inverted' need. It is interesting to note that such scepticism and immanent prescription has been found in a recent study of Scottish lay Justices of the Peace. (Bankowski *et al op cit* 92-6, 112-3, 178-80) As has been briefly stated above the needs of victims are now also recognised as requiring institutional responses. However the emerging evangelistic lobby for a new mode of criminal justice aimed at meeting primarily the emotional and educational needs of victims and offenders should itself be received with the same degree of analysis and constructive criticism.

There are a considerable number of questions and problems raised by this alternative mode of victim offender Mediation and Reparation as restorative justice. It is proper therefore to end by noting those questions:

Can such mediation be coerced on offenders and if voluntary how can one ensure its genuiness for both parties?

What should be the limits of such a mode, for example what types of offence, if any, are totally inappropriate (Shapland 1982) for what types of offence and for which offenders is there most likely to be public support for such a change of mode?

How can one ensure that victims participate fully and have their concerns given equal concern to those of offenders? (Heinz and Kerstetter 1980 Ch 8)

Is mediation only appropriate following Guilty pleas or does it have a role post- or even pre-conviction?

Does such a mode constitute a privatisation of criminal justice (like plea bargaining) and if so what relation should it have with the State's interest in criminal justice?

Is there a risk of too much random variation (beyond that already present) caused by the availability of reparation for and by individuals?

How is one to recruit and train mediators? (Davis *et al* 1987)

If the latter, are there risks to the adversarial and judicial ethos for advocates or judges?

Or are other types of professional more appropriate?

What are the risks of unsuccessful mediation; and is the deterrent rate better or worse than is currently the case?

Who gains most, and in what ways, from mediation; the victim or the offender?

Is there a risk that such a mode would lead to 'net widening' to cover delinquencies which would previously have been controlled by police discretion?

These questions all require further analysis, critical appraisal and empirical research, some of which is already occurring. They are however properly beyond the scope of this book and could indeed be the subject of another one!

Footnotes

1. Paras 2.1, 2.3, 6.10; Case Assessment 5.3.

2. Spicer's Consulting Group, 'Strategic Issues for Law
    Firms, Bulletin 6/12/1989: Quality Service - Myths
    and Realities; and see R. Rice, <u>Financial Times</u>
    18/12/1989.

3. Lord Chancellor's Legal Aid Advisory Committee 34th
    Report *op cit* paras 489, 492; <u>LAG Bull</u> 12/1973, 6;
    R. Thoresby 36 MLR (1973) 647; HC Debs <u>The Times</u>
    9/5/1975; H. Levenson, 'The Price of Justice' Cobden
    Trust (1981) 61-62.

References

Abel, R., 1 _Law and Policy Quarterly_ 1979, 5

Abel R., The Politics of Informal Justice, 2 vols, Academic Press, New York, 1981

Abel R. ed Thomas P.A., Law in the Balance, Ch 1, Martin Robertson, Oxford, 1982

Abel-Smith B., Zander M., Brooke R., Legal Problems of the Citizen, Heinemann, London 1973

Adamsdown Community Trust, Report and Analysis of a Law Centre Cardiff, 1978

Albert-Goldberg N. ed McDonald W.F., The Defense Counsel, Ch 3, Sage Foundation, New York, 1983

Alpert B.S. and Nichols L.T., Beyond the Courtroom, D.C. Heath, Lexington, 1981

Alpert G.R. and Huff C.R. ed McDonald W.F., The Defense Counsel, Sage Foundation, New York, 1983

Anderson R., Representation in the Juvenile Courts, Routledge and Kegan Paul, London 1978

Arafat I. and McCahery K. ed Rich R.M., Essays in the Theory and Practice of Criminal Justice, University of America Press, Washington D.C., 1978

Aristotle ed Ross D., Works, Vol 8, Books 10-15, Metaphysics, Heinemann, London, 1935

Armstrong S. and Graycar R. ed Cashman P., Research and Delivery of Legal Services, Law Foundation of New South Wales, Sydney, 1981

Arrow K.J., The Limits of Organisation, Norton, New York, 1974

Ashworth, A., The English Criminal Process Occasional Paper 11, Centre for Criminological Research, Oxford 1984

Ashworth, A., Sentencing in the Crown Court, Oxford Centre for Criminological Research, Oxford 1985

Atkins B.M. and Boyle E.W., 24 _Emory Law Journal_ 1975, 67

Attfield R.A. and Dell K., Values, Conflict and the Environment, Ian Ramsey Centre, Oxford 1989

Baldwin J., Pre-Trial Justice, Basil Blackwell, Oxford, 1985

Baldwin J. and McConnville M., Negotiated Justice, Martin Robertson, Oxford, 1977

Baldwin J. and McConville M. ed Baldwin J. and Bottomley A.K., Criminal Justice, Martin Robertson, Oxford, 1978

Baldwin J. and McConville M., 41 Modern Law Review 1978, 544

Barber R., 7 Australia and New Zealand Journal of Criminology 1974, 157

Barry B., Political Argument, Routledge and Kegan Paul, London, 1965

Basten J. and Disney J., 1 University of New South Wales Law Journal 1975, 168

Bay C., Canadian Journal of Political Science, 1968, 242

Bell K., Research Study on Supplementary Benefits Appeals Tribunals, Department of Health and Social Security, HMSO, London 1975

Bell K., 33 Northern Ireland Law Quarterly 1982, 132

Bellow G., 34 National Legal Aid and Defenders' Briefcase 1977, 106

Bellow G. ed Cappelletti M., Access to Justice and the Welfare state, European Institute - Sijthoff, Amsterdam, 1981

Bellow G. and Kettleson J., 55 Boston University Law Review 1978, 337

Bing, S.R. and Rosenfeld S.S., The Quality of Justice in the Law Courts of Metropolitan Boston, Committee on Law Enforcement and the Administration of Criminal Justice, Commonwealth of Massachusetts, Boston 1970

Black D., 2 Journal of Legal Studies 1973, 125

Blankenburg E. ed Blankengburg E., Innovations in the Legal Services, Oelgeschlager, Gunn and Hain, Boston, 1980

Bleiklie I., 1 Rättssociologie 1983, 55

Blumberg A.S., Criminal Justice, Quadrangle Books, Chicago, 1967

Bogoch B. and Danet B., 4 (1/3) Text, 1984, 249

Borrie G.J. and Varcoe J.R., Legal Aid in Criminal Proceedings, Institute of Judicial Administration, Birmingham 1970

Bottoms A.E. and McClean J.D., Defendants in the Criminal Process, Routledge and Kegan Paul, London, 1976

Boyum K.O. ed Boyum K.O. and Mather L., Empirical Theories about Courts, Longman, New York, 1983

Bradshaw J.S. ed McLachlan G., Problems and Progress in Medical Care, 7th Series, Oxford University Press, 1972

Bradshaw J.S., Doctors on Trial, Wildwood House, London, 1978

Brakel S.J., Judicare - Public Funds, Private Laywers and Poor People, American Bar Foundation, Chicago, 1974

Breger M.J., 60 North Carolina Law Review 1982, 282

Bridges L., Legal Action Group Bulletin 6/1982, 10, 7/1972, 12

Brill H., 31 The Public Interest, 1973, 38

Brown M. and Madge N., Despite the Welfare State, Department of Health and Social Security - Social Science Research Council, London, 1982

Bruinsma F.B., 9 Nederlands Juridik Bulletin 3/3/1990, 337

Buckle G. and Thomas-Buckle S. ed Tomasic R., Neighbourhood Justice, Longmans, New York, 1982

Burney E., 'J.P.', Hutchinson, London, 1979

Cahn E. and J., 73 Yale Law Journal 1964, 1317

Campbell C., 1 British Journal of Law and Society 1974, 13

Campbell C., Lawyers and their Public, Wilson Memorial Lectures, Edinburgh University, 1976

Campbell C.M., Lawyers in their Social Setting, Green, Edinburgh, 1976

Campbell C. ed Thomas P.A., Law in the Balance, Ch 9, Martin Robertson, Oxford, 1982

Caplan, J. ed Illich I. *et al*, Disabling Professions, Marion Boyars, London, 1977

Cappelletti M. and Garth B., 1 <u>Windsor Yearbook of Access to Justice</u> 1981, foreword

Carlen P., 'Magistrates' Justice' Martin Robertson, Oxford, 1976

Carlin J.E., Civil Justice and the Poor, Russell Sage, New York, 1967

Carlin J.E., Howard J., Messinger J., 12 <u>University of California at Los Angeles Law Review</u> 1965, 381

Cashman P., Research and Delivery of Legal Services, Law Foundation of New South Wales, Sydney, 1981

Cashman P. ed Basten J. *et al*, The Criminal Injustice System, Legal Workers' Cooperative, Sydney, 1982

Casper J.D., Criminal Justice; the Defendant's Perspective Prentice - Hall, Englewood Cliffs, New Jersey, 1972

Cass M. and Western J.S., Legal Aid and Legal Need, Commonwealth Legal Aid Commission, Canberra 1980

Cass M.J. and Western J.S. ed Cashman P., Research and Delivery of Legal Services, Law Foundation of New South Wales, Sydney, 1981

Cass M.J. and Sackville R., Legal Needs of the Poor, Australian Government Commission of Inquiry into Poverty, Canberra, 1975

Chapman S., <u>The New Republic</u>, 24/9/1977, 9

Christensen D.F., Lawyers for People of Moderate Means, American Bar Foundation, Chicago, 1970

Clark M. and Corstret A., 47 <u>Yale Law Journal</u> 1938, 1272

Clarke S.H. and Koch G.G., 11 <u>Law and Society Review</u> 1976, 57

Clayton S., 12 <u>Journal of Social Policy</u>, 1983, 213

Condren C. ed Fitzgerald R., Human Needs and Politics, Ch 14, Pergamon, London, 1977

Cooper J., Public Legal Services, Sweet and Maxwell, London, 1983

Cottrell, J., 43 Modern Law Review 1980, 549

Cranston R. ed Cashman P., Research and the Delivery of Legal Services, Law Foundation of New South Wales, Sydney, 1981

Cranston R., Legal Foundations of the Welfare State, Weidenfeld and Nicolson, London, 1985

Crow L. and Cove J., Criminal Law Review 1984, 413

Culyer A.J., Lavers R., Williams A., Social Trends, HMSO, London 1971

Curran B.A., Integrated Report, Final of 6 Reports to Assess the Need for Legal Services by the Poor, Office of Economic Opportunity Contract 4097, American Bar Foundation, Chicago 31/12/1969

Curran B.A., The Legal Needs of the Public, American Bar Foundation, Chicago, 1977

Curran B.A. ed Blankenburg E., Innovation in the Legal Services, Oelgeschlager, Gunn and Hain, Boston, 1980

Cutts L.M., 132 New Law Journal 25/11/1982, 1089

Dauer E. and Leff A.A., 86 Yale Law Journal 1977, 573

Davis G., Macleod A., Murch M., 46 Modern Law Review 1966, 328

de Charmes R., Personal Causation, Academic Press, New York, 1968

Dell S., Silent in Court, Bell, Occasional papers in Social Administration, London 1971

Derby E.S., 26 Maryland Law Review 1966, 328

Desdevises M-C. and Lorvelec S., 6 Revue Juridique de l'Ouest 1989, 6

Domberger S. and Sherr S., Economic Efficiency in the Provision of Legal Services, General Series Discussion Paper 90, Centre for Economic and Business Research, University of Warwick, Coventry 1980

Douglas R., La Trobe University Legal Studies Department, Guilty Your Worship, Melbourne 1975

Douglas R., 13 Australia and New Zealand Journal of Criminology 1980, 241

Downes D., Hopkins P., Rees W., 1 Windsor Yearbook of Access to Justice 1981, 121

Doyal L. and Gough I., 10 Critical Social Policy 1984, 6

Dworkin R., 6(1) The Hastings Centre Report 1970, 23

Edwards S.M., Women on Trial, Manchester University Press, Manchester, 1984

Egglestone E., Fear, Favour, of Affection, Australian National University Press, Canberra, 1976

Ericson R.V. and Baranek P.M., The Ordering of Justice, University of Toronto Press, Toronto, 1982

Evans F.R. and Norwood J.M., A Comparison of the Quality of Licensed and Student Attorneys, Law Enforcement Administration Agency, Washington DC 1975

Farrington D.P. and Morris A.M., 23 British Journal of Criminology 1983, 229

Feeley M.M., The Process is the Punishment, Russell Sage Foundation, New York, 1979

Feinberg J., 40 Journal of Value Enquiry, 1970, 243

Ferster E.Z. and Countless T.F., 7 Law and Society Review 1972, 195

Finman M., 1971 Wisconsin Law Review 1001

Fiocco J. and Cartwright B. ed Cashman P., Research and the Delivery of Legal Services, Law Foundation of New South Wales, Sydney, 1981

Fitzgerald J.M., Poverty and the Legal Profession in Victoria, Australian Government Publishing Service, Canberra 1977

Fitzgerald R.F. ed Fitzgerald R.F., Human Needs and Politics, Pergamon, London, 1977

Fitzmaurice C. and Pease K., The Psychology of Sentencing, Manchester University Press, Manchester, 1986

Flew A.G.N. ed Fitzgerald R.F., Human Needs and Politics, Pergamon Press, London, 1977

Fogelson F.B. and Freeman H.E. ed Wheeler S., Controlling Delinquents, Ch 9, John Wiley, New York, 1968

Foote C. ed., Studies on Bail, Philadelphia, 1966

Frankfurt H., 68 Journal of Philosophy 1971, 3

Fried C., 85 Yale Law Journal 1976, 1060

Friedman L., Journal of Social Issues, 1971, 189

Fuller B.F., 34 National Legal Aid and Defenders' Association Briefcase 12/1/1976-77, 40

Galanter M., 9 Law and Society Review 1974, 95

Galtung J. ed Lederer K., Human Needs, Ch 3, Oelsgeschlager and Gunn, Cambridge, Mass., 1980

Galtung J. and Lederer K. ed Lederer K., Human Needs, Ch 15, Oelgeschlager and Gunn, Cambridge, Mass., 1980

Gardner J. ed Cashman P., 'Research and Delivery of Legal Services', Ch 6, Law Foundation of New South Wales, Sydney, 1981

Garth B., Neighbourhood Law Firms for the Poor, Sijthoff and Noordhoff, Alphen, 1980

Garth B. ed Cappelletti M., Access to Justice and the Welfare State, Sijthoff, Amsterdam, 1981

Geerts P. ed Blankenburg E., Innovations in the Legal Services, Oelgeschlager, Gunn and Hain, Boston, 1980

Genn H., Meeting Legal Needs, Social Science Research Council - Greater Manchester Legal Services Committee, London 1982

Giller H. and Morris A., Journal of Social Welfare Law 1982, 29

Grabosky P. and Rizzo C., 16 Australian and New Zealand Journal of Criminology 1983, 146

Green E., Judicial Attitudes in Sentencing, MacMillan, New York, 1961

Greenberg J.G. ed Lerner M.J. and S.C., The Justice Motive in Social Behaviour, Plenum Press, New York, 1981

Gregory J., Crown Court or Magistrates, Cmnd 6323, HMSO, London 1975

Griffiths J., 79 Yale Law Journal 1970, 359

Griffiths J., 4 British Journal of Law and Society 1977, 260

Griffiths J. ed Blankenburg E., Research and Delivery of Legal Services, Ch 3, Oelgeschlager, Gunn and Hain, Boston, 1980

Grossmont J.B. and Sarat A., 3 Law and Policy Quarterly 1981, 124

Gurney-Champion F.G.C., 'Justice and the Poor in England', Routledge and Law Notes, London, 1926

Halbwachs M., L'Evolution des Besoin dans les Classes Ouvriers, Paris, 1933

Hanks P. ed Cashman P., Research and the Delivery of Legal Services, Law Foundation of New South Wales, Sydney, 1981

Hann, R.G., Decision Making in the Canadian Criminal Court System, 2 vols. Centre for Criminology, University of Toronto, Toronto 1973

Harper T., 130 New Law Journal 10/1/1980, 27

Heinz A.M. and Kerstetter W.A., MacDonald W.F. and Cramer J.A. eds., Plea-Bargaining, Ch 8, D.C. Heath, Lexington, 1980

Heller A. ed Lederer K., Human Needs, Ch 8, Oelgeschlager and Gunn, Cambridge, Mass., 1980

Helms P.A., 132 New Law Journal 18/2/1982, corr. 156

Herman R., Single E. and Boston J., Counsel for the Poor, Heath, Lexington, 1977

Hetherton M., Victoria's Lawyers, Victoria Law Foundation, Melbourne, 1978

Heubner M., Your Court, Lord Chancellor's Department, 6/1986

Hilgendorf L. eds Geach M. and Szwed E., Providing Civil Justice for Children, Edward Arnold, London, 1983

Hogarth J., Sentencing as a Human Process, University of Toronto Press, 1971

Holman R., Poverty, Explanations of Social Deprivation, Martin Robertson, Oxford, 1978

Homel R., 14 Australia and New Zealand Journal of
     Criminology 1982, 225

Hood R., Sentencing in Magistrates' Courts, Stevens,
     London, 1962

Hood R. and Sparks R., Key Issues in Criminology,
     Weidenfeld and Nicolson, London, 1970

Hospers J., Human Conduct, Harcourt, Brace and
     Jovanovich, New York, 1961

Hosticka C.J., 26 Social Problems, 1979, 599

Huber S.K., 51 George Washington Law Review 1976, 754

Illich I. ed Illich I., Disabling Professions, Marion
     Boyars, London, 1977

Ingleby Report, Children and Young Persons, Cmnd 1191,
     HMSO, London 1960

Johnson E., Justice and Reform, Transaction, New
     Brunswick, New Jersey, 1978

Jones P.R., Resource Implications of an Independent
     Prosecution Service, Home Office Research and
     Planning Unit, London 1983

Justice, The Litigant in Person, Stevens, London 1971

Justice, The Unrepresented Defendant in Magistrates'
     Courts, Stevens, London 1971

Justice, Witnesses in the Criminal Courts, Stevens,
     London 1986

Kandler P., 'Priorities in Legal Services', Institute of
     Judicial Administration, Birmingham 1974

Kay D., 'Tackling Tribunals', Department of Social
     Administration, University of Strathclyde 1984

Kent G., 24 British Journal of Clinical Psychology, 1985,
     259

Kilbrandon Report, Children and Young Persons, Cmnd 2303,
     HMSO, Edinburgh 1964

King M., Bail or Custody, Cobden Trust, London 1971

King M., 1 Rights 11/1976, 11

King M., The Effects of a Duty Solicitor Scheme, Cobden Trust, London 1976

Klein R., 6 Journal of the Irish College of Physicians, 1977, 88

Klineberg O. ed Lederer K., Human Needs, Ch 1, Oelgeschlager and Gunn, Cambridge, Mass., 1980

Krantz S., The Right to Counsel in Criminal Cases, Ballinger, Cambridge, Mass., 1980

Ladinsky J., 11 Law and Society Review 1976, 212

Law Forum, 6 Houston Law Review 1969, 939

Lederer K. ed Lederer K., Human Needs, Ch 11, Oelgeschlager and Gunn, Cambridge, Mass., 1980

Lee D., Freedom and Culture, Prentice Hall, New Jersey, 1959

Leffler K., 21 Journal of Law and Economics 1978, 165

Leiss W., The Limits of Satisfaction, University of Toronto Press, Toronto, 1976

Levenson H., 129 New Law Journal 15/11/79, 1133

Levenson H., The Price of Justice, Cobden Trust, London 1981

Levi-Strauss C., The Raw and the Cooked, Cape, London, 1970

Lidstone K. et al, Prosecution by Non-Police Agencies, Royal Commission on Criminal Procedure, Research Study 10, HMSO, London 1979

Lipetz M.J., Routine Justice, Transaction, New Brunswick, New Jersey, 1984

Lizotte A.J., 25 Social Problems, 1977, 565

Llewellyn K., The Bramble Bush, Columbia University Press, New York, 1930

Lucas J.R., 47 Philosophy, 1972, 237

Luckham R., 43 Modern Law Review 1980, 345

MacIntyre A., 64 Ethics, 1973, 1

Mack J. and Lansley R., Poor Britain, Allen and Unwin, London, 1985

Macaulay S., 28 <u>American Sociological Review</u>, 1963, 55

Mallmann C.A. and Marcus S. ed Lederer K., Human Needs, Ch 6, Oelgeschlager and Gunn, Cambridge, Mass. 1980

Marks F.R., 30 <u>University of Miami Law Review</u> 1976, 915

Marks F.R., 11 <u>Law and Society Review</u> 1977, 191

Marks F.R., Hallauer R.P. and Clifton R., The Shreveport Plan, American Bar Foundation, Chicago, 1974

Marshall T. and Walpole M., Bringing People Together: Mediation and Reparation Projects in Great Britain, Home Office Research, Unit Paper 33, Home Office, London 1985

Marx K., Economic and Philosophic Manuscripts of 1844, Progress Publishers, Moscow, 1959

Masotti L.H. and Corsi J.R., 44 <u>Journal of Urban Law</u> 1967, 483

Masini E. ed Lederer K., Human Needs, Ch 9, Oelgeschlager and Gunn, Cambridge, Mass., 1980

Maslow A., <u>Psychological Review</u>, 1943, 370

Maslow A., 25 <u>Journal of Psychology</u>, 1948, 433

Maslow A., Motivation and Personality, Harper and Row, New York, 1968

Matthews A. and Weiss J., 47 <u>Buffalo University Law Review</u> 1967, 231

Mayer J.E. and Timms N., The Client Speaks, Atherton Press, New York, 1970

Mayhew L. and Reiss A.J., 34 <u>American Sociological Review</u>, 1969, 309

McCabe S. and Purves R., The Jury at Work, Basil Blackwell, Oxford 1972

McClintock J. ed Cashman P., Research and Delivery of Legal Services, Ch 5, Law Foundation of New South Wales, Sydney, 1981

McDonald W.F., The Defense Counsel, Sage Foundation, New York, 1983

McKnight C., 5 <u>Law and Human Behaviour</u> 1981, 141

McKnight J. ed Illich I., Disabling Professions, Marion Boyars, London, 1977

Meeker J.W., Dombrink J. and Schumann E., 7 Law and Policy 1985, 223

Menkel-Meadows C. and Meadow R.G., 5 Law and Policy 1983, 237

Messier C., In the Hands of the Law, Commission des Services Juridiques, Quebec 3/1975

Meyer W.J., 2 Political Theory, 1974, 197

Mileski M., 5 Law and Society Review 1971, 473

Miller D., Social Justice, Oxford University Press, Oxford, 1979

Miller S. et al, 7 Transaction 1970, 38

Miller S.M. et al, The Future of Inequality, Basic Books, London, 1970

Milne J. A.J., 100 South African Law Journal 1983, 681

Morris A. and Giller H., Criminal Law Review 1977, 198

Morris P., Cooper J. and Byles A., 3 British Journal of Social Work, 1974, 301

Morris P., White R. and Lewis P. eds., Social Needs and Legal Action, Martin Robertson, London, 1973

Nader L., 88 Yale Law Journal 1979, 998

Nader R., 11 Law and Society Review 1976, 247

Nagel S.S., 55 American Political Science Review, 1962, 843

Nagel S.S., 48 Indiana Law Journal 1982, 404

Nathan N.M.L., The Concept of Justice, MacMillan, London, 1971

National Consumer Council, Making Good Solutions, London 1989

National Consumer Council/Welsh Consumer Council, Simple Justice, London 1979

Neilsen K., 6 Inquiry, 1963, 170

Neilsen K. ed Fitzgerald R., Human Needs and Politics,
    Ch 8, Pergamon, London, 1977

Nevitt D.A. ed Heisler H., Foundations of Social
    Administration, Ch 8, MacMillan, London, 1972

New Zealand Department of Justice, Access to the Law,
    Wellington 1981

O'Malley P., 11 Journal of Law and Society 1984, 91

Orbach S., Hunger Strike, Faber, London, 1986

Osler Report, Ontario Joint Committee on Legal Aid,
    Ottawa 1965

Oxley P., Access to Justice, Appendix 6, New Zealand
    Department of Justice, Wellington 1981

Pande B.B., 11 International Journal of the Sociology of
    Law 1983, 291

Parry D., J. The Law and the Poor, Smith and Elder,
    London, 1914

Partington, M. ed Thomas P.A., Law in the Balance, Ch 5,
    Martin Robertson, Oxford, 1982

Paterson A., Legal Aid as a Social Service, Cobden Trust,
    London 1970

Phillips A., 42 Modern Law Review 1979, 29

Pratt J. and Grimshaw R., Journal of Social Welfare Law
    1985, 257

Pretecaille E. and Terrail J.P., Capitalism, Consumption
    and Needs, Basil Blackwell, Oxford, 1985

Project, 86 Yale Law Journal 1976, 104

Project, 90 Yale Law Journal 1980, 122, 142

Rankin C. et al, 38 New York University Law Review 1963,
    67

Reifner U. ed Blankenburg E., Innovations in the Legal
    Services, Oelgeschlager, Gunn and Hain, Boston, 1980

Renner K.E. and Warner A.H., 1 Windsor Yearbook of Access
    to Justice 1981, 62

Renshon S.A., Psychological Needs and Political
    Behaviour, Free Press, New York, 1974

Renshon S.A. ed Fitzgerald R., Human Needs and Politics, Ch 4, Pergamon, London, 1977

Richards D.A.J., 13 Georgia Law Review 1979, 1372

Rist G. ed Lederer K., Human Needs, Ch 10, Oelgeschlager and Funn and Hain, Cambridge, Mass., 1980

Robertshaw P.E.M., 9 Proces 1983, 78

Robertshaw P.E.M., 14 Cambrian Law Review 1983, 78

Rosenberg M., 1 Windsor Yearbook of Access to Justice 1981, 294

Rossi P.H. and Williams W., Evaluating Social Programs, Seminar Press, New York, 1972

Roy S. ed Lederer K., Human Needs, Ch 7, Oelgeschlager and Gunn, Cambridge, Mass., 1980

Rueschmeyer D., Canadian Review of Social Anthropology, 1984, 17

Runciman W.G., Relative Social Deprivation and Social Justice, Routledge and Kegan Paul, London, 1966

Ryan J.P., 15 Law and Society Review 1980-81, 79

Sackville R., Legal Aid in Australia, Australian Government Publishing Service, Canberra, 1975

Sahlins M., Stone Age Economics, Tavistock, London, 1974

Sanders A., Criminal Prosecution in England and Wales, International Sociological Association Research Committee on the Sociology of Law, Madison, Wisconsin 6/1980

Sanders A. and Bridges L., Criminal Law Review 1990, 494

Schuyt K. et al, 'De Weg Naar Het Recht' Deventer 1976, cited in J. Griffiths 4 BJLS (1977) 260, 270

Schuyt K. et al, European Yearbook in Law and Sociology 1977, 25

Schwartzkoff J. ed Cashman P., Research and Delivery of Legal Services, Ch 8, Law Foundations of New South Wales, Sydney, 1981

Seebohm Report, Local Authority and Allied Personal Social Services, Cmnd 3703, HMSO, London 1968

Shane-Dubow S. *et al*, Felony Sentencing in Wisconsin, Wisconsin Center for Public Policy, Public Policy Press, Madison 1979

Shapland J., Between Conviction and Sentence, Routledge and Kegan Paul, London, 1981

Shapland J., Victims in Criminal Justice, Home Office, London 1982

Shoham S., 50 Journal of Criminal Law, Criminology and Police Science 1959-60, 327

Sigler J.A., Criminal Law Review 1974, 642

Silver C.R., 46 Journal of Urban Law 1969, 217

Silverstein L., Defense of the Poor, American Bar Foundation, Chicago 1965

Simon F. and Weatheritt M., The Use of Bail and Custody by London Magistrates before and after the Criminal Justice Act 1967, HMSO, London 1976

Simon W.H., Wisconsin Law Review 1978, 30

Skillen A., Welfare State v Welfare Society, Paper for the British Philosophical Association, 6/1984

Smith A.B. and Blumberg A.S., 46 Social Forces, 1967, 96

Smith G., Social Need, Routledge and Kegan Paul, 1980

Smith M.B. ed Fitzgerald R.F., Human Needs and Politics, Ch 7, Pergamon, London, 1977

Smith P. and Thomas P., 128 New Law Journal 6/4/1978, 324

Smith P.F. and Bailey S.H., The Modern English Legal System, Sweet and Maxwell, 1984

Soper K., On Human Needs, Harvester Press, Brighton, 1981

Springborg P. ed Fitzgerald R., Human Needs and Politics, Ch 9, Pergamon, 1977

Springborg P., The Problem of Human Needs, George Allen and Unwin, London, 1981

Stapleton W.F. and Teitelbaum L.E., Defense of Youth, Sage, New York, 1972

Stephens M., 7 Law and Policy 1985, 77

Symonds G. ed Cashman P., Research and Delivery of Legal Services, Ch 15, Law Foundation of New South Wales, Sydney, 1981

Tarling R., Sentencing Practice in Magistrates' Courts, Home Office Research Unit No 56, HMSO, London 1979

Tarling R., 25 Howard Journal, 1986, 112

Taylor J.G. *et al*, 50 Denver Law Journal 1973, 9

Thamesdown Law Centre, Juvenile Justice in Swindon, Swindon 10/1984

Thayer R., 7 Social and Economic Administration, 1973, 145

Townsend P. ed Wedderburn D., Poverty, Inequality and Class Structure, Cambridge University Press, Cambridge, 1974

Tutt N. and Giller H., Criminal Law Review 1983, 587

Twining W., 43 Modern Law Review 1980, 558

Tyler J.R., 18 Law and Society Review 1984, 52

Uhlman T.M., 22 American Journal of Political Science 1979, 22

Van Duyne P.C. and Verwoerd J.R.A., Gelet op de Persoon van de Rechter, WODC, Ministerie van Justitie, No 58, s'Gravenhage 1985

Van Koppen J. and Kate J.T., 18 Law and Society Review 1984, 225

Veblen T.B., Theory of the Leisure Class, MacMillan, New York, 1912

Vidmar N., eds. Lerner M.J. and S.C., The Justice Motive in Social Behavior, Plenum Press, New York, 1980

Vinson T. and Homel R., 47 Australian Law Journal 1973, 132

Vinson T. and Homel R. ed. Basten J. *et al*, The Criminal Injustice System, Legal Services Bulletin, Sydney, 1982

Wallace J. ed Cashman P., Research and Delivery of Legal Services, Ch 4, Law Foundation of New South Wales, Sydney, 1981

Warren D.I. ed Robertson J.A., Rough Justice, Little
    Brown & Co., Boston, 1974

Weatheritt M., The Prosecution System, Royal Commission
    on Criminal Procedure, Research Study 11, HMSO,
    London 1980

Weber T., La Trobe University Legal Studies Department,
    Guilty Your Worship, Bundoora 1980

White A.R., 87 Proceedings of the Philosophy of Education
    Society of Great Britain, Supplementary Issue, 1974,
    159

Wiggins D.W., Needs, Values, Truth, Aristotelian Society
    Service, Vol 6, Basil Blackwell, Oxford, 1987

Wilkins J.L., Legal Aid in the Criminal Court, University
    of Toronto Press, Toronto, 1975

Williams A. ed Culyer A.J., Economic Policies and Social
    Goals, Ch 4, Martin Robertson, Oxford, 1974

Wood A.L., Criminal Lawyer, College and University Press,
    New Haven, 1967

Working Party on Access to Law, Interim Report,
    Department of Justice, Wellington, New Zealand
    12/1982

Xenos, N., Scarcity and Modernity, Routledge, London,
    1989

Zald M.N., Social Welfare Institutions, Wiley, New York,
    1965

Zander M., Criminal Law Review 1969, 632

Zander M., Criminal Law Review 1971, 191

Zander M., Criminal Law Review 1972, 155

Zander M., Criminal Law Review 1972, 343

Zander M., Criminal Law Review 1976, 5

Zander M., 66 Law Society Gazette 3/1969, 174

Zander M., 126 New Law Journal 1/1/1976, 4

Zander M., 126 New Law Journal 9/9/1976, 904

Zander M., 126 New Law Journal 30/9/1976, 979

Zander M., 126 New Law Journal 2/10/1976, 1047

Zander M., 126 New Law Journal 7/10/1976, 1047

Zander M., 127 New Law Journal 22/12/1977, 1236

Zander M., 128 New Law Journal 1/2/1978, 198

Zander M., 128 New Law Journal 15/6/1978, 576

Zander M., 129 New Law Journal 1/2/1979, 108

Zander M., Cases and Materials on the English Legal System, Weidenfeld and Nicolson, 3rd ed., London, 1980; 4th ed., 1984

Zander M., Legal Services for the Community, Temple Smith, London, 1978

Zander M., Abel-Smith B. and Brooke R., Legal Problems of the Citizen, Heinemann, London, 1973

Zander M. and Glasser G., 117 New Law Journal 27/7/1967, 816

Zander M. and Morris P., 70 Law Society Gazette 3/10/1973, 2371

Zeigler D.H. and Hermann M.J., 47 New York University Law Review 1972, 159

INDEX